COMMUNITY EDUCATION: A DEVELOPING CONCEPT

COMMUNITY EDUCATION: A DEVELOPING CONCEPT

MAURICE F. SEAY
AND
ASSOCIATES

PENDELL
PUBLISHING
COMPANY

International Standard Book Number: 0-87812-067-X

Library of Congress Catalog Card Number: 73-89106

DEDICATION

During each era of educational advance there must be a group of practitioners who "make the system run." There has been — and there is today — such a group in the development of community education.

These men and women hold positions that we call Teacher, Coordinator, Director of Community Education, and Superintendent of Schools. They know and hold dear the worth and dignity of each individual. They know how to involve the people of a community in the educational enterprise that society has assigned to them. They appreciate the fact that many of our institutions — in addition to the schools — play an important role in the educative process.

To those of us who have contributed to the writing of *Community Education: A Developing Concept* Dr. Paul J. Misner is outstanding in this special group of educators. He embodies and demonstrates the leadership qualities that have been important to the development of community education.

With appreciation, respect, and yes — with love — we dedicate this volume to Paul J. Misner, our colleague and friend, and to the thousands of front-line practitioners he represents.

CONTENTS

CONTENTS *(Cont'd)*

FOREWORD

The basic documents that created these United States contain a promise — the promise of the right to life, liberty, and the pursuit of happiness. There is no promise that people shall be given these rights, only that they shall have the opportunity to seek them.

These documents, the Declaration of Independence, the Constitution, and the Bill of Rights, form the cornerstone of our educational institutions. Each of our institutions carries the charge to assist every person to reach his maximum potential in the pursuit of the promises of our basic documents.

During the past decade our educational institutions have endured a great deal of upheaval and strife. The basic causes run deep. There is great concern on the part of our citizens about their abilities to seek the promises of America.

In times of stress we in the United States have turned to education for assistance and answers. There is great question that our educational institutions, in their present lack of coordination and relevancy, can provide assistance or solutions.

For many decades the community education concept has been in the process of becoming. The concept, as defined and explained in this volume asserts that community education "dares to attempt to achieve a reasonable balance and effective use of all the institutional forces in the education of all of the people." This is truly a concept whose time has arrived.

Various contributing authors have provided specific information and examples as to how this concept can be implemented. Therefore, the volume not only provides a philosophical base for community education, but offers practical suggestions and information.

Community Education: A Developing Concept provides the student, the practitioner, and the lay public an idea which can revitalize our educational enterprise. This book explains how community education is the process whereby education can assist each citizen in seeking life, liberty, and happiness. There is no doubt that Maurice Seay

Foreword

and his colleagues have authored one of the landmark publications of the seventies.

John E. Sandberg
Dean, College of Education
Western Michigan University

PREFACE

A major purpose guided the writing of this book: to present a developing idea of education as we, the authors, have been seeing it through our different kinds of professional experiences.

The authors represent a unique combination of relationships with community education — relationships that span the history and the geography of this developing concept. Our combined experience includes work with early community school programs and leadership in developing the understanding of that movement; it includes work with the evolving programs in community education scattered through the South and Midsouth, the West and Midwest; it also includes work with Flint, the National Center for Community Education, the National Community School Education Association, and the growing number of Regional University Centers for community education. Some of the authors have developed leadership training programs, formulated basic theory, and conducted research in the field. Several of us also represent grass-roots experience with the comprehensive and school-related programs of community education.

The book, however, represents more than a symposium or collection of viewpoints. Eleven individuals have worked together for several years in several professional relationships. They have met together to discuss their outlines and later their manuscripts for the chapters which follow; and as general author, I have added sections to chapters as I believed such additions were needed for balance. Each of us now has a fresh understanding of the phrase, "Learning is lifelong." We have clarified many details of our mutual understanding about community education.

The dichotomy that exists in the usage of the term "community education" requires a word of explanation. Since community education is a developing concept, portions of its earlier forms continue to make up part of the total form presented to the world today. For example, the idea of a process which leads to a comprehensive, coordinated educational program for all the people of a community developed from the community and adult programs conducted by the community schools of an earlier period. Therefore, many comprehensive programs now struggle to free themselves from the limitations imposed by the lingering image of community education as only a unit in the public school program which offers those educational activities that fill the gaps. The concept defined and reflected in multiple exposures throughout the book will be joined now and then by reflections of the earlier, school-centered image. Such a double view is, in fact, an accurate view of the current stage in the development of the community education concept.

Because of the comprehensive nature of community education, all of the important topics could not be included in the book. Fortunately, there are many fine publications, many of which have been cited, that cover a variety of topics. Our desire is to stimulate thinking and discussion and more reading as well as research and writing by both educators and laymen. Of course, there is room for disagreement in the broad field of community education, but there is no room for status-quo thinking or practice.

The emerging community education concept has gained coherence and vitality from the active interest of several citizens who are not professional educators. There have been the philanthropists who gave both moral and financial support. Each community where the concept is being put into practice has lay leaders who make the implementation possible and effective. The nation has an outstanding lay leader in community education who is choosing to back this concept with time, energy, imagination, and an active press. The authors of this book recognize the unusual encouragement "to say it loud and clear" which they, and other community educators, are receiving today from the leading publisher of documents on that subject, Richard C. Pendell.

Personally, I thank my associates and Dean Sandberg, and the host of other friends and colleagues who, over the years, have made my experience in community education an adventure and a romance in meaningful living and service.

Maurice F. Seay

LIST OF AUTHORS

Boles, Harold W. Ph.D.
   Professor, Educational Leadership
   Western Michigan University

Heath, Paul R. Ed.D.
   Vice President for Instructional Services
   Kellogg Community College

Martin, Gerald C. Ed.D.
   Director, Community School Development Center
   and Professor, Educational Leadership
   Western Michigan University

Martinson, William D. Ed.D.
   Head, Department of Counseling and Personnel and
   Professor of Counseling and Education
   Western Michigan University

Parson, Steve R. MA
   Graduate Associate, Community School Development Center
   Western Michigan University

Seay, Maurice F. Ph.D.
   Professor Emeritus, Educational Leadership
   Western Michigan University

Seay, Ruth H. Ph.D.
   Former member of Faculty,
   Berea College

Simon, Kenneth F. Ed.D.
   Associate Dean, College of Education
   Western Michigan University

Weaver, Donald C. Ed.D.
   Professor, Educational Leadership and Coordinator,
   Mott Leadership Program
   Western Michigan University

List Of Authors

Wirtz, Morvin A. Ed.D.
   Associate Dean, College of Education and
   Professor, Special Education
   Western Michigan University

Wood, George S. Jr. MA
   Assistant Director,
   Community School Development Center
   Western Michigan University

CHAPTER I

THE COMMUNITY EDUCATION CONCEPT — A DEFINITION

THE COMMUNITY EDUCATION CONCEPT — A DEFINITION

MAURICE F. SEAY

In 1945 and again in 1953 the writer asserted in yearbooks of the National Society for the Study of Education that Americans were becoming more and more interested in "the community school." That assertion, proven to be true by educational developments in the late forties and the fifties, can now be restated in a significantly modified way: Americans in the seventies are becoming more and more interested in *community education* — the process that achieves a balance and a use of all institutional forces in the education of all the people of a community.

This growth of interest in a process, with its implication of community-wide programming, this transition from a school-centered concept to a comprehensive community-centered concept, and this emergence of the concept in the seventies as a vital and fertile emphasis influencing the entire hierarchy of education is the result of many interrelated factors. That rationale is developed in Chapter Two as part of a review of the educational thought and writing which evolved into the community education concept. A few of these factors are mentioned here because they are part of the contemporary action which has focused attention on community education. They are: (a) the publication of materials explaining and advocating this concept; (b) the work of professional associations; (c) the support of projects and demonstrations by foundations; (d) the funding of projects by states; (e) creation of new positions with responsibilities in community education; (f) the influence of school critics; and (g) the pressure of societal problems.

Publications

References are made in Chapter Two to various types of publications issued during the thirties, forties, and early fifties. Those descriptions of community school processes and programs were given wide distribution throughout America, and they proved to be convincing documentation of the possibilities inherent in community-centered education. Additional communities experimented with community school processes and variations of the earlier programs appeared in the late fifties.

Then in the sixties and early seventies the community education concept received fresh stimulation from several groups of new publications. An extraordinary assist was provided by one of these groups when the Pendell Publishing Company of Midland, Michigan, began publishing books and a journal which described and promoted community education. The books and the *Community Education Journal* contained reports from specific communities and descriptions of specific programs. This interest on the part of a publishing firm strengthened the increasing national belief and, in turn, created new interest. Richard C. Pendell, editor and publisher, reaffirmed his support of the community education concept in the following excerpts from a letter to the writer:

There is no question that I am as firmly committed, even more now, to the basic concepts of community education as a program that can aid America's social, economic, cultural and educational problems. From my travels around the country, I have become increasingly convinced that . . . government, education, the public, plus business and industry should . . . lend their combined impact upon the problems facing us [June 4, 1973].

4

Many of the books published by the Pendell Publishing Company which deal with various aspects of the community education concept are cited throughout this report. The *Community Education Journal,* first issued in February, 1971, is published quarterly and carries the following charge to its readers:

> If you are a professional educator, administrator, or educa-
> tion-oriented layman, you'll find multiple benefits from reading
> the CEJ. You'll be right up-to-the-minute on current community
> education progress; you'll gain teaching and administrative ideas
> you can use whatever your circumstance; you'll be on the "inside"
> of the fastest-growing educational concept of today.

Authors who write about community education are teaching the public that the word "education" is not synonymous with "schooling" but refers to a lifetime process of which schooling is one part. Readers, who sense in these materials a renewed confidence in the power of education, are responding with action. The thought that education can be more effective when all the contributing forces are kept in balance and are used to assist the learning of all the people – that thought is being put into action in many unexpected areas of our society because people – laymen – read about community education.

Professional Associations

Because of the highly specialized interest of most professional education associations, leaders of community education felt the need of a new organization which could recognize and emphasize a more comprehensive educational concept. Therefore, they formed in 1966 an association named The National Community School Education Association. Then state groups developed as State Associations, providing in this way a grass-roots network. These new organizations, with their staffs and their use of many different means of communication, are described in Chapter Sixteen.

Foundation-Supported Projects and Demonstrations

The Mott Foundation has been influential in bringing community education to the forefront of the educational scene today. In the thirties Frank J. Manley envisioned the opening of school playgrounds and gymnasiums during after-school hours and on weekends to be used by children, youth, and adults. He also saw the need for opening classrooms and laboratories during late afternoons and evenings for adult classes of many types and levels. This dream of the "Lighted Schoolhouse" became a reality in Flint, Michigan, because Frank Manley not only could see needs and dream dreams, he could persuade Charles Stewart Mott to give financial support to a city-wide community school program.

With continuing support from the Mott Foundation and with increasing support from the local school system, Flint has become a symbol of significant progress in the development of the community education concept. Many national workshops and special visitations to Flint and many published statements describing that program have given to thousands of laymen and educators throughout America an understanding and enthusiasm — first, for the community school in the forties, fifties, and sixties — and now, in the seventies, active stimulation toward the spread of the community education concept.

Many Mott Foundation-supported projects are described in other chapters of this report. The Mott Foundation has contributed not only financial support, but leadership and enthusiasm to these projects, and through them, to the spread of the community education concept throughout the nation.

Another Michigan foundation has given considerable financial assistance to projects which, too, have had influence upon the development and implementation of today's concept of community education. The W. K. Kellogg Foundation of Battle Creek has, since the middle forties, supported financially three series of programs which have been especially influencial: (a) the Michigan Community School Service Program (1945-53); (b) the Cooperative Program in Educational Administration (1950-1960); and (c) Leadership Education for Community Colleges (1960 and continuing).

The first series, the Michigan Community School Service Program, was sponsored by the Michigan Department of Public Instruction which assigned a member of its professional staff to the Program as Director. Eight Michigan school systems and five contiguous counties of the Grand Traverse area were involved. As a result of eight years of experimental work with interrelated community and school programs, the conclusion was drawn that people — those in small, widely separated communities, those in small communities grouped around an urban center, and those in the urban center — all wanted to improve their communities and believed that the educative process could produce such improvement. Excellent leadership was found in small communities as well as in the urban center, and that leadership welcomed interested counsel and technical assistance from outside when such help was given tactfully and sincerely. The people of these communities showed definite growth during the period of the Program in their ability to work together and to use the educative process in relating community resources to community needs as a means of solving community problems. The Program received considerable publicity and was instrumental in causing several colleges and universities to point programs more directly at community needs [Seay and Crawford, 1954, pp. 186-190].

The second series financed by this foundation, the Cooperative Program in Educational Administration, was conducted cooperatively by nine universities, at first, and later expanded to include more than fifty other universities. This program was coordinated by the American Association of School Administrators. It focused upon new strategies for educating leaders in both the preservice and inservice phases of their preparation. As explained in Chapter Five, this project resulted in a much greater emphasis upon the interdisciplinary approach in training administrators; and this emphasis, in turn, resulted in an in-depth study of the community — with consideration of such factors as its problems, its resources, and its open and hidden power structures. Many of the educational leaders trained in such programs, and introduced to the new emphasis in the fifties and sixties, now play leadership roles in programs that are implementing, or at least moving toward, the community education concept.

The Kellogg project in educating leaders for community colleges is in progress at the time of this writing. It is concentrated in ten universities and coordinated by the American Association of Community and Junior Colleges. This program places emphasis upon leadership for a definitively community-oriented institution in contrast to the more traditional view of higher education held by other regional and state institutions. A serious reconsideration of "the community" in the

7

world of higher education is being stimulated, in part, by this leadership project.

Yes, the increased interest in community education and recognition of an urgent need for greater implementation of the concept are due, in part, to successful projects financed by philanthropic foundations, particularly the Mott Foundation and the W. K. Kellogg Foundation.

State Support

Because of increased interest in the promotion of the community education concept within their borders, four states have authorized funds categorically for community education which have been administered by state departments of public instruction and allocated to local school systems on the basis of especially formulated guidelines. Other states are considering such funding. These grants are in response to growing interest among educators and community leaders, and they act as a stimulus producing more interest, state-wide, in the community education concept.

Creation of New Positions

As the community education concept has become alive, vital, and expansive, many new positions have been created. Now there is a cadre of educational leaders whose primary responsibility is to implement and research the process and the programs of community education and to disseminate information about the process and the programs. Among those leaders are community education directors, community education coordinators, staff members of community education development centers in universities, staff members of state departments of education who are assigned responsibilities for representing a state's interest in the conduct of community education programs, officers of the national and state community education associations, and university professors whose expertise is the community education concept. These educational leaders are the "avant guard" leading America from the school-centered concept of education to the more comprehensive community-centered concept that dares to attempt to achieve a reasonable balance and an effective use of all the institutional forces in the education of all the people.

School Critics

Schooling has always been a subject of interest to many people. Since almost everyone has had some experience with that subject, he can have an opinion. And criticism flows easily. Some has been quite constructive, and certain desirable changes have resulted. Within the education profession itself criticism is plentiful. There is unrest, but there is also constructive thought; many remedial projects have been planned and implemented. The community education programs described in succeeding chapters are examples of serious and constructive efforts to make education more effective for all the people.

Some of the critics are less constructive. They find some provable fault, some justifiable basis for criticism of the prevailing educational system; then a few would abolish it; others would fence it in with rules and regulations turned into law by special-interest groups. When angry critics press teachers too far, they fight back through their own special-interest groups, and the public suffers. Instruction suffers, also. And the deteriorating classroom situation prepares ground for more destructive criticism.

Fortunately for the American people, there are the constructive critics who do have plans for the improvement of educational opportunity. In the forefront of these are leaders in the community education movement.

Societal Problems

Crisis situations in American communities cause people to seek desperately for solutions. Students of our society agree that the quality of life in this country is threatened, as never before, by increasingly complex problems — pollution, depleted sources of energy, misused leisure, unemployment, scarcities of natural resources, huge programs of welfare, racism, international differences, governmental inefficiency, and problems of food, shelter, and clothing for everyone — the three "old timers" among the problems of local communities.

When in trouble, the American people have traditionally turned to education. They assume that they need more education. While "more" is not the answer today, the people are justified in their belief that education can still be depended upon to help. It is the community education concept with its principle of basing learning upon problem-solving (and the more intimate the problem the more effective the learning) that can satisfy the public demand for *help*.

Community education promises help also with some of the problems affecting the American system for formal education. Thoughtful and informed critics of the schools point out real dangers — and it should be remembered that many of these critics are educators in the system itself. They warn the public that bureaucracy is growing throughout the system. An industrial model of education is moving in as an answer to demands for efficiency, for accountability. Technological skills are being over-emphasized in our curriculums at the expense of humanistic values. Community leadership, including concerned educators, is not helpless in the face of this trend, but it does have to act. Many communities have started the action by choosing to implement the community education concept.

THE DEFINITION

Educators and laymen, faced with mounting problems and irresponsible criticism, are feeling great pressure to work together in solving societal problems. They are making many attempts to coordinate the programs of community agencies that have legitimate educational aims. Problems, of course, arise in any effort to achieve coordination of separate agencies; but some of the problems are due to differences in understanding of the community education concept. Clarification is needed.

Because of its all-inclusive nature and its breach of old habits, the community education concept is difficult to define. Definitions have a way of over-simplifying — of becoming "deadhands" to change. The writer, during the decades from 1930 to 1960, did attempt to define some of the earlier ideas dealing with education and the community.

An extensive experience in directing comprehensive educational programs for the 20,000 Tennessee Valley Authority employees and their families was summarized in 1938 as an experience in adult education. Two of the principles derived were: (a) Since education is a continuous process, it cannot be confined within fixed administrative divisions; it demands co-ordination of all of its services. (b) Educational activities should be based upon the problems, needs, and interests of those for whom they are planned (Seay, pp. 43-55).

When World War II was about to end, educators saw a chance for functional education to emerge in the postwar period. The definition of a "community school," as stated at that time by the writer, included two distinct emphases — service to the entire community, not merely to the children of school age, and discovery, development, and use of the resources of the community as part of the educational facilities of the school [Seay, 1945, p. 209].

Emphasis upon the local community was, in 1945, considered by internationalists to be isolationist; therefore, "community-school" advocates reinforced their definitions with explanations that the concern of the community school with the local community was intended, not to restrict the school's attention to local matters, but to provide a focus from which to relate study and action in the larger community — the state, the region, the nation, the world. In 1953 the writer explained further that the community school of the fifties secured its impetus from "man's new understanding of the power of education [Seay, 1953, p. 1]." After 20 years of experience with community schools, power was recognized in the educative process that could solve problems by the appropriate use of available resources. In a community, therefore, the power of the educative process could be used to relate the resources of the community to the needs and interests of the people of that community.

Evaluative studies of community-centered education made during the fifties and sixties in Michigan and in the Appalachain states have led the writer to believe that the community school concept has truly evolved into a community education concept — that numerous communities now show the concept in action — that it is a concept which can be expressed in the following brief sentence: *Community education is the process that achieves a balance and a use of all institutional forces in the education of the people — all of the people — of the community.*

The assumptions and implications of the definition are many. For example, the English language uses words having many shades of meaning; therefore, it is necessary to assume certain meanings for the words used in any definition. "Community" can refer to a number of different kinds of communities, but in community-education usage the problem is simplified by arbitrarily confining the meaning to local, geographic considerations with the extent of the area involved differing in urban, suburban, and rural communities. The word "achieves" is used with the understanding that achievement in any educational process must occur with varying degrees of success.

The implications of the words "balance" and "use" present a picture of community education in action. In Chapter Eight as well as in several other chapters, this action is described and explained. Briefly, "balance" refers to a dynamic equilibrium maintained among the contributions that various agencies make to an individual's education. The maintenance of such an equilibrium requires continuing study of the educational needs of the people, continuing planning, and continuing adjustment of the offerings of all the various educational agencies in the community. For example, if misuse of drugs becomes a problem in the community and drug-use education is needed, the school may offer the program temporarily, relinquishing it to the YMCA or YWCA or to the Department of Public Health after a planning council finds that one of those agencies can do that kind of education more effectively than can the school. The important thing is not what agency offers a needed educational activity, but that it be available when and where it is needed. Balance also requires that a program be dropped when the need for it no longer exists. In other words, balance, as used in this definition of community education, implies continuing study, planning, and adjustment of the offerings of all the various educational agencies in the community to insure a close relationship to real needs.

And the word "use" also implies continuing study, planning, and adjustment — in this case to fit together effectively the specific educational offerings and the specific educational needs those offerings are intended to meet. One of the great advantages of community education is that it offers a unique and workable process for "putting it all together."

The implications of the phrase "all institutional forces" include the idea of power which can produce an educational effect and which is organized and activated through certain agencies. The final phrase of the definition, "education of all the people of the community," implies that adult education as well as schooling for the young is part of community education — and that community education must be articulated horizontally to meet the needs of all the people at a given time as well as vertically to meet the progressive needs of each individual.

A reasonable tempering of the idealism of "all institutional forces" and "all of the people" is necessary in practice, of course. A philosophical concept may deal with absolutes — with complete and perfect totals — but educational achievement deals with partial accomplishments. Experience in setting goals and objectives and evaluating achievement teaches educators that goals — and concept — guide the educational process in the direction of the best possible achievement. And the best possible achievement for community education would be "a balance and a use of all institutional forces in the education of all the people."

Three of the implications require further comment: (a) the role of the school; (b) the growing need for lifelong education; and (c) articulation.

A major implication of the community education concept is that the public school system is one of many contributing forces in the education of the people. The role of the school is not diminished except by the need for cooperative action when it recognizes the fact that there are many educational agencies in every community that have legitimate educational aims — and that each agency has a right to serve and be served. Now, in a period of resource scarcity and criticism of waste, the possible contributions of all forces in the education of the people are more readily appreciated and accepted. Yes, the school is tremendously important, and because of its great resources of human talent and physical facilities, is most often the catalytic agent which takes the leadership role in establishing the organizational and administrative structure necessary for community-wide planning and coordination. The school is also the agency which is more likely to offer the educational services needed to provide adjustments (to add or delete) in the "balance" of community-wide educational resources.

The growing need for lifelong education becomes more and more obvious. Education for adults becomes an increasingly necessary part of community education. Schooling for children and youth is relegated to a somewhat less dominant position in the hierarchy of educational forces. Due to increasingly rapid obsolescence of skills and knowledge and even of some attitudes and ideals, and to increased leisure for great masses of adults, many forms of continuing education must grow. The elementary and secondary levels of schooling must become more of a supportive force and a preliminary phase of the comprehensive educational process. Continuing education for adults is one of the implications of the phrase in the definition, "education of the people — all of the people."

Articulation is a more important factor in the concept of community education than in the traditional concept of formal schooling because articulation must be made effective in the horizontal sense as well as in the vertical sense. Articulation has, in the past, been a concern of educators; but their efforts have been to improve the educative effectiveness of the moves a student makes from one segment of the vertical hierarchy of formal schooling to another segment. For example, a student moves from preschool to elementary school, from elementary school to junior high school, and on in this manner through graduate school perhaps, and into the more or less sporadic experiences now available in adult education. Articulation is improved for the student when the state of his horizontal learning needs — all the learning needs he confronts at a given time in his life — can be investigated and studied at each point of vertical transition. In actual practice, efforts toward better articulation of the segments of the vertical hierarchy have not been very effective, and the major reason for the failure is that the need for horizontal articulation has been ignored.

At every age level there are numerous institutional forces which contribute to a person's education. These forces grow in number and size as the population of a community grows and as the financial resources and leadership resources grow. The sad part of the story is that the research, the innovative projects, the experimentation have been conducted as if each force (elementary education, voluntary reading, summer camp, or Saturday morning's class in pottery at the art institute) were an isolated unit rather than one of many interrelated forces in the total education of an individual. When the deschoolers lambaste reading instruction or college-preparatory curriculums, they

14

ignore the totality of a person's education. Now, however, with the advent of community education and its coordinating influence, a person's education can be recognized as the totality that it has always been in fact. Research and experimentation can begin to deal with groups of interrelated forces, and the de-schoolers can improve their understanding of the total process. When such recognition of the interrelated forces occurs, the need for effective articulation — both vertical and horizontal — can begin to be met.

● ● ● ● ● ● ● ● ● ● ● ● ● ●

The action implied in the concept of community education described in this chapter can occur only when there is a plan and an organization that is granted — or that assumes — responsibility for some programming. The plan and the organization must have innate authority and power to implement this responsibility, and because the plan and the organization have been formulated by democratic procedures they do have the necessary authority and power — derived directly from the people of the entire community. The formulation of the plan and the organization are accomplished through the involvement of representatives of the people — leaders who are concerned, who have insight and confidence in the educative process, and who can influence the use of agency resources (staff and facilities) for programming. Community education based on this kind of innate authority has power to coordinate, to plan, to evaluate, and to promote comprehensive programs of education for all people of a community.

CHAPTER II

HOW THE CONCEPT GREW

HOW THE CONCEPT GREW

MAURICE F. SEAY

The current American concept of community education has developed out of three centuries of experience with schools and with nonschool agencies that have performed various educational functions for the people of communities. Originally, of course, the American school grew out of the desire of small communities to augment the teachings of the home and church by providing somewhat more formal opportunities (in classrooms) for agents of the community (teachers) to stimulate and guide the learning of young citizens.

As communities grew larger, the demands upon individuals became more complex and their educational needs grew in proportion. The American school grew larger and more complex. It offered a rapidly increasing variety of programs within its span of a 12-year public school system plus higher education, but the total educational needs of individuals proliferated at an even faster pace. No longer did the combination of family-taught precepts and formal schooling meet all the educational needs of all people in all their social and vocational relationships — and at all the ages of their lives.

It should be remembered that the American people have believed in education. When they, individually or collectively, have come face to face with a gap in their knowing, they have sought professional guidance of their efforts to solve their problems. As citizens and voters they have called upon their schools to transmit the knowledge, skills, and attitudes that would guarantee the American way of life — at its best — for everyone. The nation's educational leadership responded with a variety of reform movements intended to bring forth a more complete fulfillment of the American dream.

EARLY DEVELOPMENT OF THE COMMUNITY EDUCATION CONCEPT

The nineteenth century saw the work of such men as Horace Mann, Henry Barnard, and Caleb Mills who made the public schools more responsive to the conditions of their time. During the early years of the twentieth century a broader representation of the nation's educational leadership asked how the traditional system of formal schooling could be improved. In 1900 John Dewey was already writing from his experience in developing an experimental school at the University of Chicago. In his widely read *School and Society* was the sentence, "Learning certainly, but living primarily, and learning through and in relation to this living [p. 37]."

"Individualized instruction" became a watchword, and techniques developed by Carleton Washburne in the Winnetka, Illinois, schools were adopted widely. The "project method of instruction" was advocated by many educators, including William H. Kilpatrick of Teachers College, Columbia University, who recommended "projects" as a means of replacing textbook-centered subject matter with purposeful work through which students would use and master all essential learnings. "Progressive education" was given a strong voice through the Progressive Education Association; it became a controversial movement stimulating a variety of innovations and vigorous public interest in all the activities of the public schools.

In the meantime, from 1914 to 1917, the nation fought a war to make the world "safe for democracy." The high idealism of the post-World War I period was reflected in the books of such educators as Joseph K. Hart who wrote, in his *Discovery of Intelligence*, "Education is not apart from life . . . The democratic problem in education is not primarily a problem of training children; it is a problem of making a community [1924, p. 382]."

By the time of "the great depression" of the thirties, teachers, principals, curriculum supervisors, and superintendents had become well acquainted with the concepts of early twentieth-century educational reform through college classes and professional journals, and some of them had conducted experimental programs in their own schools during the decade of the twenties. Experimentation was considered evidence of professional competence; innovation was rewarded with journalistic attention. When innovation became an economic necessity, many of these teachers and administrators were ready with skills and enthusiasm to implement the need.

The stock market collapsed in 1929; businesses failed and jobs disappeared. The banks closed in 1931. The country was partially paralyzed by the economic disaster. People were forced to apply their knowledge and inventiveness to the resources they could find in their immediate vicinities. The local community became, abruptly, the setting for a dramatic human struggle to survive.

Emergence of the Community School

Many communities turned to the schools for leadership during the emergency. The schools had buildings and equipment which were centrally located for the convenience of families; they also had a staff of teachers and administrators, some of whom were acquainted with innovation. The results were varied, but the pattern was being worked out by individual schools and communities as they cooperated in planning and using their combined resources to solve community problems. The pattern appealed to leaders of communities throughout the nation.

Samuel Everett edited a book which dealt with the "community school" as it was defined in the thirties. This book, *The Community School* (1938) provided detailed reports on techniques used in school-community problem-solving programs with examples drawn from community-wide programs in the states of Washington, Georgia, California, Missouri, and Michigan. The student-made community study figured prominently in this material. For example, the junior and senior

21

high school students of Seattle studied the city, state, and region in which they lived. The first unit of the course was an airplane trip which took students out of the classroom into the sky and let them see the contours of land and water and the appearance of urban occupancy – a youth-capturing approach to community study.

The South – especially the rural South – recognized school-community cooperation as a practical step toward more effective use of limited resources to solve serious economic and educational problems. In 1929 Elsie Clapp agreed to direct, as principal of the Ballard School near Louisville, Kentucky, an "experiment in rural education [Clapp, 1940, p. 6]" which developed during the next five years into one of the early community schools. In fact, the opening sentence of the report on this program states confidently, "It was in Kentucky that we came to an understanding of the nature and functioning of a community school [1940, p. 3]."

The federal government recognized the special emergency in the South by establishing in 1933, in addition to many work programs, the Tennessee Valley Authority as a planned program of conservation, resource-use, and stimulation through educational programs of a more stable and prosperous life in the area. The Highlander Folk School of Summerfield, North Carolina, attempted to improve the economic position of the community's mountain farms by establishing a cooperative. Soon after a federal grant of $7000 had been acquired to help pay initial expenses, protests from angry citizens, including a labor union, caused the grant to be withdrawn. Students and teachers refused to be defeated, won the support of organized labor, and brought about the needed economic improvement plus "a strong upsurge in community morale [Everett, pp. 265-297]."

Residents of cities saw, in several instances, school-community cooperation as an educational necessity. Paul J. Misner described the "community educational center," which he was directing during the middle thirties in Glencoe, Illinois, as including in its membership all persons living within the community. This community education center provided the means by which "the needs and responsibilities of the community may be formulated in relation to the demands of a changing civilization for the continuous growth and enrichment of children and adults in the Glencoe community [Everett, p. 80]." Frank J. Manley, who had gone to the Flint, Michigan, public school system as physical education instructor in 1927, saw children after school hours playing in the city streets while the school playgrounds remained not only empty but closed. His role in securing financial assistance from Charles S. Mott and in guiding early developments in the Flint community schools has become well known (Minardo, 1972, p. 13).

While the few leaders whose names have become synonymous with community education were starting their work, many others whose names have been forgotten were working in classrooms and in administrative positions to implement an idea which was taking shape in the unique mixture of economic emergency and philosophical idealism that characterized the thirties. Few periods in American history have shown so clearly that ingenuity carries no consistent relationship to financial affluence.

Recognition of the Community School

When World War II precipitated another national emergency, a large number of communities responded with school-community cooperation. People of specific communities discovered, for example, that the leadership of school administrators and teachers did help a community handle rationing of scarce foodstuffs and gasoline more effectively. And the same school-community cooperation proved to be vital as a learning procedure for elementary and secondary school students. When the school stayed open for adult evening classes and volunteer war service projects, and when the school library served all members of the community — whatever their ages — the community school was again serving in a time of national emergency. Many different kinds of communities found they could use the cooperative procedure. The plain logic of the educational possibilities in such cooperation caught the attention of philanthropists and of many other socially-sensitive leaders. Several of them helped community schools directly and enlisted the help of government, national educational associations, and various other educational agencies in promoting the community school idea.

Toward the end of the war years, individuals responsible for educational planning at the national level looked ahead to a new day. After the war the mistakes of the past could, perhaps, be corrected. The year 1945 saw the publication of a two-volume study, *American*

Education in the Postwar Period, by the National Society for the Study of Education. The editor expressed the sense of mission which educational leaders were feeling at that time in his opening sentence of the Preface: "It is the purpose of the present yearbook to provide the most serviceable guidance possible for the replanning of educational programs that will obviously be required to meet postwar demands upon the schools [Henry, p. V.]."

A large number of references to school and community cooperation appeared throughout the two volumes. For example, H. T. Morse wrote, "Cooperative planning of the many different agencies is to be encouraged on as broad a scale as possible [Part I, p. 54]." George Gant wrote that resource-use education must use "the community . . . as a laboratory [for the study of] man's unsuccessful adjustment to the natural environment [Part I, p. 199]."

The title of one chapter in the two volumes was "Community School Emphases in Postwar Education." In it the present writer described two distinctive emphases, "service to the entire community, not merely to the children of school age; and discovery, development, and use of the resources of the community as part of the educational facilities of the school [Part I, p. 209]."

In Part II, which was primarily concerned with structural reorganization, Chester S. Williams insisted that the postwar school must go beyond its limited sphere into the community and provide leadership in an unostentatious promotion of incentives for adult learning [pp. 76-77]." And Agnes Samuelson wrote, "The reconstruction of the educational program in terms of changing curricular emphases and new groups to be served brings into focus the relationships of the schools to other agencies rendering educational and social services [p. 187]."

The immediate postwar years of the late forties saw a development of interest in the community school which justified references to a "community school movement."

The interest could be expected to flourish in professional groups of educators, but several organizations which were not primarily educational in their purposes devoted issues of their publications to the subject. For example, Community Service, Inc., an organization formed by the well-known engineer, A. E. Morgan, to promote the interests of the community as a basic social institution, devoted its September-October 1953 issue of *Community Service News* to "The Community School."

One article in the periodical mentioned in the preceding paragraph holds special interest because of light it throws on the evolutionary nature of the community education concept. This article, "The School in the Community" had been written twelve years earlier — just before World War II — by Howard Y. McClusky of the University of Michigan; it had first appeared in the April 1941 issue of *The North Central Association Quarterly*. In it McClusky wrote:

> To fasten the whole burden of education on the school is to delegate to a part of society that which only society as a whole can achieve. . .This. . .does not propose that the functions which society is trying to pass on to the school are not legitimate objects of education, nor does it mean that the school should not share some responsibility for them. It merely illuminates the nature of the relationship which the school should maintain. To elaborate: The school may well be the most important single agency in society to improve the community, but the primary function of the school should be that of helping the community to help itself. The community school then becomes the instrument whereby the superior resources of the community are mobilized for self-improvement. It becomes a catalytic agent and coordinator. It would help the community discover, funnel its power into extra-school agencies. Thus the school must work **in** and **with** the community and only **for** the community when it can contribute some unique service which no other agency possesses [1953, pp. 150-151].

Two different kinds of organizations for the study of education, the NSSE and the Educational Policies Commission of the National Education Association, were among the professional groups which devoted time and money to extensive research on the community school role. Publication of the findings of their studies appeared in the early fifties.

The 1953 NSSE yearbook, Part II, was entitled *The Community School*. Seventeen chapters dealt with distinctive features such as the program, the staff, organization and administration, international examples, and overcoming barriers to the development of community schools. Since several references will be made to this publication later in this chapter and in other chapters, more specific references will be omitted here.

The Educational Policies Commission published, in 1954, a 42-page brochure entitled *Strengthening Community Life*. The small size tended to hide the thoroughness of a year's study and the quality of a carefully written report. Prominent educators made the study, choosing six community schools to be the evidence that schools could be and had been instrumental in helping people develop stronger communities. One was the Pasadena, Texas, Independent School District which had helped to meet the problems associated with mushroom growth from farming community to suburban industrial community. Another was the Philadelphia school system which played a prominent role after 1947 in the city's struggle to become "a strong constellation of improving communities in which citizens, teachers, and pupils work together in building community [p. 31]." A third was the Norristown Community, a small rural area in Georgia. A fourth was Lyons Falls, New York, where a community council brought new life to a village of 1200 people; and a fifth was Mesick, Michigan, mentioned earlier as one community cooperating in the Michigan "Community School Service Program." The sixth was the Bronx Park Community Project in New York where the leaders found they must build on a feeling of community, as well as a school-community organization.

Increasing Polarization of Viewpoints

The high hope of the late forties faltered during the uneasy years of the American "cold war." Russia's Sputnik brought fear reactions in the United States, and pressure grew from citizens who thought the schools should be more efficient, more "accountable." Financial incentives were used to increase the number of scientists and mathematicians prepared in the schools. But the Supreme Court decision of 1954 also came during those uneasy years. Many people recognized that it was time to "play fair" with black-skinned people. Other minority groups were recognized. And the issue of racial equality opened the door for other humanitarian issues. Clean air began to seem more important than three cars at every back door. A nation paved with concrete began to look undesirable. Human beings reached a self-conscious understanding of the fact that male and female were equally human. Their elders were pictured in a newly humanitarian press as people also. Social upheaval in the sixties demonstrated the fact that the economic and political views of the American people were pulling away from the center of the statistical curve and grouping toward the two ends: the somewhat extreme positions of (a) human needs subordinated to technological needs; and (b) technological needs subordinated to human needs.

Polarization of educational viewpoints became recognizable. One influential group of leaders in government, the military, and business and industry demanded that education agencies serve the national expansionist needs in areas of bigger defense, bigger technology, and an annual increase in the gross national product. "Bigger and better" was assumed to be one of the tenets of natural law.

Another influential group of leaders represented humanitarian interests such as civil rights and protection of the ecology. "Bigger is not better!" was one of many slogans used to persuade the public toward a more humanistic point of view. And these leaders pleaded with educational agencies to transmit the humane values in the American culture along with the technological skills.

Emergence of the Community Education Concept

Certainly the community school was concerned with humane values and humanitarian issues. Educators and other community leaders turned to it as the educational answer to increasingly complex problems. By the sixties, however, communities had become increasingly urbanized and their members were more expectant of educational services in great variety for everybody throughout his life cycle. And larger numbers of agencies appeared with educational programs aimed toward diverse education needs within the community.

The community school concept had always recognized the programs of other educational agencies in the community, but in the sixties educators began to see the school as one among many

27

educational agencies. Obviously, they said, education is a comprehensive thing, a social institution. Community leaders began to think in terms of community-wide, institutionalized forces which were performing — and could be expected to perform better — the functions society entrusted to education. They saw that the time had come for the school-centered concept to grow into a community education concept.

SIGNIFICANT THREADS FROM
THE COMMUNITY SCHOOL MOVEMENT[1]

As the concept of community education evolved, it incorporated many threads that ran through the community school movement. The various kinds of publications appearing between 1938 and 1954 which have been reviewed in this chapter — and others not mentioned here — support the selection of the following six threads as significant ideas in the movement.

1. The community school recognized in actual programming the basic fact that education is a continuous process.

2. Educational objectives were stated in terms of desired changes in behavior.

3. Educational activities, supported by appropriate instructional materials, were based upon the problems, needs, and interests of those for whom they were planned.

4. The school served the community and the community served the school.

5. A local community provided a focal point for understanding other, larger communities of people.

6. The community school challenged school and community leaders.

These threads are as clear and strong in community education today as they were in the community school. When they are applied to community education, however, the phrase "educational agencies" or "institutional forces" should be substituted for the word "school." The

1. An earlier reference to "Threads" was published in the *Community Education Journal*, 1972, pp. 16-19.

following commentary on the educational reasoning and practice involved in each of these six significant threads from the community school movement probes more deeply into the philosophical development of the community education concept.

Education a Continuous Process

In Everett's 1938 report of community school programs, he wrote, "An analysis of the programs presented in this book indicates that an acceptance of the community approach to education involves the acceptance of fundamental positions in both educational and social theory.... All life is educative.... Education requires participation .... Adults and children have fundamental common purposes in both work and play.... Public-school systems should be primarily concerned with the improvement of community living and the improvement of the social order [pp. 435-442]." Everett urged teacher-preparatory institutions to prepare youth and adults to carry on a community type of public education.

Also reported in 1938 was a unique educational experience in the Tennessee River Valley where the TVA was helping the people of the region develop their economic future and their social institutions as well as controlling the river's flood stage and producing a by-product: electrical power. As director of the Training Division of the Authority from 1934 to 1937, the present writer described the first four years of the educational program. TVA needed electricians, for example, but the residents of the Valley were farmers. Training began before any construction work could start — training in all of the skills needed for the tremendous task that was ahead. And at the same time elementary and secondary schools and adult programs were established for all the families in the new communities. Pressed for immediate action and staffed with trainers and teachers, innovation was inevitable. The guide was an educational philosophy which all shared. The following excerpt indicates the kind of philosophy it was:

An electrician does not have an 'education' to make him an electrician, another 'education' to cause him to use his leisure time profitably. An electrician has *an* education to which all of his experiences contribute ... [This concept] does not eliminate study of specialized subject matter or practice in highly technical skills, but it relegates such study to a subordinate position — a part of the whole educational process for an individual ... The conception that education is continuous is, of course, not new. However, the application of this conception is to a planned program of education for all age levels of a community has seldom been attempted [Seay, p. 46-47].

Seven years later (1945) Edward G. Olsen wrote in the preface to his book, *School and Community*, "From many sources one learns that all life is educative." The view of education as a continuous process was accepted quite generally after the thirties. Schooling patterns became somewhat more diverse, but the most dramatic evidence appeared after World War II with the development and proliferation of adult education, continuing education, and the two-year community college. The community school had played a pioneering role as it implemented the idea with programs of school-community problem solving.

Formulation of Objectives in Terms of Behavior

Learning is a highly personal process. The learner perceives a problem and applies available resources to its solution. He learns from working out his solution. People of all ages learn when they recognize problems and apply available resources to their solution. In this process human behavior is changed. Educators, therefore, plan educational programs in terms of the behavior change that can be expected to result from specific learning experiences.

The community school grew out of direct efforts to help people meet problems. The economic emergency of the early thirties, for example, called attention to the fact that many people were going through hungry winters because they had no way of preserving the quantities of food they were growing in the summer. Schools could get money to equip canneries, so a school-community partnership developed around these canneries. The objective was, at first, canning food that people could eat during the winter. Later, the objective included new skills to make canning safer and more successful. School leaders realized that other educational objectives could be served through this cooperative relationship between the school and the people of the community, and classes were organized to help people solve other problems. The teaching objectives began to be "appreciation of literature" or "understanding political processes," or perhaps, "improved family communication."

The people of the community — those who were of school age and those who were not — were urged to use the school library after they had finished canning their surplus food and when they came to the school for community meetings or regular classes. They were also urged to enjoy the recreational activities sponsored by the school. In each case the educational objective was some kind of change in behavior. And these objectives were far from superficial. The writer has referred to a change in behavior as "a change that permeates the whole fiber of the individual. It becomes part and parcel of his body of understanding as well as of his basic way of doing things [Seay, 1953, p. 8]."

Community school leaders of the thirties, forties, and fifties recognized that an educational objective requiring changed behavior could be achieved only through the learner's participation in learning experiences related to the solving of problems — preferably the problems found in the learner's own experiencing of community life. Community educators of today agree with them.

Selection of Educational Activities

Ralph W. Tyler, in *Basic Principles of Curriculum and Instruction* (1950), refined into classic definitions some of the mid-century professional thought on the educative process and learning behavior. He referred to "the interaction between the learner and the external conditions in the environment to which he can react [p. 41]" as a learning experience. Skillful selection of learning experiences gave a student an opportunity to practice the kind of behavior implied by the results expected. And in addition to providing practice, well-selected learning experiences gave a student satisfactions from carrying on the kind of behavior implied by the results expected. Of course, the selected experiences must be within the range of possibility for the student involved, and many particular experiences could be used to attain the same results.

The community school implemented the educative process with straight-forward attacks upon real problems. For example, a project might involve a major community problem of sanitation. Students acquired valuable skills, values, and insights while working on the major problem. They (a) collected facts concerning the problem and the related resources in their community; (b) set up demonstrations and experiments attempting to find answers to various aspects of their problem; (c) participated in group deliberations involving study, reporting, planning, and decision-making; (d) observed other community situations, discussed recognized problems, and considered ways of solving them; (e) worked on individual and group projects bearing on a selected sub-problem; and (f) used a variety of instructional materials to find and organize a solution to the major problem.

A community school usually did not relinquish subject-matter organization of curriculum when it planned a program built upon local problems and resources. It merely shifted emphasis. English was still taught, but taught through use in problem-solving and with the understanding that it would be used by the learners in further problem-solving. Language, science, and arithmetic provided knowledge that gained much value in direct application.

Varied and interesting materials were found in the search for information that would help solve the problem at hand. Other materials were developed when a special need called for them. The instructional materials were usually of four types: (a) commercially-produced materials such as textbooks, library books, and films; (b) special-purpose materials designed to meet specific needs with specific resources in mind (Public Health Department bulletins, for example); (c) school-made materials prepared by teachers and pupils as part of their study of local problems (posters, collections, exhibits); (d) the physical and cultural environment of the community school (the brick of a 100-year-old building and the ruins of the local brickyard where the brick had been fired, or the retired Congressman who was happy to describe certain intricate steps in the functioning of local, state and federal government).

One experiment which studied the effect of special-purpose instructional materials upon community problems of food, clothing, and shelter was the Project in Applied Economics, sponsored by the Sloan Foundation. The part of the experiment related to dietary practices was administered by the University of Kentucky and functioned approximately ten years (1939-1949). This part became known as "The Sloan Experiment in Kentucky."

Various threads of the community school movement ran through the Sloan Experiment. For example, among the basic assumptions upon which the experimental procedure was built were:

1.   School programs which emphasize community problems are effective for teaching skills of learning.

2.   If children are to receive the ultimate benefits from a program of education in community problems, instruction should begin in the first school year and should continue throughout the period of schooling. All children should be taught, as early as possible, the resources available for solution of their problems.

3.   Recruiting and utilizing local resources and abilities would contribute towards the success of the experiment [adapted from Seay & Meece, 1944, p. 10].

During the first year of the experiment in Kentucky, a need for instructional materials was recognized. The textbooks in use at the experimental schools included some topics related to food, but an analysis of the textbooks revealed that the content was general and often impractical for rural areas. Those who were guiding the experiment agreed that "if children are to learn how to live success-fully . . . they must have instructional materials . . . concerning problems of their community and the local resources available for improvement of living in the community [Seay & Meece, 1944, p. 19]." The major emphasis of the experiment became the preparation and evaluation of new instructional materials focused upon a community problem and the resources available for the solution of that problem. By the year 1945 the Kentucky center had produced 39 readers which were used to supplement the textbooks at the elementary level already in use in the experimental schools. The authors of these readers were the regular teachers who had been teaching in these schools. They took a leave of absence, came to the center, and were assisted in their writing by a professional editor.

In 1945 the Project in Applied Economics, which sponsored experiments at that time in Florida and Vermont as well as in Kentucky, prepared materials on food, clothing, and shelter to be used in English and social studies classes. That experience was reported by Hillis (1948) in *The Preparation and Evaluation of Instructional Materials on Community Agencies.*

Travers (1973) described the rationale for the emphasis on special-purpose instructional materials in the Sloan Experiment. He wrote:

> The underlying idea was that the children would take home information that they might discuss with their parents, and that the parents in turn would heed the advice [and practical information] given. The materials were designed . . . to have impact on the quality of life in the community and were not limited to materials of literary interest alone . . . . The plan would have been a credit even to today's scientists who live in an age that has seen the development of sophistication in the field of evaluation [pp. 986-987].

Travers also categorized as the same type of experimentation in a more recent project, *The Alaskan Readers,* developed under the auspices of the Northwest Regional Educational Laboratory. He comments:

> The development of the readers was based on the analysis of the skills to be learned, a theory of the development of grapheme-phoneme relationships, the identification of culturally relevant materials, the careful selection of decoding exercises, and so forth [p. 985].

The Battle Creek School System (Michigan), under the direction of Superintendent Harry R. Davidson, has a unique plan for supplementing the regular textbooks with school-made instructional materials. A teacher with ability and interest in writing has been allocated released time from teaching to prepare readers containing descriptions of important Battle Creek industries, institutions, and problems. Some titles of these readers, which are used at different grade levels, are: *Battle Creek, Cereal Capital of the World; Battle Creek City Government; Township and County Government in the Battle Creek Area; Federal Government in the Battle Creek Area; Home Ownership in Battle Creek.*

The determination of the proper balance in the use of the four types of instructional materials, listed in a preceding paragraph, is a task for each school. Many community schools found the planning toward a better balance of such materials to be excellent in-service education for teachers. Materials-preparation projects were established; and these teacher-made materials were sought eagerly by those who taught in other community schools. New school-community relationships were initiated. Libraries were strengthened by the addition of several kinds of materials, and teachers comprehended more clearly the meaning of the term, "community school."

Reciprocation of Service between School and Community

The Community School Movement viewed school-community cooperation as a two-way street. The school helped solve community problems and the community provided resources for the instructional program of the school. Of the six "significant threads" this perhaps was the one most publicized during the forties. The stories of several of the early community schools appeared in inexpensive brochures which circulated widely among teachers and administrators of that period — particularly among those who were emphasizing or wished to emphasize similar kinds of problem-solving in their own school system. Such brochures featured case histories of innovative, reciprocal programs. The following examples are illustrative.

Parker High School Serves Its People was written by the faculty of the Parker District High School in Greenville, South Carolina. The brochure was published in 1942 with assistance from the Southern Association of Colleges and Secondary Schools. An introduction listed extensive plant facilities which accommodated 1400 school-age youth and many adults of the community. A caption explaining two excellent photographs, which showed people of varying ages working as operators and maintainers of large looms, said, "One part of the school's Vocational Department is equipped as a small cotton mill where pupils and adults are trained. Pupils from these courses are prepared to go on the job in one of the community textile mills [p. 2b]."

In addition to these facilities, the pupils in the high school were encouraged to find and use other educational facilities in the district and in the City of Greenville. By using the school bus, pupils were able to visit institutions throughout Greater Greenville. They went into mills, foundries, packing houses, and gas and electric plants; they inspected farms near the school; they visited banks, the post office and the various social agencies. In other words, they studied the life of their community. A faculty member said, "More and more the community is becoming our school. As we try to meet the varied needs of the boys and girls in our school, we find ourselves turning to the community for help; and as we do so, we see numerous opportunities for helping our students by assisting them to become an important part of the community and of its efforts to improve [p. 60]."

Similarly, *The Story of Holtville*, published in 1944, described developments from 1938 to 1943, the years during which Holtville Consolidated School in Deatsville, Alabama, participated in the community school study made by the Southern Association of Colleges and Secondary Schools. Two questions were given particularly revealing answers in the brochure: (a) How were the teachers prepared for the new program? and (b) How were funds secured to equip and maintain new buildings and services?

The sixteen Holtville teachers were typical of the teaching staff of the average rural Alabama consolidated school of 150 elementary and 350 high school students. Most of them had received college training in Alabama institutions. Five had earned M.A. degrees. Their salaries were slightly below the state average, which in 1940, was $1031 per year. But the relationship between principal and teachers was good; democratic ways of working had developed among teachers and students. Although the program of the school was conventional before 1938, students were sharing in making some plans and decisions, particularly those affecting extra-curricular activities. And for several years before 1938 the students had maintained an excellent record in scholarship as shown by tests and by the achievement of those who went on to college. This evidence of student ability and productive teaching was an important factor in the confident attitude throughout the school which was necessary for participation in an experimental program. Students and teachers also knew their community had confidence in the school. The teachers accepted the new way of working as a challenge. They studied, held many faculty meetings, and spent a great deal of extra time on their school work. Members of the staff of the Southern Association Study assisted by working with faculty and students throughout the school year and during the summer.

Funds were indeed limited at Holtville. The brochure quotes the Principal as saying, "We are constantly harassed by money matters and always at work on ways to make ends meet [p. 165]." The school tried to make use of all available resources, particularly those of Federal agencies such as the Farm Security Administration and the National Youth Administration. The faculty, student body, and people in the community found ways to raise money. For example, one group of boys set up a barber shop; a group of girls opened a beauty parlor. But the need to expand school facilities pressed constantly.

Attention should be called to the fact that the Holtville School did not continue to operate services or industries after they were established and the accompanying financial arrangements had been fulfilled. Such "going" businesses were released to the community. Some further expansion included a large frame building which was built to provide room for a photography group, space for a community tractor and power-spraying machine, a printing room, a woodwork shop, a refrigeration plant, and a hatchery. It was not long before a group of students and teachers had discovered a need in the community for a canning plant. A wing was added to the new building to provide for this service to the community. Later the school built a building for arts and crafts, a pottery plant, a junior high school home economics cottage, and houses and pens for a quail-raising project. Sometimes when new materials or equipment proved expensive, money was obtained from some department on the campus which was receiving money for services rendered, or money was borrowed on the assumption that the new department could be made self-supporting through its services.

A Michigan "Community School Service Program" was described in Chapter One in connection with the support given the community school idea by the W. K. Kellogg Foundation. Of interest here are the kinds of specific improvements made in eight local communities during the years of the Program, 1945-1953. The improvements were the results of coordination of various local agencies and local interests, and of many hours of committee work. Examples were the Hobby House in Concord, the industrial survey in Elkton, the Health Center in Mesick, the playground in Rockford, the truck-drivers' school in Stephenson, and the home-crafts industry in the Grand Traverse Area, (Described in Seay and Crawford, 1954, pp. 177-78).

Several brochures represented a regional emphasis in school-community reciprocation, while others emphasized planning for wise use of natural and human resources. Frequently the two emphases appeared together as they did in *Learning by Living*, a report on a "Resource-Use Education Project," published in 1959 by the Southern States Work Conference and the Committee on Southern Regional Studies and Education. Teamwork was the theme. The preface of the report explained that literally thousands of teachers, pupils, administrators, supervisors, and other leaders were involved in the school and community programs which were described. The programs themselves ranged from a study of fire danger in the forest surrounding a school (which led various classes to gather materials and eventually to plant ten acres of the school campus in pine trees) to "Lollypops: a study in nutrition [p. 14]."

Another type of publication appearing frequently in the early fifties represented industry-education cooperation. Usually these brochures were financed by a cooperating industry and were prepared by a public relations firm after consultation with community school leaders who were working with the local industry to solve certain community problems.

The United States Office of Education published several bulletins directed toward encouraging the development of community schools. Bulletin No. 5, published in 1951, followed the pattern of the earlier, locally published brochures by describing the town of East Hampton, Connecticut, delineating the more unusual of the school activities, and explaining that "the school is a meeting center for many local organizations, for all town meetings and town businesses; the doors are open at all times for its continued use by the townspeople. In like manner the facilities of the factories, the bank, the foundry, and local government are open to the use of school children. These agencies have helped immeasurably to develop in the children an understanding of their own community and an increasing participation in community life [p. 3]."

Comprehension of Other, Larger Communities

Leaders of the community school movement believed that a neighborhood provided a logical focus for the study of specific problems of the home community, the state, the region, the nation, and the world. The need for starting a learning activity with a concept or perception already familiar to the learner had long been recognized by teachers. They knew that learners comprehended new information more readily when they could relate it to known information. Thus, students could deal with problems at the state, national, and world levels more adequately when they had used various kinds of problem-solving techniques in dealing with the real problems of their familiar neighborhood.

Paul Hanna (1953, p. 233) diagrammed this idea as a series of concentric circles. He explained that each neighborhood, unique among all the thousands upon thousands of such communities throughout the world, is the common center for all the concentric-circle communities which lie outside. A community school holds membership in all of these communities — and is a member of all of them simultaneously. A community school, therefore, "while properly devoting a larger share of time and effort to the home community, will not neglect its responsibility in improving living in the state, the regional, the national, and the world communities [1953, p. 235]."

The 1954 statement of the Educational Policies Commission, mentioned earlier, emphasized the necessity for building strong local communities as a means of safeguarding the American way of life. The statement warned:

Although we have grown beyond the local community, we have not outgrown our need for it. In the twentieth-century world the individual still finds his focus in a locale. Indeed he cannot serve best as a citizen of broader communities-of-living without the home base of a strong local community. Modern man needs the personal touch in his day-to-day relationships — a touch that can best be given by face-to-face contacts in the places where he lives and works [p. 4].

Recognition of Challenge

The community school concept challenged administrators and teachers to stimulate ideas which the people of the community could recognize as valid. Leaders also were challenged to recognize ideas which members of the community brought to them. The challenge demanded that leaders plan, listen for feedback, act and then listen for more feedback; and then repeat this process patiently in increasingly complex combinations.

Planning meant working with students, with parents, with representatives of other agencies, with many different interest groups in the community. It meant getting them interested, informed, involved — and it always meant listening to them. The ideas, feelings, background information, and even the prejudices of the people of all ages from all parts of the community played a part in the work of the community school leader.

Harold D. Drummond wrote in 1953 that the desired interaction between the school program and community life could be achieved by a professional staff which had "the qualities of mind and spirit which are possessed by good teachers everywhere. Supermen are not required. . . . Through cooperative pooling of abilities, the professional staff of the community school makes the best possible use of each individual's capacities [p. 106]."

Ruth Strang (1953) discussed a "good" leader's group-work skills, commenting that the leader does not obscure the real significance of the discussion by "forcing the members' statements into inappropriate categories . . . . The leader helps all the members to feel free and easy; he focuses attention on the goal they want to attain; he helps certain members to think more specifically and to the point; he does not evaluate or judge their remarks, although he may sharpen, emphasize, and relate the ideas they express [p. 173]."

Democratic procedures were used by community school leaders because such procedures were more practicable for helping groups of people work out solutions to real problems. And because of such democracy in action, the programs of the community school were remarkably relevant. The democratic method of achieving group action was found to be an effective method when it made use of the following three conditions:

1. The group is willing to use an expert or a consultant whose opinion or recommendations are weighed on their merits.

2. The group will, before making a decision, consider facts as secured from surveys, from such agencies as public health, city planning commissions, Agriculture Extension, and of course the Census Bureau.

3. There is an atmosphere or climate of feeling that causes each member of the group to be free to express his opinions and his interpretation of facts without any fear of reprisal by those in power or any fear of embarrassment in the presence of those who do not agree with his viewpoints.

The community school challenged leaders to be innovative. They had to be innovative in the beginning of the period between 1930 and 1960 because they were working with a new, untried idea. Innovation invited criticism, of course, from those who preferred traditional ways or who had vested interests in the status quo and from all those who feared change. Community school leaders were accused of rocking the boat. But the boat had to be rocked. Social change was then as inevitable as it had been before. If schools were to function in a changing society, community school leaders were challenged to go out into their communities and learn to know the issues and the people so well that they could, working in cooperation with other leaders, bring constructive action out of the criticism and disturbance.

Leaders discovered that the use of democratic procedures, with careful evaluation of feedback, actually worked. The democratic method of achieving group action produced close school-community relationships. People learned to see real community needs, and they learned to plan, support, and carry out solutions to real problems. People also learned that their state, nation, and world faced problems — community school leaders believed that procedures used for solving local problems could and would be used by the people of the community for dealing with such matters as war and peace, land utilization, problems of state and national government and of human justice.

Idealism colors much that is written and spoken about educational leadership. The leadership of community schools and community education has been subjected to a particularly idealistic spelling out of goals; and an individual who is inclined to interpret statements literally could well be dismayed at what seems to be expected of him. It is true that a certain kind of magic is expected, but this does not mean that a community education leader has to be superman. What he does have to be is a believer in the power of education. A person with good, average ability can, when he is "turned on" by his vision of opportunity, be great.

SOME THOUGHTS ABOUT
THE PAST AND THE PRESENT

When community education is defined as a process which achieves a balance and a use of all institutional forces in the education of all the people of a community, a certain cooperation on the part of "all the people" is assumed. The process promises comprehensive opportunities to learn through solving real problems and assumes that people of all ages throughout our complex society will meet the challenge, will grasp the opportunity to learn. There are dependable indications that many people will. People tend toward being self-actualizing. People with open, inquiring minds recognize that they individually (and in their group) have problems, and they welcome educational help in bringing together the necessary resources to solve the problems.

Several aspects of the American experience suggest, however, that many people have learned other ways of responding to challenge. Those who plan the action of the community education process will need to recognize this fact if they are to plan realistically. They will need to understand the implications of the Ducktowns in the American experience.

Ducktown, Tennessee, offered three generations of Americans a particularly vivid lesson in ecology. That lesson lay along the side of a road in the mountainous corner of the state where the eastern border touches North Carolina and the southern border touches Georgia. The lesson was spread out over dozens of square miles for all the people to see — and the people drove by and looked. A generation later that lesson was described in forceful words for all the people to read — and the people read. Here is one of those descriptions:

> Industry came to Ducktown. . . .Copper ore was discovered; mining began; a smeltery was built. One of the resources of this remote region was being developed; it meant new jobs, income to supplement farming and forestry. But the developers had only copper in their plans. The magnificent hardwood forests to a distance of seven miles were cut and burned as fuel for the smelter's roasting ovens. The sulphur fumes from the stacks destroyed the thin cover that remained; not only the trees but every sign of living vegetation was killed and the soil became poison to life.

> The dead land, shorn of its cover of grass and trees, was torn mercilessly by the rains; and the once lovely and fruitful earth was cut into deep gullies that widened into desolate canyons twenty and more feet deep. No one can look upon this horror as it is today without a shudder. Silt, swept from unprotected slopes, filled the streams and destroyed fish life. The water was robbed of its value for men, for animals, and for industry, while farther down the stream a reservoir of a private power company was filling with silt. One of Ducktown's resources, copper, had been developed. But all its other resources had been destroyed in the process [Lilienthal, 1944, p. 53].

This Ducktown has been salvaged in recent years, but other Ducktowns horrify America today. The Ducktowns of polluted rivers and dying lakes, the Ducktowns of needless war, the Ducktowns of human slums — these Ducktowns are in every community today. And the problems they represent are not only spread out for everyone to see — they are growing. What are the implications of the Ducktowns in the American experience?

Philosophers seek to understand how this kind of destruction can happen among thinking human beings. Ducktown was not the only early example of destruction. Several generations of intelligent people have been looking at thousands of such lessons. Why did people not learn how to solve this kind of major societal problem? Why? Is it because the social institution of education had been failing through several generations to teach a few of civilization's most important lessons?

Will and Ariel Durant asked what determines whether a challenge will or will not be met and gave their own answer from their lifetime study of civilization. They said, " . . . the answer is that this [meeting the challenge] depends upon the presence or absence . . . of creative individuals with clarity of mind and energy of will. . .capable of effective response to new situations [1968, p. 91]."

Do people need more than an opportunity to learn from the lessons spread out before them? Has an increasingly complex society so complicated the motives of individuals and of groups that people must now be helped to learn new ways of understanding and of coping with their problems?

For many years the people from nearby Copperhill and Knoxville — and from other communities all over the United States — looked at Ducktown's disaster, read about it, were shocked; then they became used to the problem, turned their attention to other interests, and left Ducktown for someone else to solve. A homespun, unplanned variety of lifelong family-church-school and incidental education had taught the American people that there was nothing they could do except to remove themselves and their loved ones from the unpleasantness. Here and there, for short periods of time, community schools helped a few people to learn how to use community resources to solve community problems — and several individuals saw in this learning experience a process they and their group could use in attacking and solving other, larger problems.

The people as a whole, however, chose to leave the big problems to big organizations which, the people reasoned, had the knowledge, money, and authority to cope with such things. The unstudied, unplanned variety of lifelong education (which had served quite satisfactorily in an uncomplicated, predominantly rural society) had taught the American people that this was the way it was done in the United States. Nothing in their education had taught them that the basis for their reasoning was false. Nothing had taught them to know — to sense in every fiber of their being — that the authority was innately theirs to exercise through group process. Nor had their education taught them that working out a way to have industry without an industrial by-product of Ducktowns was a matter of life and death — for themselves, perhaps, and certainly for their children and grand-children.

Of course the people were scolded through all of this time because they did not, somehow, suddenly rise up and turn their communities and their nation into a beautiful Utopia. But they were also scolded into buying certain products, into paying more taxes, and into keeping their lawns free of crabgrass. The people could see how to do the small things, but they could not see any way to correct industry's bad habits without endangering their own paychecks. Thus the people became irresponsible as caretakers of their communities, not from lack of good intentions, but from lack of clear vision of their real self-interest and from lack of knowing how to use the power they had.

Will community education use its great opportunity for the purpose of merely transmitting a heritage of irresponsibility? Or will the leaders of community education sharpen the clarity of their own vision and help all the people to see more clearly — and to know how to do something about what they see?

Jack Minzey and Clyde LeTarte referred to "community self-actualization [which occurs] when a community is capable of the initiative and sustained action necessary for attacking and solving its own problems, and when it is moving in the direction of the fulfillment of individual and community needs and community potential [1972, p. 33]." And they pointed out that a community can become "self-actualized [p. 29]."

Four assumptions made by Minzey and LeTarte are listed as prerequisites for self-actualizing communities. Assuming (a) that communities are capable of positive change, (b) that social problems have solutions, (c) that one of the strongest forces for making change is community power, and (d) that community members are desirous of improving their communities and are willing to contribute their energies toward such ends — assuming those basic conditions, communities can fulfill their possibilities [adapted, pp. 32-33].

These far-reaching assumptions rest upon other assumptions. It must be assumed, for example, that "positive change" is change in the direction of meeting the truly major, long-range interests of the people of a community and of the larger communities of which they are also members. It must also be assumed that people can determine their most important individual and group interests in a complex and changing society.

Community education offers the best hope now visible in American society for developing these assumptions into foundations for sustained action upon complex societal problems. And the success of community education depends upon "clarity of mind and energy of will," to use the words of the Durants. Clarity of mind, particularly, is essential, and that quality among the members of groups of people is largely dependent upon education.

The challenge to leaders who are guiding the process of community education is one of the great challenges of contemporary civilization. Today the local community is a complex unit. Leadership today is a more complicated function than it was in the communities of Parker District High School and of Holtville. But the principles of leadership are similar. If a leader is to understand his role and its vast opportunities, he needs to understand and apply substantiated theory. The explanation in Chapter Four of a theory of educational leadership and the discussion of leadership training in Chapter Five are applicable to school and community leadership in the process of today's community education.

CHAPTER III

INSTITUTIONS, COMMUNITIES, AND
THE AGENCIES OF COMMUNITY EDUCATION

INSTITUTIONS, COMMUNITIES, AND THE AGENCIES OF COMMUNITY EDUCATION

HAROLD W. BOLES
AND
MAURICE F. SEAY

> True education ... emerges from an understanding of the social order and of the nature of man, and from no other source.
>
> — Sizer (1972, p. 34)

Community education leaders and potential leaders should have an understanding of the social order and of the nature of man. They must see the society in which they function in terms of its institutions and of the agencies which, in their local communities, carry out the functions of the education institution. A definition of institution is a starting point.

DEFINITION OF INSTITUTION

Like every other society, American communities have many institutions, but the term is used so loosely and with such varied meanings that some agreement on a definition seems essential.

Common Usage

If one says that a person spent some time in a mental institution, everyone knows that the word "institution" indicates a specific *type of place*. An article to the effect that the institution of penology needs drastic overhaul makes it clear that the reference is to a *total philosophical idea and the agencies responsible for it*. A comment that Wall Street represents the financial institution is interpreted to mean that a specific agency is representative of certain institutional *transactions*.

If the University of Notre Dame is said to be an institution that almost invariably fields a good football squad, it is evident that institution means a particular *physical plant*. Savings and Loan Associations are understood to be a part of the institution of banking, and thus the word "institution" is equated with particular *practices*.

Most adults cope with many uses of the word "institution" without a second thought as to its ambiguousness. Yet, if people are asked whether it is learning, education, schooling, teaching, instructing, or training that society has institutionalized, most are unable to reply. Even most educators do not know because they have never thought seriously about the matter; nor do most of them have any criteria by which to judge. To establish criteria, educators may find it helpful to consider the definition of social institutions according to sociologists.

Sociologists' Definition

According to Eisenstadt (1968): Social institutions are usually conceived of as the basic focuses of social organization, common to all societies and dealing with some of the basic universal problems of ordered social life. Three basic aspects of institutions are emphasized. First, the patterns of behavior which are regulated by institutions ["institutionalized"] deal with some perennial, basic problems of any society. Second, institutions involve the regulation of behavior of individuals in society according to some definite, continuous, and organized patterns. Finally, these patterns involve a definite normative ordering and regulation: that is, regulation is upheld by norms and by sanctions which are legitimized by these norms [p. 409].

Sociologists usually list five to ten spheres of influence, or *social institutions*, in which regulative principles structure the activities of individuals into definite organizational patterns. Of these social institutions, the most common are the domestic, the economic, the educational, the political and the religious. Some persons substitute either the occult or the scientific for the religious institution, depending upon the individual and the culture.

The functions for which social institutions have primary responsibility vary in number from seven or eight to twenty or more. Some of the more important of these, along with the present writers' judgment of which institutions are responsible for them in United States society today, are shown in Table 3-1. The functions of the educational institution should be particularly noted.

Criteria for Institutions

Institutions constitute a part of the basic organization of society and are essential to the existence of order in it. If one accepts as criteria for an institution the regulation of individual behavior, the ritualization of that behavior, and the existence of norms to which sanctions are attached, five facts become evident that are not clear from Eisenstadt's definition. One, the matter of values is involved, otherwise norms could not exist; two, the term institution is used to refer to: (a) general patterns of expectations for social behavior, and (b) individual groups in which this behavior is embodied; three, there is great overlap of responsibility among institutions; four, any major social institution functions through one or more agencies; and five, any social change requires alteration of one or more major social institutions.

Definition Used Herein

An idea, practice, or belief must be valued by an individual or a group if it is to be continued. The child who repeatedly engages in a particular type of play must find sufficient satisfaction in the activity to wish to repeat it, or he will choose another activity instead. The same is true of the teenager who takes drugs or the adult who engages in volunteer hospital work.

51

Table 3-1. SOCIAL INSTITUTIONS AND THEIR FUNCTIONS

SOCIETAL FUNCTION	INSTITUTION AND RESPONSIBILITY				
	Domestic	Economic	Educational	Political	Religious
Produce new members	1				
Individualize each member	1		1		2
Give each member a sense of purpose	2		3		1
Relate each member to society	1		2		3
Maintain order in the society				1	
Distribute influence & power		2	3	1	
Produce & distribute goods, services, & satisfactions		1			
Relate each member to his physical environment	2		3		1
Teach kinship	1		3		2

Key: 1—indicates a primary responsibility for a function.
    2 or 3—indicates a secondary or tertiary responsibility for a function.

A society that cares enough, individually and collectively, about having the young learn what the elders know makes provisions for learning activities. Importance must attach to having others experience satisfactions that adults have experienced or they will make no provision for the creation and preservation of artifacts which transmit some record of their experience, such as sculpture, paintings, and books. Repetition and perpetuation require effort, loyalty, and commitment; people devote effort and give loyalty or commitment only to what they value for some reason. The fact that they may not be aware of the reason does not really matter.

The reason for institutionalization, therefore, is that members of some group value something enough to make attempts to assure its perpetuation. This leads to the definition of social institutions as *ideas, practices or beliefs to which society attaches sufficient value to assure their perpetuation.* Education is such an idea, practice, or belief.

INSTITUTIONS AND CHANGE

The idea of change is implicit in the idea of interaction among people. In its most concrete form, social change means that the present generation is engaging in activities different from those of preceding generations; the changed activities indicate a change of values. The persons who comprise the complex network of patterned relationships, in which all people of a community participate to varying degrees, all act, interact, and react differently from time to time — or from day to day. No normally-functioning person ever engages totally in ritualized behaviors. Automatons, robots, and computers always do; normal humans, never totally.

Since people act, interact, and react differently from time to time, change permeates society. Social institutions change, the structure of their agencies changes, the positions within a particular organization change, the holders of positions change, the person holding a particular position changes. Statuses and roles change. All such changes, collectively, constitute social change.

Desirability of Change

The nature and rapidity of social change depend on how well-pleased people are with things as they are. People in some communities seem satisfied with their customs and struggle to perpetuate them, shielding their young from "contaminating" influences. At the opposite extreme are the revolutionaries of the world, who seek change for the sake of change but seldom have constructive alternatives to propose.

Inevitability of Change

Because people do not engage in totally ritualized behaviors, change is inevitable. How rapidly change occurs depends on whether people devote effort to causing or preventing it, or whether they are apathetic. An institution imposes limits on the behavior of individuals and it exists to perform that function, among others. When an institution gives up a function for which it has been responsible, some other institution usually assumes or is given the function by society, but when there is a vital function for which no institution or representative agency has responsibility, institutionalized limits sometimes disappear. Limits on some elements of the social structure may also disappear, as Halle (1963) indicated:

Pluvis said he could sum up the evolution of our society in a phrase: the disappearance of limits. The limits on the size of our communities disappear, so that our cities spread and multiply their cells without control. The same thing happens to our governments, which go on growing even after their growth has reduced them to floundering helplessness, like dinosaurs in a swamp. It happens to our population when the limits that disease and the food supply have set to its growth are removed. It happens to our weapons of war when the chemical limits on their potential power is removed. It happens to the jurisdiction of government when the limits of natural law disappear from among us. It happens to musical composition when the limits set by traditional scales and harmonies disappear; and to art when the limits set up by the requirements of representation disappear. . . .[pp. 93-94]

Social change, therefore, is inevitable when vested interests deliberately plan it and people at large either support the change or care so little that they do not oppose it. Much unplanned social change also is inevitable, particularly in areas where there are no limits or the limits are disappearing.

Planned Change

Proponents of certain planned and purposeful changes have always been vocal, and there are many proponents on the contemporary scene.

Skinner (1971) went further than most of his contemporaries in suggesting planned social change — further in terms of the long-range and pervasive nature of the proposed change because he proposed going "beyond freedom and dignity" of the individual in order to achieve a "better" society. Proposed changes often become issues, and protagonists and antagonists gather around each issue. Perennial tugs-of-war develop and continue. A few current issues are legalized abortion, sex education in schools, legalized drug usage, euthanasia, eugenics, government aid to nonpublic schools, bussing to achieve racial integration, and conservationist ecology.

Planned social change is brought about by people through their social institutions, utilizing one or more agencies. Any proposed change is a threat to persons whose interactions would be affected, and the change may be resisted by those people. Early advocates of the school as an agency of social change, for example, suffered much abuse for their views. George Counts and Harold Rugg were two educators who suffered abuse for their advocacy of change which has taken place a few years after their day of leadership. As recently as July 1951, Rugg's appearance on the campus of the Ohio State University set off a furor. His publicly-stated views received national press coverage and resulted in a Board of Trustees screening policy intended to keep "subversives" off campus! Yet, at this writing, the boards of education of metropolitan Detroit are under court mandate to achieve racial balance on an unprecedented geographic and numerical scale. In dozens of other cities, thousands of school children are being bussed away from neighborhood schools for the same purpose. Schools now *are* agents of social change, by court mandate.

Unplanned Change

Change not deliberately planned will, nevertheless, occur when pressures become strong enough. Supreme Court Justice William O. Douglas (1970) made that point chillingly succinct in regard to government when he said, "There are only two choices: A police state in which all dissent is suppressed or rigidly controlled; or a society where law is responsive to human needs [p. 92]."

Justice Douglas advocated in this 1970 manifesto (pp. 92-94), changes which do not seem radical of themselves, and it is difficult to see how his proposals were in any way subversive. However, because the document advocated planned change, it threatened certain people, and they conducted serious and impassioned talk of impeaching its author. These people did not see that, in the absence of planned change, they would inevitably be affected by unplanned change; nor did they see that the effect of unplanned change could be more adverse than that of planned change.

Reciprocity

Since social institutions are represented by agencies through which humans interact, the idea of reciprocity within and among roles has face validity. Reciprocity is inherent in the definition of interaction; that is, when two people or institutions interact, one acts and the other reacts. If a woman undertakes a role in an economic agency, for example, her role in the family changes – of necessity. When the fields and factories no longer needed children, the role of children in the educational institution changed. When the production of goods moves from the family or tribe to the factory, family or tribe and corporation roles change. When responsibilities of state or national government increase or expand, those of local communities contract or disappear. When common problems are solved or disappear, the focus must change to new problems or the sense of community is lost.

COMMUNITY

The term community means things held in common – things ranging from real estate to beliefs and customs. Usually, when one speaks of *a* community he means a set of people who have many elements in common. Many of the communities in the larger society are based on the ethnic considerations of country of origin, race, or religion. Thus we speak of the Italian or Greek community, the black community, or the Jewish community. The fact that people are members of more than one community (the neighborhood and the state, the nation, and the world) was mentioned in Chapter Two.

Many other definitions are possible, but the one to be used here is: "A community is a geographic clustering of people that makes possible human interaction in solving problems of concern to all." In rural areas, the geographic clustering may be by townships, or even by counties in sparsely populated areas. Clustering may also be in villages or towns. In the urban setting, clustering may be by ghetto, neighborhood, or suburb.

Reasons for Communities

Coleman (1966) listed and attributed to Tonnies important activities that usually require human interaction for completion, namely:

work

education of children

religiously related activities

organized leisure activities

unorganized social play of children

voluntary activities for charitable or other purposes

treatment of sickness, birth, death

buying and selling of property

buying consumable goods (food and clothing, for example)

saving and borrowing money

maintenance of physical facilities (roads, sewers, water, light)

protection from fire

protection from criminal acts [p. 674]

Such activities bring about *shared patterns of living* — cultures or subcultures. The activities are necessary to carrying out institutionalized functions of the larger society; and some of the activities, and the agencies which provide them, themselves become institutionalized. Sandlot baseball, for example, is a form of institutionalized activity that provides unorganized social play for children.

Reasons for Disorganization

There are at least six reasons why clusters of people, close enough in geographic proximity *to act*, sometimes *do not act* as a community. The six are: (a) the really meaningful problems that can muster the all out energies of people have been solved, (b) the people perceive no common problems, (c) there are no persons willing to lead in problem solution, (d) the individual energy required for collective efforts is greater than people are willing to invest, (e) there is collective effort, but two or more sub-groups are pulling in different directions, and (f) the structures necessary for collective efforts do not exist.

In an established community, the problems that can mobilize the all out efforts of people may have been already solved. There may be schools, fire departments, police, and departments of public utilities in existence. People find it difficult to get as worked up about litter in the streets as about getting a community's first and only hospital. Too, with the high degree of mobility of our population today, individuals often do not stay in one place long enough to learn the nature of the pressing problems of their communities.

A geographic cluster of people of all age strata, from newly-weds through retirees, may not perceive any common problems. The childless young may be concerned about tennis courts and swimming pools, the young marrieds about schools, the middle-aged about crime in the streets, and the retirees about lower taxes.

Leaders are always in short supply. Leadership takes commitment, guts, and quality of "joyously enduring stress."[1] A leader has to stick his neck out and say, "Here is a cause in which I believe. Who will

---

1. Harold E. Sponberg, in an address to The Michigan Association of School Administrators Conference, Cobo Hall, Detroit, September 1965, coined this phrase.

llow me?" Only a few people in any group can be expected to possess ese attributes; and contemporary mobility narrows the field still ore. When all of a person's roles in the domestic, economic, ucational, political, and religious social systems were concentric, ntered about the place where one lived, the sense of affiliation with e place of residence was stronger, and leaders were much easier to 1d. Now, many men and women with leader propensities earn their 'ing miles from their bedroom communities.

Coleman's imaginative tale (1966, p. 680) of the hotel cornice ricks about to fall illustrates the fact that the consequences of each erson's action or inaction must, somehow, be felt by him if he is to 1ake the effort required to take action:

> Suppose there are some bricks loose in the cornice of a hotel, and I see them from my hotel room. These bricks could fall, injuring or killing a passer-by on the sidewalk below. If action is to take place, I, out of concern for the passer-by or the hotel, must report this to the desk clerk, the desk clerk must report it to the manager, and the manager must call a brick-layer to have the loose bricks repaired. All this is no simple matter, for it requires a chain of organization: from me to the desk clerk to the manager to the repairman. Each person in this chain must be sufficiently motivated to carry out his particular action, or there is effectively no organization.

The witnesses in the infamous Genovese murder case, and others who "didn't want to get involved," simply could not see enough "what's in it for me?" to make the effort worthwhile. The same lack of personal realization of what the outcome means hinders clear perception of community problems by some members of communities.

Factional fights, where there is plenty of collective energy devoted to "us against them" struggles, abound in almost every community. Lots of adrenalin flows but few problems get tackled, and fewer yet get solved. Much energy is wasted; much time is lost; much interpersonal goodwill is destroyed.

If existing agencies for human interaction cannot provide, or are not perceived as providing, for the resolution of a particular problem, that problem is likely to go unsolved. Inertia sets in. Abundant experience with group inertia has shown that awesome amounts of energy are required to initiate and bring to fruition any new structure for interaction.

Lack of Community

Social problems often go unsolved when there is lack of "community" among geographically-close clusters of people and all forms of education — particularly the schools — usually become the whipping-boy of society. Following every war since the Franco-Prussian, the losing side has invariably said, "If only our men had been better educated, we would have won." This is true even of the Cold War of the 1950's. After Sputnik I, the tired cliche was the same, and *the schools, as the only generally recognized agency of the educational institution,* were charged with the "defeat." The school curriculum was beefed-up with more mathematics, more science, and more foreign languages.

The degree of institutionalization of education determines the climate in which its agencies function. The structures necessitated by those agencies constitute the social milieu in which educational leaders lead or fail to lead. Those structures are called organizations.

ORGANIZATIONS

The structure or framework in which people who are significant to each other interact in order to perpetuate a shared pattern of living is an organization. The word "organization," to the minds of many persons, conjures visions of giant factories, stiff-necked boards of directors, and endless red tape. As the following anecdote illustrates, organization may have other guises:

I was appraising some rural property in northern California when I came upon a commune, an abandoned farm where a group of young people were "doing their thing." A bearded youth was cultivating a row of beans. A young woman softly strummed her guitar. A pleasant-looking man was painting an ancient barn.

I struck up a conversation with the barn painter and found him affable and articulate. "We seek total freedom here," he told me. "We are trying to escape the clock-oriented, regimented life-style of modern society."

At this point we were interrupted by the ringing of an old-fashioned school bell. The bearded gardener dropped his hoe and sauntered off in the direction of the bell. The guitar player stopped her strumming and followed.

"You'll have to excuse me now," said my new friend. "That bell means it's ten o'clock, and we all have to meet at the house to get our work assignments for the day."[2]

Even the least formal, the most protesting, way of life results in some organization. Organizations are the agencies — the medium — through which institutions perpetuate values.

Organizations as Agencies

People collect into and work in groups in order to accomplish those things which they cannot do alone, or to accomplish them better than they could do alone. The degree of organization of groups varies tremendously, but even the least formal group has a loose organization. Thus, organizations serve as agencies of institutions and make possible certain activities from which individuals can benefit.

According to Hicks (1967) and others, all organizations, or agencies, have these five common characteristics: (a) they involve people, (b) the people interact, (c) interactions are to some degree ordered and prescribed, (d) each individual sees the organization as in some way helping him, and (e) the interactions help to achieve some joint objectives that are related to individual goals. An agency of community education must have certain core elements if it is to exhibit these characteristics.

---

2. Robert A. Moss in "Life in These United States." *Readers Digest*, September 1972, pp. 76-77.

Core Elements

Hicks (1967) indicated that humans, interacting purposefully, are the "core elements" of any organization. Jay (1971) pointed out that a corporate organization is dependent on people who find in it "rewarding work, status, vigorous activity in the company of their peers, a channel for aggresive instincts, and an identity (p. 302)." People must find these same satisfactions in an agency of community education. The people working in the agency need certain working elements just as the people working in a corporate organization do.

Working Elements

A community education leader must be fully aware of the resources available to the people and programs for which he is responsible. Those resources are the "working elements" of the organization, and they may be either human or nonhuman. People are resources to the extent of their ability *to do* necessary tasks, *to influence* others, and *to use concepts.*

Nonhuman resources that are necessary to every agency of community education include materials, facilities, and a means of interacting with some elements of the larger society. For example, some of the materials necessary to an adult high school completion class include books, paper, and pencils. Facilities needed include enclosed and heated space, furniture, and media devices. Without some interaction with the society, students would be unavailable. However, because of interaction with the society, some survival elements must be built into any organization.

Survival Elements

In order to survive, the elements of strength, faith in purpose, vigor, and cohesion must be built into or acquired by an organization. Such elements of survival are as necessary to a school as to any other agency. The organization must develop an "apparatus of permanence" (Jay, 1971, p. 260) to keep it from being destroyed by outside enemies or torn apart by internal strife, from rotting away through vitiation of individual energies, or simply from falling apart as community bonds come unglued.

The apparatus of permanence is achieved through a series of multi-level, overlapping, interlocking social systems. That apparatus is complicated by the fact that, while each individual in the organization is a member of one or more of its internal social systems, he simultaneously is a member of some "communities" or social systems outside the organization.

AGENCIES OF COMMUNITY EDUCATION

It was pointed out earlier in this chapter that the educational institution is one of several major social institutions, each of which has numerous agencies charged with responsibility for carrying out institutional functions. However, there are at least three misconceptions that are rife in our society today and they make acceptance of these agencies very difficult for most people.

Common Misconceptions

The first common misconception is that the *school* (one agency of the institution) can be equated to the *educational institution*. Thelen (1960) spoke tartly to this:

> The false belief that the school is the community's sole educative agency leads to a rather serio-comic state of affairs: every group or individual with any kind of vested interest in education immediately gets out its snickersnee and goes out after the schools! Service clubs, religious groups, merchants, police safety squads, charitable institutions needing pennies, colleges wanting students — not to mention the 100 percent Americans, the regional chauvinists, and the foundations with pet notions about education [pp. 54-55].

For as long as people persist in the false belief that "the school" (including the college and the university) is society's only educative agency, they will continue to condemn to lives of failure and feelings of worthlessness those people who fail to fit the mold of the school. The present writers have no wish to halt the search of the schools for better means of reaching and teaching more people, but all the members of society need to understand that people can learn and are learning outside "the school" as well as in it, and that there are many ways of getting an education — some without having an *instructor!*

A second common misconception is the long-held perception of "the school" as the sole educative agency of society. The limited view of education as a school-based pre-vocational activity of the young — an activity which terminates at an age somewhere between the late teens and the early twenties, depending upon the occupation for which the individual is preparing — must be changed.

The age of technology is forcing everyone to realize that education is a process in which every person must engage himself throughout his lifetime, that occupational information and skills are but a small part of the total education to be acquired, and that more than increased income is to be found in education. The journalist Mayer (1961) pointed out what should have been obvious: ". . . there is something sickening about the spectacle of a society which can reach children's minds only through their stomachs or their vanities [p. 131]."

The third common misconception is that one agency (namely, the schools) is or can be solely responsible for all the *functions* which society demands of the educational institution. One need only examine the following partial-listing of functions to see the impossibility of this.

Primary Functions of Community Education

Functions for which the educational institution, through its many agencies, has primary responsibility in our society include:

1. *Transmitting the culture.* This function was, originally, the responsibility of the family, the church, the artisans, the craftsmen, and the tradesmen. This is a conservative function.

2. *Social reform.* Reform can occur either through force or through persuasion and rationality. If rational means of reform are to prevail, some education — some learning for a purpose — is essential. This is a liberal function, hardly found in closed societies.

3. *Discovering new knowledge.* This, too, is a liberal function, supposedly characteristic of open societies. Each individual is supposed to be free to explore, to find his own truth.

4. *Rehabilitation.* Remolding deviant individuals is a manifest or primary responsibility – to help those who have erred against their fellowmen and those who feel that they are less than whole people.

5. *Making children into adults.* This function resulted as European countries came, about 400 years ago, to regard childhood as a special period of life. The child's world of fairy stories, games, toys, and special books for learning was invented (Plumb, 1972). The school, as a distinct agency for helping the child to learn values and judgment, to gain information, and to become an adult, had existed for centures, but its functions changed when childhood was "invented." As humanitarian concerns and a steadily-shortening life in the work force took children out of agriculture, industry, and the trades, there was concomitant concern that they learn salable skills prior to their induction into the labor force! Responsibility for teaching skills passed from the family, tribe, or "master" to other agencies. Today, the responsibility seems to rest almost entirely with the schools, a state of affairs that has developed by default.

6. *Assisting the use of leisure time.* Perception of responsibility for what people do with their leisure is of comparatively recent origin. Educational assistance in this area has become an important function to assure that every adult uses his ever-increasing nonwork time in ways that are not inimical to society.

7. *Individualization.* This emphasis resulted from the Judeo-Christian professed belief in the dignity and worth of the individual. Society has an obligation to help the individual develop his uniqueness and discover who he is.

Secondary Functions of Community Education

Functions for which the educational institution presently has secondary responsibility include:

1. *Baby sitting.* Children who could no longer go into the fields or the factories with their elders needed some agency to keep them occupied, and the task fell to the schools because of the Puritan ethic that "the devil finds work for idle hands." This function is doubly important today since many families have both parents employed outside the home.

2. *Teaching sexuality.* The home once taught boys to be boys and girls to be girls, but this responsibility has now been forfeited to the advertising world. If sexuality is to be purposefully and objectively taught, current family patterns seem to indicate that the school and other educational agencies must do the job. It remains to be seen whether the unisex movement is more than a passing fad.

3. *Providing a courting ground.* Responsibility in this area has developed since most families no longer have the intimate kinds of interaction with other families once provided by such social activities as husking bees and barn raisings; and since, for many families, the church is no longer a focus of major social activity. Thus, for boy to meet girl and for nature to take its inevitable course to assure procreation, new meeting-grounds are essential.

4. *Controlling the labor supply.* A function of the school and other educational agencies is withholding the young from the labor market until about the age of twenty-two in order to assure more jobs for those who are older. This function is of comparatively recent origin. Community education also has the functions of assuring that there are enough people with the proper skills to get society's work done, of re-training individuals as necessary, and of assuring that the older worker learns something that will help him continue to feel useful when he is ejected from the work force at an ever-earlier age.

5. *Providing a sense of purpose.* This is the evident responsibility of the religious and domestic institutions, but it has become a partial responsibility of the educational institution.

6. *Relating the individual to society.* A task formerly accomplished by the family, this responsibility is another that educational agencies now share with the family.

7. *Teaching kinship.* Helping the individual to learn how he is related to other human beings is another family responsibility that often falls to educational agencies by default.

8. *Allocating influence and power.* This is a recently-assumed responsibility that educational agencies, particularly in a technological education-oriented society, share with the political institution. No one denies that education is important to such allocation.

9. *Relating to the physical environment.* A function that is related closely to finding a sense of purpose, namely, relating human beings to their physical environment, is being given a renewed importance. From earliest recorded times, man has searched for his relationships to his environment; today many agencies of education have the function of aiding in this search.

10. *Teaching the importance of standards.* The disappearance of standards was discussed earlier in this chapter. If standards are to be developed and maintained, an educational function is implied.

Perhaps all of the above-listed primary and secondary functions of educational agencies could be subsumed under the function of "socializing the individual" or "community education." The agencies of education, despite their wide diversity, all have certain elements in common.

Elements of Education Agencies

If an organization is to carry on in behalf of individuals or of the society, activities that will help or affect what individuals learn for certain purposes (and this is the definition of an educational agency), certain elements seem essential to its structure. First of all, an educational agency must include *learners*. Second, it must include *persons* who are *to help learners*. *Purposes for learning* also must be apparent, and they may be seen from the viewpoints of society, of the community, of the learner, or of the agency itself; purposes generally indicate what is to be learned and why. *Facilities* are also essential, as are *resources,* and so is a *structure* within which people can interact. Some *communication with the outside* is the last of the common elements.

If these elements of an educational agency are used as criteria to determine whether a particular organization is an agency of education, horizons inevitably will extend far beyond "the schools." If a community education leader is to function effectively, he must be able to conceive how *all* of the agencies and the particular agency that employs him fit together and into the overall pattern. To gain such a concept, some understanding of the sources from which people can get information is essential.

Sources of Information

The following catalog of information sources available to any individual, regardless of age, may seem overly simplified, but the categories do not appear to be affected by one's belief as to what constitutes "education." It seems that advertisers have learned to make far more effective use of many of these sources of information than have educators. The sources are a person's:

1. *Action* — his own explorations in an environment either natural or man-made — in the form of:

   — direct experience, either at play or at work;

   — purposeful study and observation.

2. *Interaction* with other people — or with their recorded images — in:

    — informal relationships with (a) peers; (b) persons of more experience (parents and neighbors, for example); or (c) persons of less experience;

    — formal relationships with those individuals whom society imposes upon the learner for the express purpose of imparting information to him (teachers and master craftsmen for example).

3. *Reaction* to the ideas of people as recorded in:

    — printed or written words;

    — symbols, charts, diagrams, statistical tables, and similar devices;

    — artifacts;

    — pictorial illustrations;

    — voice recordings.

Types of Agencies

Then instead of considering the school the sole agency of community education, leaders need to look at the entire gamut of agencies through which the above-listed sources of information may be utilized. Thelen (1960) spoke also to this:

It is no doubt as flattering to the egos of schoolmen as it is relieving to the anxieties of parents to believe that schools educate our children. Nothing of course, could be further from the case. The school, like the meat market, pool hall, church, and streetcar company, contributes *something* to the education of children, no doubt, but one would be hard put to know just what, how important it is, how central in the student's life, and how much it contributes to the overall development that we refer to as education. In our society it is the community's responsibility to educate its children — one way or another. Our pious assumption that the educational job is done entirely by the schools is patently false as judged by our knowledge of what really goes on [p. 54].

Informal. There are several agencies of society which may provide no formal instruction but which nevertheless provide opportunities for an individual to learn, and are thus *educational agencies* in the broad meaning of that term. A recapitulation of them may clarify the total scope of education. Most of these informal educational agencies have been considered agencies for educating children, but most of them could provide opportunities for anyone, regardless of age, who has a mind that is trying to reduce its uncertainties.

1. *The self.* Pestalozzi, Dewey, and others who advocated "learning by doing" brought about an awareness that the self is important to learning, and the formal schools have taken some recognition of this fact in the recent trend toward again providing for independent study. The self is, of course, the educative agency used by the laboratory researcher — and by the infant who must feel, bite, and taste everything that he can see or touch.

2. *The family.* In the home, the family serves as an agency of education. What and how the family teaches in contemporary United States life are quite different from what is learned in many societies or from what was learned in ours in an earlier era; there can, however, be no question but that the family, regardless of its composition, is a potential source of learning.

3. *Social groups.* An individual learns, albeit informally, from playmates, whether they vary from time to time or consist of a regular "gang"; he learns from them in clubs and at dances, or at skating, swimming, pizza, bridge, or cocktail parties.

4. *Neighborhood haunts.* In a social group or alone, in a secluded sylvan retreat or in the middle of a busy street, the individual is learning something.

5. *Occupational groups.* From the historical time when a child was "bound out" or apprenticed to a master to learn a trade

up to and including the present time when an apprenticeship or professional internship is included in the training of adults, people have recognized that a neophyte learns from those who are more experienced than he at a particular skill or trade. A neophyte also learns other things from those who are more experienced than he when he associates with them during coffee breaks, at work, or over lunch.

. *Personal media.* Although not often mentioned, personal media — media serving one or a few individuals — also serve as agencies of education. Personal media would include conversation, questions and answers, photographs, color slides, scrapbooks, diaries, letters, family documents, and individual learning systems. All such informal educational agencies have tremendous impact on the learning of individuals.

Nonformal. A useful designation of nonformal education, separat- ing it from both informal and formal, was made by Paulston (1972), who defined the nonformal

. . . as structured, systematic, nonschool educational and training activities of relatively short duration in which sponsoring agencies seek concrete behavioral changes in fairly distinct target popula- tions. It is, in sume, education that does not advance [one] to a higher level of the hierarchical formal school system [p. ix].

Agencies of nonformal education, by this definition, abound in our society. They include the following:

1. *Mass media.* Certainly advertisements are "structured, sys- tematic, nonschool . . . activities of relatively short duration in which sponsoring agencies seek concrete behavioral changes in fairly distinct target populations." Perhaps the same is true of all media messages aimed at large segments of the population. Thus, books, newspapers, magazines, church services, political and civic meetings, records, tapes, radio,

television, billboards, and signs of all sizes and descriptions may be considered agencies of nonformal education.

2. *Church schools.* Church school groups, whether of the "daily vacation" or the year-round type, provide learning opportunities for countless individuals of widely varying age levels. The story of these "schools" and their purposes provides some interesting insights for the student of educational history.

3. *Youth-serving groups.* Many groups have been organized for young people of varying ages, and each has, either overtly or covertly, one or more specific aims for which it provides learning opportunities. The list is extensive, and varies from community to community, but typical of the groups which reach large numbers of people are Scouts, Little League, Rocket Football, 4H Clubs, and Y.M.C.A. – Y.W.C.A. Overall, there are some 250 such organizations on a national scale.[3]

4. *Armed forces.* For centuries nations have armed certain of their citizens and have taught them to use arms. Increasingly, the service branches have turned to providing education of an ever-broadening nature on both required and elective bases. Clark and Sloan concluded, after their study of *Classrooms in the Military* (1964) that in peacetime the average serviceman often spends 80 to 85 percent of his waking hours in educational endeavors. They also reported that, at that time, more than 1 million servicemen all over the world were studying over 2500 USAFI courses. Cohen (1967) showed total enrollments in the armed forces to be expanding from one million in 1967 to a projected three million in 1970, and to level off there. With the advent of all-volunteer forces, it remains to be seen whether this figure is at all accurate.

5. *Special governmental programs.* At least from the time of the Freedmen's Bureau just following the Civil War; through the C.C.C., N.Y.A., and F.E.R.A. of the Great Depression; to and including the Peace Corps, Job Corps, Work-Study,

---

3. See No. 4108, Paulston, *op. cit.*

O.E.O., VISTA, and similar programs of post-World War II years, the federal government has provided numerous learning opportunities not directly connected with "the school."

6. *Government schools.* There are literally hundreds of schools that are operated either directly or indirectly by various departments, bureaus, and special agencies of the federal government. Examples are the Indian schools run by the Bureau of Indian Affairs, schools for law enforcement officers which are provided by the FBI, and the school for meteorologists under the auspices of the U. S. Weather Bureau.

7. *Civic and cultural centers.* Citizenship schools, art centers, museums, theaters, libraries, and concert halls are among the agencies serving nonformal educational purposes.

8. *Social organizations.* Many organizations have functions which provide opportunities for people to learn something for a specific purpose, and they are, thus, educative agencies. They range from fraternal organizations to service clubs, professional organizations, labor and credit unions, penal institutions, ameliorative associations (e.g., cancer and respiratory disease associations, Goodwill Industries, and the Salvation Army) and government welfare organizations.

9. *Company schools.* Industry pioneered the trend for organizations to educate their employees by setting up "training programs" to provide individuals with specific job skills. The booming expansion of these programs into virtually all areas attests to attempts to fill a void in the almost insatiable and universal appetite for learning. A few major industries now provide programs comparable in variety and scope to some universities, and several enroll more students than do some universities! In some programs, not only employees but members of employees' families are enrolled. Cohen (1967) projected an enrollment of 12 million in company schools for 1970 and a whopping 17.5 million for 1974! He also projected additional 1974 enrollments of 18.1 million in "professional and technical training" and 6 million in "on-the-job training."

10. *Special-needs schools.* Most people are not even aware of the schools which have been developed to meet peculiar and pressing needs in certain industries and occupations. Such schools are controlled by no one company. Since no catalog of them appears to exist at the present time, it is not possible to indicate the entire gamut which they cover, but perhaps two examples will suffice to indicate their variety. Poultry raisers cooperated to provide a "school" in which the exotic art of chicken sexing is taught, and graduates of the relatively short course earn more than do most public school teachers! A school which trains' jet pilots has a long waiting list of persons willing, and presumably able, to pay the shockingly dear tuition for this highly specialized training.

11. *Proprietary schools.* Almost any employee of the public schools would be amazed at the extent and variety of the listings to be found under "Schools" in the yellow pages of the telephone directory of any sizeable urban community. Clark and Sloan's *Schools on Main Street* (1966) included discussion of both proprietary and special-needs schools.

12. *Correspondence schools.* Cohen (1967) reported that enrollments in correspondence schools rose from one million in 1940 to 2.4 million for 1965, and he projected enrollments of 2.8 million for 1970 and 3.2 million for 1974. Although Pfeiffer and Sabers (1970) reported some dismal statistics regarding attrition in and completion of correspondence courses, many learners continue to utilize these agencies.

Formal. As Mead (1961) and Goodlad (1971) indicated, every society has designated certain agencies as responsible specifically for transmitting knowledge to its younger members. Thus has society institutionalized education. In the United States, society has developed numerous agencies, each of which is charged by some segment of society with responsibility for transmitting knowledge, but we commonly have recognized only those that are formal in nature, such as the following:

1. *The school.* Once, the school consisted of the "common" or "grammar" school, which taught the 3 Rs to a privileged few

74

for a few months in each of one or two years. Today, everyone is required to attend, and the school is in session for at least five days per week and nine months per year; and there is some serious discussion of and experimentation with extending both the school day and the school year. Many schools offer adult education classes. A burgeoning movement for "Community Education" encompasses many programs, some of which fall in the formal category. There are also some area vocational schools which function as offshoots of the public schools. Increasingly, both informal and nonformal agencies of education are being considered as alternatives to the school, as Saxe (1972) has indicated.

2. *Alternative and free schools.* According to *Newsweek,*[4] in early 1973 there were 900 privately financed free or alternative schools operating in at least 39 states, plus somewhere between 400 and 1,000 alternative schools being run by public-school systems. These must be classed as agencies of formal education since the learners who attend them undoubtedly are and will be accepted by other units of the hierarchical system. As the *Newsweek* article[5] pointed out, the big difference between this and earlier reform movements is that learners, parents, and teachers are deciding for themselves — on an unprecedented scale — what is the best program to meet their specific needs. Graubard (1973) analyzed the reasons for disaffection with the public schools, and it seems clear that the public schools must change or they must face increasing competition from the alternative and free school movement.

3. *Vocational and technical institutes.* Numerous vocational and technical institutes exist, and they usually enroll learners at the post-secondary level. Whether they are agencies of formal or nonformal education is a moot point since few of their graduates "advance to a higher level of the hierarchical formal school system." However, since it is possible in most cases for those graduates of the institutes who wish to

4. Schools with a difference. *Newsweek*, 1973, 81(17), 113.

5. Ibid., p. 114.

advance in the formal school system to do so, the institutes are classified here as formal agencies.

4. *Community and junior colleges.* The junior college pattern seems to be waning while that of the community college is expanding. Several states now have systems of community colleges so extensive that virtually any citizen of the state is within reasonable, if not easy, commuting distance.

5. *Four-year colleges.* Although plagued by financial and enrollment ills because many of them are private and lack substantial endowments, the four-year colleges still abound and are recognized as necessary components of our traditional pluralistic system of education.

6. *Universities and graduate colleges.* Most universities in this country consist of a graduate college plus several other colleges, but there are some graduate colleges that exist independently of universities. Together, the universities and graduate colleges comprise the capstone of formal education. Alternatives here, also, are under consideration as Coyne and Hebert (1972) indicated, which would mix the informal and the nonformal.

The agencies of formal education are generally recognized as public, parochial, independent, or private, depending on their sponsorship.

SPONSORSHIP AND COORDINATION OF AGENCIES

There are many reasons for the sponsorship of the numerous agencies of education. In order to understand their sponsorship, one needs to consider the purposes served, the levels of organization, and the sources of agency support. Purposes were discussed in Chapter Two as part of the development of the community education concept, and further mention appears earlier in this chapter. Levels of organization and sources of support are described briefly in the following sections.

Levels of Organization

Some educational agencies are organized at a single level, some at two levels, and some at several levels. At the *local level* are public, parochial, private, and proprietary schools; private colleges; radio and television stations; and newspapers. Some of these are found also at other levels. At the *area level* (larger than local, smaller than state) are intermediate or county public school systems, diocesan parochial school units, and some community colleges. At the *state level* are several types of special schools, penal institutions, state colleges and universities, state departments of education (usually regulating public, private, and parochial schools), some private and parochial school units, most of the examining boards and most compulsory accrediting agencies.

Accrediting agencies which provide services for those agencies who seek accreditation voluntarily are organized usually on a *regional*, multi-state basis; for example, the Southern Association of Colleges and Secondary Schools and the North Central Association of Secondary Schools and Colleges are multi-state organizations.

At the *national* level there are the many government schools, and, of course, the U. S. Office of Education.

Some agencies which have educational along with other purposes are *international* in scope. These include UNESCO, the International Red Cross, the World Health Organization, international labor unions, scouting, Y.M. – Y.W.C.A., and service clubs. All these except UNESCO and WHO have national units, also.

Sources of Support

A vital question in sponsorship of agencies is finance. Who pays? Agencies are in perpetual competition for dollars, and all appear to get their finances from one or a combination of the following sources.

Taxes. Taxes have been used to support public elementary or "common" schools since about 1832 and to support public secondary schools since about 1874. Community colleges, state universities, and state and local schools for the handicapped all engage in political activity and compete for tax dollars. All of the national government schools and many libraries and museums also derive support in whole or in part from this source. The numerous court cases pending in 1973 and the concerns expressed by many federal and state legislators indicate that vast changes may be imminent in funding through taxation.

Tuition and Fees. Direct costs are charged to learners by most private, parochial, and proprietary schools and colleges. Most state colleges and universities use tuition and fees to supplement tax-fund allocations. Many museums, galleries, and concert halls charge fees, also.

Endowments. Donations in perpetuity have been and continue to be of considerable help in the support of many colleges and universities, both public and private. Libraries and museums also benefit from endowments.

Membership or Admission Fees. Fees are a principal source of support for many unions, concert halls, galleries, and museums.

Voluntary Contributions. Donations from friends and patrons keep numerous libraries, theaters, galleries, and concert halls in operation.

Product Sales. Sales support most of the book publishers, schools in industry and business, publishers of tests, and manufacturers of learning systems. Sales are of considerable help to newspapers and magazines also, when combined with advertising fees.

Advertising Fees. Advertisers are the chief source of support for radio and television stations, and they are a major source for newspapers and magazines.

Many suggestions regarding the sponsorship of various types of educational agencies may be found in the *Yellow Pages of Learning Resources* edited by Wurman (1972).

Coordination of Agencies

Inasmuch as every community has a wide variety of agencies that can be used by learners, it behooves community education leaders to try to get them coordinated. Since agencies inevitably engage in the political and economic struggles for resources, it would be wise to avoid waste of resources and unnecessary duplication of services and facilities. The emphasis here is on *unnecessary* duplication, as the present writers are in no way suggesting the abolition of our pluralistic system of agencies.

The Norm. The norm is that no one in a given community has any catalog or other tangible evidence of all existing agencies. The one attempt at the present writing, that even aims toward conceptualizing and calling attention to the plethora of agencies is the *Yellow Pages of Learning Resources* (Wurman, 1972). The pathetic waste that results from lack of coordination is exemplified in many cities by school playgrounds that stand vacant during summer months while city recreation directors scrounge for funds and staff to provide playgrounds. Also exemplifying the norm are Boys' Clubs and Scout troops desperately seeking facilities while school buildings stand vacant many hours of every day, or schoolbased adult education classes that hunt for enrollees while Y.M.C.A., Y.W.C.A., or other classes of the same type have unfilled seats. In order to help obviate such conditions, some school districts have turned to "Community School" programs.

Community Schools. Community School programs attempt to use school facilities for more hours of the day than required by the regular instructional program. They often provide classes for persons of nonschool age and recreational activities for those of preschool, school, and post-school ages.

Programs that reach beyond the usual instructional program and the 9 a.m. to 3 p.m. day have been tried many places, and many have continued for several years with varying degrees of success. The schools of Flint, Michigan, (mentioned in Chapter Two), have operated community school programs since the 1930's. These programs, strengthened by the enthusiastic support of the Mott Foundation, have attracted hundreds of visitors yearly from throughout the United States and numerous foreign countries. Many other systems have instituted programs based on the Flint model, and some have gone further by attempting to make their schools all things to all people. At the opposite pole are critics of the schools whom we have characterized as de-schoolers.

The De-Schoolers. In full cry at the heels of school teachers, administrators, and board members are various critics led by those who would abolish schools entirely. Critics of the schools are not new on the educational scene, but de-schoolers are. Men such as Goodman (1962), Reimer (1971), and Illich (1971) insist that schools do not carry out the functions entrusted to them and should be totally abolished, with their responsibilities being taken over by other agencies. Holt (1972) has now joined them, and Coyne and Hebert (1972) have described alternatives to formal higher education.

Close behind these leaders are contingencies demanding accountability, performance contracting, alternative schools, or the choices permitted by a voucher system. All have some justified criticisms of the schools. Few have constructive plans for carrying out all of the institutionalized functions of education. Among those who do are some of the leaders in the Community Education Movement.

The Community Education Concept

One major purpose of community school adherents has been to use school buildings for more than the daytime instructional program. Some few community school directors have been and are guilty of trying to organize classes and activities for this purpose alone, without regard for the needs and wishes of local residents. This action is understandable if the only criterion used by school systems and by community residents for judging a director's accomplishment is the number of people he gets into a building.

By contrast, most community education leaders follow the belief that any community should use all of its educational agencies to foster individuality while helping individuals to recognize their commonality; to help all its citizens learn to identify and solve common problems. Community education had its origins many years ago in such diverse localities as Appalachia, Florida, New England, and in Michigan's upper and lower peninsulas. Sometimes in concert with and sometimes discrete from community schools, the community education concept has spread, and the community education process has served many communities. Through the National Community School Education Association and the University Centers for Community Education, the movement enjoyed unprecedented growth in the early 1970's. The editors of *Phi Delta Kappan* saw fit to devote an entire issue to the movement in November 1972.

Community education and the free schools movement both stand somewhere between the "School is All" and the "De-Schooled Society" poles; community education, particularly, would use every educational agency in a community — recognizing the school system as often the largest and most important educational agency of the group. The concept is a comprehensive one. No one can presume to speak for all of community education; however, any educational reform must recognize that accountability, effectiveness, and efficiency are all needed in a process of effective education. The community education concept is leading the way in the development of a process that promises to help all people of a given community learn more effectively and more efficiently than has been possible with uncoordinated community educational resources.

CHAPTER IV

**COMMUNITY EDUCATION
LEADERSHIP: A THEORY**

COMMUNITY EDUCATION LEADERSHIP: A THEORY

HAROLD W. BOLES
AND
MAURICE F. SEAY

> The development of theory from which to test the assumptions and hypotheses underlying the community education concept is essential to the survival of community education as a viable process.
>
> — Weaver (1972, p. 154)

RELATIONSHIPS

Many people seem to believe that theory is a worthless academic exercise, of no use to practitioners in the field. Nothing could be further from the truth. John Dewey once said, "There is nothing so practical as a good theory." The great advances in the sciences and in technology have resulted from theory development. Advances in community education must also result from theory development.

A theory is a framework for raising intelligent questions about a phenomenon and about data which might be relevant to those questions, and for relating those questions to what is already known or assumed. A theory is really a search for relationships between the unknown and the known.

Man's Search for Relationships

The history of mankind is the history of man's search for meaningful relationships in his physical environment, between man and his nonhuman environment, and, more recently, between and among men and societies of men. The physical sciences, the biological sciences, and the behavioral and other social sciences have all resulted from this search. Men have recorded their own and have built upon each other's guesses, conjectures, speculations, suppositions, hypotheses, and investigations. They have combined these into theories, have researched, restated and restudied, until a body of principles and laws has been developed. Always, there has been a problem of sorting out the irrelevancies to make the investigative tasks easier. Recently, systems analysis has been used as a way of sorting out irrelevancies, *sometimes by simulation before the actual system exists!* In an attempt to reduce the number of possible variables in a given system, man has resorted to definition.

The Objectives of Definition

In the continuing search for order and relationship in and with their surroundings, people are forever plagued by the matter of relevance. As every student of probability knows, if there are many variables in a situation, the possible numbers of relationships grow to astronomical proportions. An investigator can make a situation manageable for investigation only by *restricting* the elements of the situation to those that are relevant to his pre-conceived *purpose.* He starts by defining his terms. His choices of definitions depend on his values.

Values are determined not only by man's activities as he pursues the eternal quest for order and relationship, but by the choices that he makes as he performs those activities. Sometimes he has no choice. Not all relationships can be investigated. Those that cannot be become part of the *institutional process.* Those relationships that can be investigated ultimately become parts of the *instrumental process.* Both institutional and instrumental processes result in things and ideas that men prize and hold dear — in values. Definition is necessary to both processes.

In groping from the unknown to the "known," man utilizes statements of at least eight different kinds, as shown in Table 4-1. Each kind of statement is defined in the table. Of the eight kinds of statements, two are accepted as facts, or what is known. Theory utilizes assumptions and hypotheses to discover new knowledge that is related to what is known.

What is Known

The statements that are generally considered "facts" are of two kinds, as shown in Table 4-1: (a) the principles or concepts which derive from the institutional process and (b) natural laws or constructs which *can be proven* in the instrumental process. The latter result in "hard data"; the former never do.

Principles. Lacking any "hard data" on which to make a decision, one may, as Wheelis (1958, p. 184) suggested, pray, consult dogma, or refer — perhaps unwittingly — to existing practices or beliefs. In such circumstance, man calls on "facts" that transcend the evidence at hand. Such values reign where empirical methods have not yet provided answers, and such maneuvering is called the *institutional process*; it often calls on "principles." An example would be a community education director who, lacking data regarding what community residents believe that they need, institutes a recreation program because that is what a neighboring community is doing.

Research Evidence. The *instrumental process* on the other hand, is a series of actions of investigation of order and relationship that uses the scientific method. The "facts" that this method establishes have transcultural validity. They derive from tool-using, observation, and experimentation. For most of the decisions of life, however, most people cannot wait until they have clear-cut answers from research. Thus, for problems that will not wait, decisions are apt to be made by reference to "principles" or conventional wisdom. When the instrumental process *is* used, an investigation is undertaken that is based on the as-yet unknown. An example would be a community education

TABLE 4-1
The Place of Theory in Progressing from Guess to Fact

Theory			
	The "Known"	Principle or Concept	a statement of order or relation so rational or so logical that it is generally accepted as unvariable under varying conditions and seems unlikely to be disproven
		Natural Law or Construct	a statment of order or relation that has been or can be demonstrated to be unvariable under given conditions
	The UnKnown	Hypothesis	a statement of possible order or relation accepted tentatively as true for the sake of obtaining evidence
		Supposition or Assumption	a statement of possible order or relation accepted tentatively as true for the sake of argument or exposition
		Speculation	a statement of possible order or relation
		Conjecture	a statement of opinion or judgment
		Surmise	a statement based on imagination or suspicion
		Guess	a statement based on little or no evidence

director conducting a block survey to learn the kinds of problems people perceive.

The Unknown

In man's search for relationships, he may use, as shown in Table 4-1, a guess, a surmise, a conjecture, a speculation, a supposition or assumption, one or more hypotheses, or some combination of these. These are perceived by the present authors to be listed in an ascending order of importance if one wishes to arrive at new "facts."

Most guesses probably do not advance knowledge very far because they seldom relate to evidence. One could *guess* at how one leads in solving the problems that are of concern to the residents of a given community, but if the guess proved accurate, it would only be by chance. However, if one made a *surmise* on the same subject because the lives and work habits of residents in his community appear to be similar to those in a near-by community, he might come closer to the truth. A *conjecture*, based on the opinions or judgment of several experienced community education directors, might come closer yet. A *speculation* relating the judgment of a leader in a particular community to the experience of leaders in similar communities might also be used. Or, one might make a certain *assumption* in order to set about leading in solving community problems. Of most use in arriving at new "facts" would be hypotheses which could be tested and either confirmed or rejected.

Tying the Unknown to the Known

Theory, then, ties the unknown to the "known," as indicated in Table 4-1. As hypotheses and assumptions are accepted into the realm of "facts," those that have a data base and can be demonstrated as unvariable are called "laws." Those that transcend the evidence at hand but are so rational or so logical that they nevertheless gain general acceptance become "principles."

Theory relating to leadership in community education must explain how people structure their interactions in order to solve common problems. The structuring is done, of course, through

89

organizations of one kind or another. Theory must tie what is known about organizational structures and social systems to what is only hypothesized or assumed.

Organizations and Social Systems

In order to survive, the elements of strength, faith in purpose, vigor, and cohesion must be built into or acquired by any organization or group. An organization must develop an "apparatus of permanence" (Jay, 1971, p. 260) to keep it from being destroyed by outside enemies, being torn apart by internal strife, rotting away through vitiation of individual energies, or simply falling apart.

The apparatus of permanence is achieved through a series of multi-level, overlapping, interlocking social systems. That apparatus is complicated by the fact that, while each individual in any organization is a member of one or more of its internal social systems, he simultaneously is a member of several social systems outside the organization.

Analytic thought about the systems with which one is familiar leads to discovery of the key elements that characterize all systems, namely unity and interdependence. Digestive system, circulatory system, plumbing system, sewer system, system of roads, school system, distribution system, and so *ad infinitum;* in each system there is a unity of purpose and an interdependence of parts necessary to its functioning. Then a social system consists of parts (people) who are interdependent. The actions of one affect others. If an individual is to be useful to an organization, he must have a feeling of belongingness, commonality, or *community,* and he must feel that the rewards which the social system can provide are "worth it" to him.

If a group wants to operate as a "community," every individual must feel that he belongs not only to a neighborhood or division, but to the total entity. Some kind of communication generates the feeling of belonging, but a communication system, according to Jay (1971), only transmits a picture of a social system. The picture is composed of, first, some addition to the identity of the people involved. Even a badge or pin has "powerful magic" if it represents a status that people value. The picture also tells people how individuals are treated, and this information is gleaned through both formal channels and "the grapevine." The perceived picture of a shared pattern of living – a subculture – must provide something that individuals prize. The individual member must be able to believe in the central faith of the community. The goal must be one in which he can believe, and he must understand the doctrine, share in the rituals, be aware of group purpose and limits, participate in folkways, and use the special jargon. Regardless of the size or purposes of the community, individuals must accord an earned respect to its leaders, whether they are elected representatives, the tribal elders, or the powerful elite.

Even more important to the individual than the sharing and the respect is the knowledge of what the community can do for *him*. A member who believes that the deck is stacked so that he cannot "make it" as well as the next, or so that his problems will never be considered, will never feel that he belongs.

Every social system has certain inputs, one or more processes, and certain outputs. These elements as they pertain to a community social system will be discussed later in this chapter.

The structures of community organization can be informal or formal, flexible or rigid, temporary or enduring, specified or unspecified. The concern in this consideration of community education leadership is primarily with the formal, enduring, specified structure; either flexible or rigid. There is secondary concern with informal structures, or interacting groups, within formal organizations, and cognizance is taken of discrete informal unspecified structures. It is the belief of the writers that the process of leadership is little different in the latter than in the former. However, understanding of the social milieu in which community educational leadership occurs depends in large measure on understanding formal and more-or-less enduring structures.

THEORY DEVELOPMENT

It is odd that little attempt has been made to formulate theory regarding community education leadership. The nearest approach seems to have been in the NSSE (1953) yearbook on *The Community School*, prepared by a committee with Seay as chairman.

An excellent guide to theory development was presented by Weaver (1972, p. 155), who said that if one wishes to systematize what he believes about a particular phenomenon, he typically: (a) defines the phenomenon with which he wishes to deal, (b) describes the conditions within which he expects to investigate the particular phenomenon, (c) synthesizes what is already known about the particular phenomenon based upon both research and practice, (d) posits assumptions and hypotheses which follow logically from synthesizing what is already known, (e) tests the assumptions and hypotheses, and (f) modifies the theory according to the results obtained from the testing of assumptions and hypotheses. Each of these steps in theory development will be discussed briefly as it relates to the field of community education.

Definition of Community Education Leadership

Definitions can be argued to infinity, but if one is to develop theory, the use of stipulated definitions is essential. Leadership, as the concept is developed, investigated, and taught at Western Michigan University, is a *process*. Not a skill, not a group of high status people, but a process. Community education, too, as taught in this university, is a process, not a program. Perhaps, then, separate definitions should be presented, and later combined.

Leadership is a process in which an individual takes the initiative to help a group to move toward goals that are acceded to by group members. For the purpose of considering community education leadership, the reason *why* group members assent will be considered as voluntary, although we firmly believe that leadership can, and often does, occur when assent is grudgingly given.

Community education, as defined and explained in Chapter One, is a process that achieves a balance and a use of all institutional forces in the education of all the people of a community. In community education, activities are based upon the problems, needs, and interests of those for whom they are planned. The solutions of the problems may be individual, but the problems are common to numbers of the group. For example, young people may have the problem of recreation. Several dozen solutions may be provided, but the problem is common to many youth of the community.

Then *community education leadership is a process in which an individual takes the initiative to help a group in using available resources to learn to solve problems held in common.* An example would be a director who, having conducted a survey to discover interests and needs, helps group members find and utilize resources to meet their needs.

Constraints

The first step suggested by Weaver has now been completed, in that the phenomenon of community education leadership has been defined. The second step outlined was "describes the conditions within which he expects to investigate the particular phenomenon." The constraints of community education leadership are of two types, namely (a) those of the leadership process, and (b) those of community education.

Taking initiative is not enough to assure that the leadership process will occur. The process really consists of two separate types of actions, held by Lipham (1964) and others to be diametrically opposed — leading and administering. The authors of this chapter believe that either can occur without the other, but that the leadership process necessitates both. Each has two discernible goals, and thus four basic goals are involved, as illustrated in the following model.

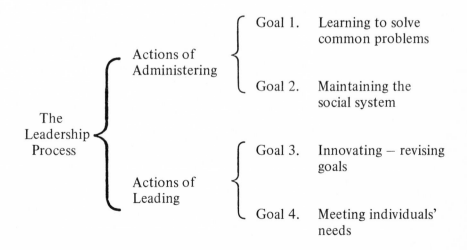

The Leadership Process

Actions of Administering

Goal 1. Learning to solve common problems

Goal 2. Maintaining the social system

Actions of Leading

Goal 3. Innovating — revising goals

Goal 4. Meeting individuals' needs

One person may perform the actions of administering and another the actions of leading, or a skillful leader may do both. However, if only goals 1 and 2 are achieved, the status quo is maintained and no progress is made. If only goals 3 and 4 prevail, problems may remain unsolved or the social system may disintegrate, and in either case movement toward goals 3 and 4 comes to a halt. Then community education leadership must operate within the constraints of seeing that actions are taken to reach toward all four of the above listed goals.

To both the sociologist and the layman, the term "community" refers to things held in common — things ranging from real estate to beliefs and customs. There are many communities in the total society, usually based on geographic proximity or on the ethnic considerations of country of origin, race, religion, or sex. Thus there is the residential community, the Italian community, the black community, the Jewish community, or the Women's Liberation community.

Then community education leadership must operate within the constraints of (a) involving people who are geographically clustered close enough to interact and (b) including people who have common interests and problems. But the solution of problems requires commitment and energy, so there is the third constraint that people must *want enough to solve problems* that they are willing to devote time, energy, and perhaps other resources to the task.

If education is defined as *learning for a purpose*, then there is the further constraint that people must be learning for the purpose of solving problems.

Synthesis of the Known

The third step in theory development is synthesis of what is known about the twin phenomena, "leadership" and "community." This is a vast undertaking, so only some of the major "knowns" will be described.

Principles. An excellent illustration of *unproven*, but generally accepted, statements, or principles, are those of Maslow (1954) relating to the levels of need at which people operate, as shown in Table 4-2.

94

TABLE 4-2

A Possible Hierarchy of Human Needs and Satisfaction

Level of Need			Nature of Satisfaction
Psychological	Ego	AESTHETIC	beauty
		SELF–ACTUALIZATION	self–esteem autonomy privacy knowing understanding
		ACCOMPLISHMENT	order successful task completion pride of workmanship involvement––service to others realization of potential

	Social	SECURITY	freedom from threat, or loss of:
			    income and other perquisites
			    protection
			    privacy and other rights
			    affiliation
			    status
			    admiration
			    respect
			    indulgence of idiosyncrasies

		STATUS	recognition of the influence one has praise credit for work done feeling needed
		AFFILIATION	feeling loved or wanted feeling accepted identity loyalty conformity to expectations

Physiological		PROTECTION	(from uncertainty) habituation, ritual
			(from territorial invasion) privacy,
			    with numerical reinforcement if needed
			(from enemies) shelter, fire, light,
			    group strength
			(from the elements) shelter, clothing

		SURVIVAL	activity sexual expression sleep, warmth air, water, food, bodily elimination

Adapted from Maslow (1954)

Understanding of this table is basic to several statements about both leadership and community that seem to be generally accepted and unlikely to be disproven. Among them are these:

1. Many of the problems that once gave people a sense of community have already been solved.

2. When people interact, each is trying to influence other members of the group.

3. Communication is necessary to the exercise of any form of influence.

4. If any social system is to be maintained, someone must assure that interaction occurs, that membership does not change too rapidly, and that people get enough satisfaction from the group to want to stay with it.

5. Change is necessary to growth.

6. The introduction of change often causes individuals to feel anxious and threatened.

7. Individuals have needs that can be conceived of as constituting a hierarchy, and when needs at one level are satisfied, an individual then tries to satisfy needs at "higher" levels, as suggested in Table 4-2.

8. Until an individual is able to satisfy his physiological needs, he is unlikely to be much interested in his other needs.

9. Influence, authority, and power are different denominations of the same "currency."

10. The purposes for which society institutionalized education can be identified.

Discussion of these and other purposes follows later in this chapter.

Research Findings. There are numerous research findings that seem to have implications for the consideration of theory of community education leadership. Among the findings that may be generalizable to populations other than those used in the research samples are those summarized as follows:

1. People seem to get their satisfactions from things such as recognition, further opportunity, involvement, and task completion as opposed to pay, attractive surroundings, or shorter hours (Herzberg *et al,* 1959, 1965, 1966, 1968).

2. The message sender, the message, the medium, the receiver, and feedback are all important in the communication process (Hovland *et al,* 1953; and Lerbinger and Sullivan, 1965).

3. In any group, certain individuals have more "idiosyncrasy credit" than others (Hollander, 1958, 1967).

4. Individuals all have different perceptions of what is happening in interaction among them (Berelson and Steiner, 1967).

5. The ways in which change, or innovation, can be effectively diffused are known and can be applied (Hägerstrand, 1968).

6. A leader is more effective when his motivational level corresponds to the motivational level of his followers (Graves, 1966).

Stating the Unknown

Theory development requires relating the unknown to the known, and according to Weaver (1972), the fourth step in theory development is: "posits assumptions and hypotheses which follow logically from synthesizing what is already known." This is a way of suggesting unknown areas to be explored. The number of assumptions and hypotheses which might be posited is almost infinite, but here only ten of the more important are suggested. Investigation of any hypothesis might add greatly to what is known about community education leadership.

97

Assumption 1. A leader is a person who uses influence, authority, or power in his interactions with other people. *Hypothesis 1.* Any individual who can establish a basis for influence, authority, or power in a community can be a community education leader.

Assumption 2. A status position in an organization can aid an individual in establishing an influence base. *Hypothesis 2.* A person who has *positional* authority (see later discussion) in a school system or a city government can be more effective than a person who relies solely on the *personal* authority of what he knows or can do.

Assumption 3. When people interact, they engage in a process of social exchange in which each gets something in return for something he gives. *Hypothesis 3.* What a community member gives and what he gets in the exchange process can be identified, as can be what the community education leader gives and what he gets.

Assumption 4. Understanding the social exchange process can help one to become a leader or to be a better leader. *Hypothesis 4.* Understanding the social exchange process will improve one's skills as a community education leader.

Assumption 5. Improved communications skills can make one a more effective leader. *Hypothesis 5.* An individual with high-level communications skills will be more effective as a community education leader than one with lower-level skills.

Assumption 6. An authority or power base in a total community can make a leader more effective than a base in a sub-unit of that community. *Hypothesis 6.* A community education director in a city government will be a more effective leader than will a community school director.

Assumption 7. Understanding social perception and the reasons for individuals' differing perceptions can help one to lead people better. *Hypothesis 7.* A community education leader who understands perceptions will be more effective than one who does not.

Assumption 8. Understanding the needs and motivations of people can help one to be a more effective leader. *Hypothesis 8.* A community education leader who understands his own and others' needs and motivations will be more effective than one who does not.

Assumption 9. Influence and authority have both rational and emotional bases; power has only an emotional basis, in that the sanctions that can be invoked as a result of power always involve hope or fear. *Hypothesis 9.* An appeal to the emotions of people will be more effective for a community education director than will an appeal to their rationality.

Assumption 10. Institutionalized education (learning for a purpose) can and does occur in many places other than schools. *Hypothesis 10.* Community education leaders will be more effective if they try to coordinate the various educational agencies than if they concentrate on schools.

Testing Hypotheses

The fifth step in theory development, according to Weaver, is the testing of hypotheses. The practitioner of community education should collect and analyze data relating to the foregoing and other hypotheses. Results should be reported to the University Centers for Community Education and disseminated through periodicals, special reports, and other publications.

Graduate students and university faculty members who expect to be or are working in community education should be doing research projects, theses, and dissertations that collect and analyze data relating to hypotheses such as those suggested in the preceding section.

Modifying Theory

The University Centers for Community Education should each designate someone responsible for receiving feedback from practitioners and students. Data should be carefully studied and analyzed there as well as in the field. There should be an up-to-date file of data relating to any and all aspects of community education leadership.

As findings warrant, re-statements of theory should be disseminated to the field. As hypotheses are verified or rejected, those facts should be made known. New hypotheses should be suggested, and areas needing research but for which no hypotheses have yet been developed should be high-lighted.

Because University Centers exist, the community education movement is in a unique position in regard to being able to promote the exploration of hypotheses, to solicit feedback, to collect and analyze data, to modify theory relating to the field, and to disseminate results.

The remainder of this chapter is devoted to discussion of some further elements of theory as viewed by the present writers. Numerous further hypotheses are implied and might be extracted for investigation, and samples have been randomly suggested.

PURPOSES OF COMMUNITY EDUCATION

The viewpoint from which one considers community education determines the purposes that he perceives. Some educators believe the purposes of community education to be congruent with those of society, others think the purposes should be those of the specific community, others see community education as fulfilling the purposes of all of the many agencies of education, others consider the purposes of community residents paramount, and still others limit the purposes to those within the purview of the schools, colleges, and universities. Like the seven blind men of Hindustan who went to "see" the elephant — all of them were right, and all of them were wrong!

As more consideration is given to the theory of leadership in community education, some thought about each set of purposes seems essential.

Purposes of Society

In Chapter Three there is an extensive discussion of the many agencies that exist for carrying out the functions of the social institution of education, considering why they exist, by whom they are sponsored, and from what sources they are funded.

Our society expects that, among them, the various agencies of education will carry out the functions of: transmitting the culture, social reform, discovering new knowledge, rehabilitation of deviant individuals, making children into adults, individualization, providing child care while parents work, teaching sexuality, providing a courting ground, controlling the labor supply, relating the individual to society, teaching kinship, allocating influence and power, relating the individual to his physical environment, and teaching the importance of standards. These may not be all of the purposes that society has for education, but they are among the most important, and they are discussed in some detail in Chapter Three.

A Community's Purposes

If a community consists of people who hold something in common, then any social system is a "community." There is a unity of purpose and an interdependence of people. Here, too, some assumptions and hypotheses can be developed that could help to discover new knowledge that relates to what is already known. *Sample Assumption:* The unity of purpose lies in utilizing resources to help people learn to solve problems that are common to them; thus, the "community" for solving problems of unemployment is not necessarily the same as the "community" for providing recreation for children, or the "community" for combating crime in the streets. *Sample Hypothesis*: The purpose for which people come together to learn and work determines a "community;" the community is not a monolith that decides purposes and then pursues them.

Extensive discussion of possible reasons for formation of various communities can be found in Chapter Three. However, the concept of purposes as the uniters of the many different communities is essential to the development of theory in community education leadership that is concerned with a comprehensive and balanced program of education for all the people of a *geographic* community.

Purposes of Agencies

The purposes of educational agencies as viewed by the agencies themselves seem to include:

Carrying out institutionalized functions prescribed by society. Examples of agencies having this purpose include public schools and colleges.

Meeting special-purpose needs of some segment of society. Examples of agencies pursuing this purpose include parochial schools, church-related colleges, occupation-related "schools" such as those for bricklayers' apprentices, scouting, and Y.M.-Y.W.C.A.'s.

Meeting individual's needs. Most of the legitimate proprietary schools that have listings in the yellow pages of telephone directories have this purpose.

Diffusing propaganda. Propaganda as used here refers to the spread of doctrines and is not meant to be pejorative. *Sample Assumption*: The diffusion of propaganda is a purpose of a multitude of such diverse agencies as exemplified by church sects, advertisers, the American Legion, the news media, Common Cause, and the service academies. *Sample Hypothesis*: Propaganda-diffusing agencies are interested primarily in providing or affecting *what* the individual learns.

Profit making. Profit is a purpose of most legitimate proprietary schools, and many owners recognize that profit making can be accomplished only by also meeting individuals' needs. "Fly-by-night" schools have only the profit purpose.

Regulation. This is a purpose of some agencies which provide *no* learning opportunities and only regulate those who do, through various forms of accreditation.

Purposes of Learners

The purposes for which learners patronize the myriad agencies of education are quite varied, and they include but are not limited to:

Meeting legal requirements. If truth were told, many children and youth are in some schools only because the law requires them to be there.

Becoming more socialized. Society provides many powerful compulsions for individuals to accept values held in common by those around them. To the extent that the individual does so, he accepts the purpose of becoming more socialized.

Becoming more individualized. To the extent that one wishes to foster his uniqueness and learn who he is, he accepts this purpose.

Reducing personal uncertainties. The individual who accepts this purpose needs no external motivations, and has found "the joy of learning."

Enjoyment. Those who have experienced the exhilaration or the sense of power that comes just from *knowing* may patronize agencies which can help them to know, whether it be knowing great books, biochemistry, the arts, or some humble craft skill.

Inspiration or self-renewal. Some learners seek agencies that can lift melancholy, reduce despair, or provide new or renewed sense of purpose.

Learning job skills. The agencies that can provide job skills have always been popular with learners, and are now more popular than even because of technological developments that require periodic retraining for many people.

Some agencies of the educational institution exist for the purposes of society, some for a special community of learners, some for their own purposes, some for the purposes of individual learners, some for two of these, and some for all four. The purposes which people hold in common determine the "community" for that particular bit of education.

Roles of Schools, Colleges, and Universities

Sample Assumptions: (a) Community education and those individuals who lead in the activities necessary to achieving its goals and objectives are concerned with cradle-to-crypt or womb-to-tomb learning for everyone; (b) community education must be addressed to problems that concern groups of people without regard to age, months of "the school year," days of the week, or hours of the day. *Sample Hypothesis*: The success of community education programs is measured in terms of numbers of people helped to problem solutions rather than in credit hours produced or in grade point averages.

By contrast, schools usually are concerned with children from the age of four or five to and including youth ages fifteen to eighteen, from September into June, from Monday through Friday, from about 8:30 or 9:00 A.M. to about 3:00 or 3:30 P.M. Colleges and universities serve a select group of students in the age bracket from seventeen or eighteen to about twenty-one to twenty-three, with a sprinkling of the more mature. They, too, are basically concerned with a September to June "year" although they generally have more provisions for summer programs than do "schools." Colleges and universities sometimes extend their week to include Saturday morning, and they often start earlier on the week days and provide classes later on those days than does the "regular school" program. Whether in a school, college, or university the individual learner finds his search for problem solutions circumscribed by limited offerings and "requirements."

Schools, colleges, and universities have significant roles in the education of a limited number of learners during a sharply restricted portion of those learners' lives. Community education, by contrast, should play a significant role in the learning of everyone throughout his life.

AUTHORITY

How an individual comes to have or can gain authority is important to whether and how far he can lead in community education. As yet, no one has cataloged what is known or has developed multiple hypotheses for learning more about authority, but it is a fertile field in theory development, as these examples indicate.

Sample Assumption: A person based in a school can be a community education leader. *Sample Hypothesis*: A community school director can, through investigation of the problems plaguing people of nonschool age, extend community education programs to meet their needs.

The terms influence, authority, and power have been used to the point of vulgarization, but many of the uses have been ambiguous. Some clarification may be achieved by considering influence, authority, and power as varying denominations of the currency that is used in the process of exchange in social systems, an idea adapted from Lerbinger

(1965). Influence, it seems, is the most common denomination of the currency, authority next, and power the rarest. Everyone possesses and uses influence, fewer persons possess and use authority, and fewer still possess and use power. An illustration of these relationships may be found in Figure 1.

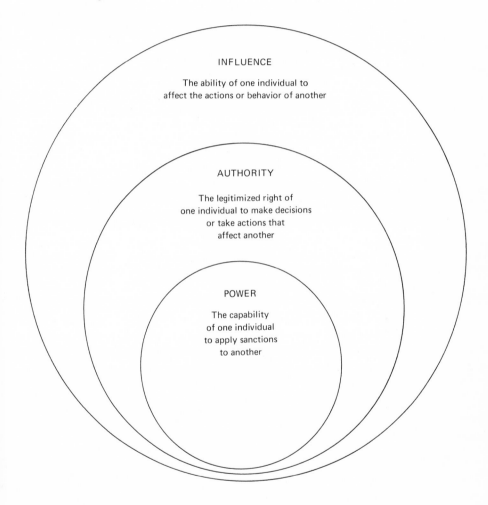

INFLUENCE

The ability of one individual to
affect the actions or behavior of another

AUTHORITY

The legitimized right of
one individual to make decisions
or take actions that
affect another

POWER

The capability
of one individual
to apply sanctions
to another

Figure 4-1. SOME POSSIBLE RELATIONSHIPS

Influence is a relationship in which the person influenced "gives" a change of action, inaction or belief and "gets" reduction of some uncertainty that he has. Influence might be compared to the one-dollar bill — it is possessed by everyone, used in most transactions, and "buys" relatively little. The influence of a given individual is likely to reach more people at more remote distances in the social systems in which that individual functions than will either any authority or power that he has.

Authority is the next "larger" denomination of influence currency. "Authority" indicates more about the social relationship of persons that it involves than does "influence." Authority is a larger denomination in that it is possessed and used by fewer persons, but it "buys" more. It might be compared to a twenty-dollar bill. Its use between individuals who have no group interaction is very rare.

What Authority Is

Authority is a relationship in which one person legitimizes another person or group to make decisions to take actions that affect him in return for some relief from responsibility. Authority is based on the dependence-independence conflict which psychologists recognize as ever-present in each human being. Even in the rare "self-actualizing" individual, there is the urge sometimes and in some situations to allow others to relieve him of responsibility for his own actions. At such times, the individual is willing to surrender some rights in exchange for the relief of uncertainty promised by the social currency called "authority."

The legitimization of authority much more often is an overt and conscious action by the receiver of a message than is the recognition of influence, and thus it has a rational base. The motive for concession (the need to enter into, continue in, or return to a state of dependency) may or may not be recognized, but the normal individual who does not sometime heave a sigh of relief at being able to turn over to someone else partial responsibility for his own decisions or actions is rare indeed.

Communication is even more essential to authority than it is to less-specific forms of influence. Only if the receiver of an "authority's" message can find some credible basis for believing that the authority figure can better direct his actions or thoughts than can he himself will he exchange the right to make decisions that affect him for relief from responsibility. A community education director will be ceded authority only if people are convinced that he can help them solve problems that they have not solved without him.

Where Authority Comes From

The recognition that one individual sometimes must concede authority to another probably has existed since the first two primitive men physically confronted each other. A *personal authority* based on specialization has been recognized since there has been a division of human functions, and has been discussed in the literature at least since 1926 (see Demos). Weber (1922), four years before that, distinguished between but did not elaborate on two types of legal-rational authority. All people rely on the personal authority of others constantly in daily routine — for example; to learn whether a TV program is worth watching, where is a good restaurant, or whether John Doe is a good employee.

Positional authority has been in the conceptual realm of most people from their first acquaintance with a simple organization that had positions that differed in status — perhaps the family. Personal authority has been explicated in admirable detail by Barnard (1938) and others. Leaders often lead by combining the authority of a "line" position and personal authority. Some leaders use only one or the other, because that is all they have or can acquire.

In order to make understandable the seeming paradox of free men legitimizing others to make decisions or take actions for them, as is necessary in community education leadership, some amplification of the concepts of personal and positional authority seems apropos.

Who Has Authority

Personal authority seems to derive from either physical or psychological qualities. An individual may be perceived as having a credible basis for making decisions that will affect others because of such inherited physical qualities as blood ("royal lines"), appearance, voice, or skin color. He may evidence authority (sheer power) through inherited size (witness Goliath!), acquired strength or skill (witness

David!), tone or quality of voice, or contrived appearance (witness the war paint used in tribal wars; the use of cosmetics; the garb of religious, military or other figures).

A credible psychological basis for authority may be found in emotional regard for the authority figure based on admiration; on affection or liking; on love; on identification of the figure with a familiar figure, with a cause, or with an organization; on personality; or on persuasive ability. Regard also may be due to such rational factors as demonstrated physical or intellectual ability or knowledge, commitment or dedication to an idea or a cause ("the true believer"), commitment to an organization ("the organization man"), to courage, to social prestige or status, to professional accomplishment, to name (Taft, Roosevelt, or Kennedy, for example), to wealth, or simply to a demonstrated willingness to assume responsibility.

Any writer attempts to establish a personal authority by demonstrating knowledge of his field. Good speakers and teachers do an analogous thing when they qualify themselves in regard to the task at hand through their opening remarks. Indeed, communications research indicates that this ritual is essential to having the message received and attended. Perhaps the most cherished and most difficult to establish basis for personal authority among rational people is that of sheer elegance of logic or brilliance of ideas.

Name-droppers attempt to establish personal authority through implied association with influential figures. Persons who include their position titles or academic qualifications in "letters to the editor" on topics totally unrelated to the presented credentials are attempting to counterfeit images as authorities.

Most people today seem to agree that there is an amorphous quality, described and named "charisma" by Weber, which relatively few individuals possess. To date, it has not been adequately identified, described or defined, although it seldom has, in these days of secular disillusion, the supernatural element formerly attributed to it. As presently perceived, the phenomenon seems usually to involve the factors of admiration, affection, or love; advocacy, or persuasive ability; and commitment to a cause. Appearance or name also may play a part, and willingness to assume responsibility almost always characterizes the charismatic individual, as it does any leader. Although charisma is a phenomenon of personal authority, the authority figure may possess positional authority also, or his charisma may help him to gain it.

Positional authority is always found where there is a hierarchy of positions, and indicates a continuing relationship of individuals. Anyone in a "higher" position is supposed to have the automatic right to make decisions affecting subordinates. However, the right is "nominal"[1] unless it is recognized as legitimate by subordinates, regardless of who granted it or how the position was obtained. The ascribed right to make decisions affecting them is recognized as legitimate or "authentic"[2] by subordinates only if they find a credible basis for *personal authority* in the position-holder or if he wields *power* over them. Positional authority has limits that include the permanency of the situation as well as the ego-involvement, age, and social maturity of the individuals involved.

If authority can be exercised only through use of implicit or explicit sanctions, the next larger denomination of the social exchange currency − power − is involved. Coercion, either overt or covert, and rewards are parts of any social exchange that depends on power.

Power is a relationship in which a person gives another person or group obedience or conformity in return for implicit rewards or under threat of explicit punishment. Power might be compared to the fifty-dollar bill − possessed by few people, used in few transactions, but a very potent persuader. The power exchange usually takes place in an organization, although it can occur on an interpersonal level between individuals who are not even members of the same group, or who are members of a social system that exists only fleetingly. An extreme example would be a holdup. Here, a fleeting social system is formed in that the actions of one individual are likely to affect the actions of others. Here, power accrues to the holder of superior force.

Table 4-3 summarizes the actions of both follower and leader when any of the "currency" denominations is used in the exchange process.

---

1. Richard Gowell used these terms in this manner in an unpublished paper at Western Michigan University, 1968.

2. Ibid.

Table 4-3. The Use of Social Exchange Currency

When the Currency is	The FOLLOWER		The LEADER	
Influence	Gives:	Some change of action, inaction, or belief	Gets:	Someone to do something he desires
	Gets:	Reduction of uncertainty	Gives:	Direction
Authority	Gives:	Someone else the right to make decisions that affect him	Gets:	Legitimization to make certain decisions to take certain action
	Gets:	Relief from responsibility	Gives:	Direction
Power	Gives:	Obedience of conformity	Gets:	Conformity to his wishes
	Gets:	Reward or punishment	Gives:	Direction and reward or punishment

Securing More Authority

Sample Assumption: Many community education leaders would like more authority than they possess. *Sample Hypothesis*: The only basis on which a greater amount of *authentic* authority can be secured by an individual is through (a) getting more people to legitimize the leader's right to take actions or make decisions that affect them, or (b) gaining more capability to impose sanctions on others. These statements may be so self-evident as to be "principles."

The individual who secures a promotion within an organization gains more *nominal* authority, but it does not become authentic until followers recognize that the individual has some right to exercise it. If the promotion entails increased capability to give pay raises, to promote others, or to fire subordinates, it will soon be legitimized because power is involved.

Sample Assumption: A community education director can secure authority that does not depend on his position. *Sample Hypothesis*: The offering of a learning opportunity that solves a problem of concern to a number of people will cause them to recognize the authority of the person responsible for the offering.

How Authority Is Exercised

Authority is exercised by *giving* direction in return for some relief from responsibility; by *getting* legitimization to take certain actions or make certain decisions in return for taking the actions or making the decisions (see Table 4-3).

Sample Assumption: People who seek problem solutions often do not want to be solely responsible for them. *Sample Hypothesis*: A community education director who assumes responsibility for getting a group to work on the problem will be "authorized" by group members to take necessary actions or make necessary decisions.

The remainder of this chapter is devoted to a general summary of our beliefs about who leads whom, and makes no attempts to distinguish the known from the unknown. While the discussion is not in reference to community education *per se*, it may suggest hypotheses that can be explored in that kind of setting.

WHO LEADS WHOM?

In a system that is available to investigators or observers, inputs, a process, outputs, by-products, and feedback are discernible and can be identified, depending on certain limitations imposed. Corresponding factors appear to exist in a social system.

A social system exists for a specific function to which relationships of people in both formal and informal sub-systems are important. The process in a social system is one of interaction, or social exchange, between role-players. In that process, communication, authority, and perception all play important parts. Roles are determined by positions, or allocations of tasks to be performed, and to each role certain expectations and reciprocal sanctions attach. Expectations reflect

111

values. Each individual in a social system tries to influence each other individual to the extent that will help to satisfy the influencer's own needs, and this makes leading possible. One or more of the positions in a social system involves the tasks of both leading and administering. To understand how those tasks can be compatible, a unifying theory is essential. If people are to learn to be leaders, the theory must be not only explanatory of what is and has been, but predictive as well.

A theory of leadership must explain the relative pulls of individuality and conformity on the persons of both leader and follower. It must also consider factors in the leader, in the led, and in the situation. It must heed certain warnings that have been given in regard to the acceptance of theory. It must meet criteria for a theory.

The Leader

A social system consists of two or more human beings in interaction. An individual who influences others, for whatever reason, is the leader in that situation. The inputs of a social system consist of the patterned actions, or behaviors, of all of the individuals in the system, plus certain expectations originating outside the system but relating to it. In carrying out the function assigned by the larger culture that was responsible for the social system's formation, the system members may use *facilities*, sometimes including one or more physical systems.

The coping behaviors of an individual are caused, they are goal directed, and they are motivated. They result from the individual's needs and his values, combined with the expectations held for him at one or more cultural levels because of one or more roles that he occupies in social systems. Numerous social systems exist to perpetuate education, or *learning for a purpose*, which has been imbued with value sufficient to warrant its perpetuation.

The Led

In every social system there are individuals who, for their own various reasons, prefer at times to be dependent on others. At those times, they become the led.

Variant and deviant behaviors of group members are of concern to a leader if they disrupt or seriously interfere with the functioning of the social system in which he is leading. Nonconforming behavior usually is a sign of some kind of conflict, although limits of what may be considered nonconforming for a specific individual may depend on his group-granted "idiosyncrasy credit."

An individual's knowledge of anything outside himself depends on his senses and their stimulation, but nonobservation, malobservation, faulty memory, inaccurate recording, or predisposition can greatly affect one's selection and awareness of possible stimuli. Every functioning individual adds to or subtracts from raw sensory stimuli to obtain what he perceives as a coherent picture of the world, and in perceiving people he takes his cues from both situations and persons. In social interaction, the matter of whether two persons have similar predispositions in terms of value orientations may be quite important to how they perceive each other, and communication certainly is important in that regard. Sensory deprivation or perceptual deprivation studies have profound implications for our society and for any individuals subjected to prolonged deprivation.

The Functions of Leading

Inputs, consisting of the behaviors of individuals in a social system, are converted to outputs through the process of social exchange, to which every member contributes effort, skills, devotion, allegiance, influence, authority, and power in varying amounts. Every member receives from the system according to his psychological needs. The social exchange process is one of interaction, and is dependent upon initiating actions, perception, and communication.

Characteristics of the *functional* leader in a given situation, regardless of who has been designated as leader or by what means the designation was made, are (a) who contributed most, (b) who initiated most actions, and (c) who was the sender of the most messages that influenced the group.

Every person uses communication in order to exercise whatever influence, authority, or power he possesses, but there are many cultural limits of communication. Significant research exists in regard to the message sender, the message, the medium, and the message receiver.

In membership groups, the currency of power, authority, and influence is used most frequently, although it may be used outside such groups. In the power relationship, hope or fear is ever present and thus the exchange always involves some coercion or duress, whether or not the use of power is considered legitimate. In the authority relationship, some independence is surrendered by an individual in return for relief from having to make certain decisions or take certain actions himself, and the reasons for one being willing to make such a surrender range a wide gamut. In the influence relationship, one "gives" a change of action, inaction, or thought, often evidenced by a changed attitude, in return for removal of some uncertainty. Reasons for one being willing to make the exchange may be as numerous as one's uncertainties. Outputs of a social system include a product, a satisfier of human want; this is intended to satisfy the needs of the larger society, to do which the social system was formed. Production entails specification of what is to be done, "quality control" or checking what *is* done, and feedback. The product is the only output of a social system to the larger society.

Outputs of a social system that are internal to the system include organization-maintenance and both group and individual needs-satisfaction. Organization-maintenance requires that group members learn their responsibilities, coordination of individuals' efforts, conflict resolution, group agreement on goals, and feedback. Need satisfaction of individuals applies to the leader as well as to followers, and includes acceptance by the group, morale, and satisfaction with the group (identification, belongingness and rationality of expectations). Individual satisfiers are believed likely to lie *in what is being done,* while dissatisfiers are more likely to be found in *conditions under which the group works.*

By-products among a social system's outputs *may* include new theory, research, improved practice, and dissent; they seem always to include risk of some kind.

Constraints

In the exchange that occurs in any social system, the leader, whether he be a status leader or an emergent leader, has a particular job to do. That job includes some or all of the steps in the administrative process; whether the leader wills it or not, organization, even at the most informal level, necessitates some administration.

Innovation is certain to occur in most systems, and it can result from invention (basic research), creative synthesis (theory), diffusion (practice), or applications of technology (applied research). Innovation from any of these sources may originate with any member of a social system, and not just with the leader. However, leaders often have "preferred outcomes" that may result in innovation.

The imperative of leading combined with the imperative of administering appears to pose a dilemma for the leader, who must do both, but the dilemma is more imaginary than real. Empirical research has been done that can help the leader to bring about change, although many leaders have functioned and are functioning without benefit of research. Some pragmatic guidelines on how to bring about change or reduce resistance to it can help, also.

Problems are solved only by the making of decisions, and decision-making must be followed by other administrative or managerial actions if system outputs are to be achieved. In addition to decision-making, the administrative process includes the actions of programming, communicating, coordinating, and appraising.

The Risks

Risk is a concomitant of leading, and results from many causes. Among the causes of risk are lack of skills, injudicious or ill-timed decisions, conflicts, threats, lack of concepts, pressure groups, and timing of innovation. While risk is a by-product of a social system's process of social exchange, more risk inures to the leader than to any other system member because of his heightened visibility.

However, any time that change is proposed, some risk to the social system becomes a distinct possibility. If the anticipated gain seems to be outweighed by costs, whether in money, time, or effort, the change will be resisted and the risk is thereby increased.

Hypothesis: The number of followers who can be depended on by a community education leader may be inversely proportional to the perceived amount of risk to the group, as indicated in Figure 2.

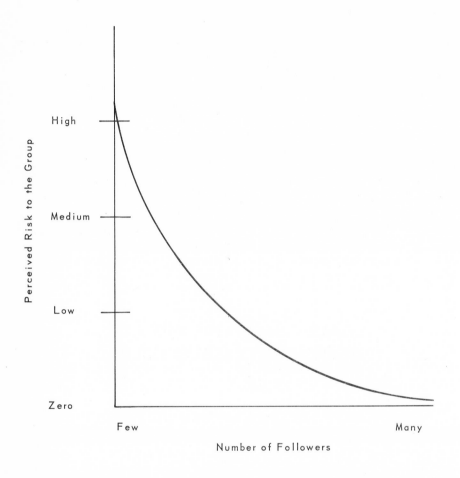

Figure 4-2. Effect of Risk on Number of Followers

The foregoing statements concerning relationships, theory development, the purposes of community education, and authority present a framework for raising intelligent questions about community education. The statements on authority, particularly those concerning the leader and the led, are related to the subject of the following chapter on leadership training.

CHAPTER V

**LEADERSHIP TRAINING IN
COMMUNITY EDUCATION**

LEADERSHIP TRAINING IN COMMUNITY EDUCATION

DONALD C. WEAVER

AND

MAURICE F. SEAY

Implementation and dissemination of the community education concept require leaders. They must be people who are personally and professionally qualified to give leadership to community education — the process that achieves a balance and a use of all institutional forces in the education of all the people of a community. While the personal requisites to success as a leader may depend somewhat upon qualities of the individual personality which are not directly subject to modification through the educative process, the professional skill requirements can be learned. Community education leaders can and must train themselves, with the help of leadership training programs, to be professionally skillful in meeting their responsibilities to all the people of a community. This chapter deals with those skill requirements and with the quality and extent of training programs designed to meet them. The chapter will (a) review a background, (b) describe current training strategies and programs, and (c) discuss trends which indicate likely leadership training programs of the future.

A BACKGROUND

To see clearly the present problems and future possibilities in community education leadership requires some understanding of recent historical developments. American educational history shows that, prior to 1950, efforts to improve the effectiveness of educational administration consisted primarily of sharing successful techniques among those administrators who were practicing in the public schools. There was little talk about theory of educational administration; there were few efforts to develop principles of educational administration against which to test current practice. However, by the fifties, educational and civic planners in the United States and Canada recognized that demands upon the schools required the educational administrator to do more than merely manage the technical details of the school. Leadership was needed desperately. School administrators were pressed to develop the competencies necessary to lead one of the fastest growing and most unanimously patronized community agencies in the nation: namely, the school.

Two Antecedents

During the fifties the W. K. Kellogg Foundation made grants totaling approximately seven million dollars for the purpose of improving the training of educational administrators in the United States and Canada. The universities, state departments of education, and professional organizations which received the grants developed a group of programs which functioned actively and cooperatively during more than a decade. The groundwork for these programs was laid in the late forties by four professional organizations: the American Association of School Administrators, the National Conference of Professors of Educational Administration, the Council of State School Officers, and the Canadian Education Association. Approximately sixty university centers in the United States and Canada developed the programs. The entire cooperative venture, which became known as the Cooperative Program in Educational Administration (CPEA), was the beginning of a concerted effort to professionalize the role of the educational administrator.

A Kellogg Foundation report (1961) cities the results of the CPEA as follows:

1. There is greater emphasis on recruitment and selection.

2. The orientation of students to the field of educational administration is receiving much more attention than formerly.

3. New teaching methods (such as case study and interdisciplinary approach) are being introduced.

4. Courses are no longer based largely on the mechanics of administration, but are grounded in principles and theory.

5. There has occurred a breakdown of the barrier between preparation programs for elementary and secondary principals and those for superintendents.

6. Internships are receiving wide and varied use.

7. Other forms of field service have become highly important.

8. Evaluation of the students has come to include appraisal of both knowledge about administration and use of knowledge in real situations.

9. Faculty members of the institutions now have wider backgrounds from social science disciplines.

10. There is more concern for guidance of students [p. 17].

Another important outcome of the CPEA was the creation of the University Council for Educational Administration (UCEA), which was organized for the purpose of improving the preparation of administrative personnel in education. Membership in the Council consists of major universities in the United States and Canada. The Council conducts research, prepares and disseminates materials for use in administrator-preparation programs, and coordinates the efforts of participating universities. Much of the Council's work in recent years has been directed toward the development of training strategies and materials including simulation, case method, laboratory training, gaming, and the internship.

The CPEA and the UCEA have served to establish the importance of the environment within which the administrator practices. Once the importance of the environment was accepted in the field of administrator preparation, the consequent need for emphasis upon the behavioral sciences had to be accepted. As a result, preparation programs for educational administrators were redesigned with an inter-disciplinary approach which included meaningful study of the social sciences.

Management and Leadership Functions

Another development which has contributed significantly to understanding of the administrative process in recent years is the separation of the administrative role between those behaviors which serve a *management* function and those which serve a *leadership* function. The fact that the educational administrator must perform a management function is generally recognized. Clearly, he must maintain the organization. Regardless of the outcome from manipulation of the human variables within the organization, there is an expectation placed upon the educational administrator that he will maintain the organization at all costs. The maintenance of the organization obviously requires specific skills of organization and management.

At the same time that he is maintaining the organization, the administrator is required to provide leadership; that is, he releases and channels energy within the organization toward the accomplishment of goals. According to Halpin (1966) leadership is situational. Depending upon the situation in which the leader finds himself, he is required to (a) initiate structure or (b) demonstrate consideration. Halpin describes leader behavior in terms of the two dimensions, explaining that when the leader is initiating structure, he (a) makes his attitudes clear to the staff; (b) tries out his new ideas with the staff; (c) criticizes poor work; (d) speaks in a manner not to be questioned; (e) assigns staff members to particular tasks; (f) maintains definite standards of performance; (g) emphasizes the meeting of deadlines; (h) encourages the use of uniform procedures; (i) makes sure that his part in the organization is understood by all members; (j) asks that staff members follow standard rules and regulations; (k) lets staff members know what is expected of them; (l) sees to it that staff members are working up to capacity; and (m) sees to it that the work of staff members is coordinated.

When the leader is demonstrating consideration, he (a) does personal favors for staff members; (b) does little things to make it pleasant to be a member of the staff; (c) is easy to understand; (d) finds time to listen to staff members; (e) looks out for the personal welfare of individual staff members; (f) treats all staff members as his equals; (g) is willing to make changes; (h) is friendly and approachable; (i) makes staff members feel at ease when talking with them; (j) puts suggestions made by the staff into operation; and (k) gets staff approval on important matters before going ahead [adapted from pp. 88-89].

Whether administration and leadership are, as Lipham (1964) suggests, "mutually exclusive [p. 141]" processes or, as Hanlon (1968) indicates, "leadership is a necessary part of the process of administration [p. 87]" is not at issue here. What is of importance to those concerned with training of educational administrators is the development of skills which permit effective management of the organization and, at the same time, make it possible to provide efficient leadership which moves the organization toward the accomplishment of its goals.

An Interdisciplinary Approach with Emphasis upon Organization Theory

Administrator-preparation programs of the fifties, which were directed toward the development of a theory of administration, drew heavily upon disciplines outside education; and, as indicated before, leadership training continues to do so, drawing particularly upon the social and behavioral sciences. Indeed, such concepts as "situational leadership [Stogdill, 1948, p. 40]," "social systems in administration [Getzels, 1958, p. 151]" and "defensive vs. participative administration [Gibb, 1967, p. 60]" are dependent upon such fields of study as communications theory, sociology, and psychology.

Trends in the early seventies indicate that future efforts to understand the administrative process are likely to continue to depend upon inputs from the social and behavioral sciences. However, these trends also indicate that administrative theory development in the seventies and eighties will focus attention upon the field of organization

123

theory — particularly the empirical studies under way in the field of industrial management. There is a growing awareness on the part of those attempting to develop administrative theory that the organization itself poses administrative problems entirely aside from the nature of the personnel involved or the environment within which the organization operates. Such problems appear to be intensified as the size of the organization increases. As Leavitt (1972) observes, ". . . the large organization superimposes some special difficulties on these others [problems of individuals, of relationships, or small groups], difficulties that seem to be the product of large industrial organizations [p. 257]."

Most educators are aware that problems inherent in the management of large organizations are not limited to industry. In fact, many large educational organizations appear to have become unmanageable in recent years despite efforts to apply the best principles of administration and leadership known to date. It is possible, therefore, that administrator training of the future will require increased emphasis upon the structure of the organization as it relates to organizational manageability.

Training Needs in Community Education

The view that the work of the educational administrator included two functions, management and leadership, applies to the administrator of a program in community education as well as to the administrator of a school or of a public library. A community education administrator performs many of the same functions that other educational administrators perform; his role quite obviously includes both managing and leading functions.

In 1953 few schools employed an administrator whose prime responsibility was the administration of a community education program. However, Drummond indicated at that time a need for specific competencies within the professional staff of a community school. Recognizing that many staff members would be involved in activities other than those directly related to administration, Drummond suggested that they possess, as a group, the following competencies:

1. A point of view which merges living and learning, which recognizes in-school and out-of-school living experiences as a continuum which is educative.

2. Sensitivity to social problems and trends based on wide reading by staff members and participation in discussion groups which identify and consider social needs.

3. Ability to live and work with others based upon a demonstrated respect for human personality and a willingness to consider the ideas of all community members. The staff needs to have those qualities of personality which make the establishment of good human relationships easy: a good sense of humor, tact, patience, and a spirit of tolerance.

4. Knowledge of the community and of techniques for studying the community which can provide the staff with knowledge of human and natural resources available.

5. Breadth of interest and educational preparation which enables staff members to be, at one time, competent specialists in their teaching area and competent students of community needs.

6. Physical health and emotional stability sufficient to withstand the greater-than-average expenditures of effort that are normally associated with community and school leadership.

7. Ability to apply what is known to the solving of identified community problems. This ability rests heavily upon an ability to marshal the forces of communication in a community.

8. Knowledge of children and youth which is as important in a program which includes adults as in one which deals only with children and youth.

9. Flexibility which permits adjusting an educational program to the changing conditions and problems of the community.

10. Faith in people which enables a staff to believe that people of good will become eager to improve the living conditions of their community when leadership in that direction is available. Such faith involves also a belief that people are able to achieve what is desired through application of reason and cooperative action (adapted from pp. 106-109).

Distinction between Process and Program

A definition of the specific management and leadership skills required of an administrator depends to a great extent upon the definition of his job; and there is some disagreement among writers on community education regarding the role of the community education administrator. The following writers have described various aspects of the administrative role in community education. The chief differences in their points of view lie in their varying emphases upon *process* as contrasted with *program*.

In the early fifties Seay referred to community education (exemplified at that time in the community school) as a process involving the relating of community resources to community problems. The following statement appeared in 1953:

The community school, by means of the educative process, relates the resources of people and communities to the problems of people and communities in order to accomplish a higher standard of living. The force which puts this process in motion is the understanding by educational leaders and laymen of the power of education in promoting social progress. The use of the educative process in relating problems and resources makes possible the achievement of the goals of the community school [p. 13].

Minzey and LeTarte (1972) supported the earlier position of Seay by giving community education a process emphasis:

Community education is a philosophical concept which serves the entire community by providing for all of the educational needs of all of its community members. It uses the local school to serve as the catalyst for bringing community resources to bear on community problems in an effort to develop a positive sense of community, improve community living, and develop the community process toward the end of self-actualization [p. 19].

In keeping with this description of community education, Minzey and LeTarte indicated training needs for community education leaders under four general headings: (a) understanding the community education philosophy; (b) technical skills for implementing community education; (c) humanitarian concerns; and (d) general administrative skills [p. 176-178].

Totten and Manley (1969), on the other hand, saw the community educator in a more restricted program role within the school:

> The director comes on duty at noon during each school day, stays on the job until late evening, and is at work on Saturday and throughout summer weeks. Except for the formal instructional program for children during the afternoon, the director is responsible for organization, coordination, supervision and administration of all programs and activities during the time he is on duty [p. 144].

This view of the director of community education spells out the personal and professional qualifications for the job in terms of health and vigor, personality, attitude, dedication, missionary zeal, skill in recreation and sports activity and English usage.

Observations in the field indicate that, to date, most community education activity in this country is limited to programs offered within the school. For this reason, the present role of the community educator is limited to a narrow range of management functions, clerical and custodial primarily. He organizes programs, recruits and assigns staff and student personnel, and supervises activities. Little progress has been made in actual fact toward providing for the processes recommended by many of the writers in the field.

The difficulty encountered by community educators in providing for the processes of community education may be understood better after differentiating carefully between program and process. The two ideas set up a dual responsibility for the administrator in community education. Management and leadership are involved in both parts of the dichotomy.

Speaking to a conference of community educators, Weaver explained this dichotomy in terms of goal expectations. He said, "*Program* is activity directed toward a goal — the activity usually restricted by time, place, and clientele. That is, a high school completion program is offered on an arbitrary time schedule, in the school, to serve a specific group. *Process,* on the other hand, is activity directed toward a goal, but usually not subject to the limitations of time, place, or clientele. The process of group leadership can be practiced wherever there is recognized need for such leadership [Unpublished paper presented at regional seminar, January 11, 1973]."

Both parts of the process-program dichotomy are important. A successful community educator soon learns that one part does not function without the other. Indeed, it is to be hoped that community educators learn to utilize their skills of leadership and management to help the people of communities meet their individual needs and solve their community problems whenever and wherever such skills are indicated. Sometimes their skills will be used in the leadership and management of process; sometimes in the leadership and management of program.

There is evidence, however, that successful functioning as a leader in the process role requires competencies different from those required of the program leader. In fact, some evidence suggests that those who function well as programmers find it difficult to leave the relative comfort of the program restrictions to provide process leadership in the community at large.

There is also evidence that failure to realize the potential of the process approach to community education may relate directly to the nature of our leadership training programs. Observation of these programs would indicate that considerably more effort is spent in training people in the management aspects of community education than is spent in training them in the leadership functions. Hence, the community educator feels he is better prepared to deal with program than with process. Furthermore, the selection of people entering leadership training programs in the field of community education has emphasized potential for development in the management skill areas at the expense of potential for development in the area of leadership skill. These observations would suggest thoughtful review of training needs in the areas of both process and program and courageous revision as needed at the leadership-training level.

The prime task of the community educator of the future is likely to be that of providing leadership — releasing and channeling energy within the organization toward the accomplishment of goals. In this role the community educator is primarily concerned with the processes of initiating structure and demonstrating consideration through such activities as coordinating, communicating, and surveying. He will demonstrate his ability to manage, as well as lead, the organization as he plans, directs, and supervises the programmatic aspects which develop out of his work as a community leader.

Community Education Goals

A national study of community education goals conducted by Weaver (1972) provides further data upon which to base predictions regarding skill requirements for community education leaders. These data are shown in Tables 5-1, 5-2, and 5-3.

Table 5-1 indicates the goals of community education reported as primary by 50 percent or more of the respondents in the national survey. The respondents, all of whom were professionally involved in the field of community education in either the public schools or at the college level, selected the 23 primary goals listed in Table 5-1 from 40 possible goals taken from the literature. It will be noted that, with the exception of seven goals directly related to providing programs, most of the goals involve what Minzey and LeTarte (1972) have defined as process — coordinating, surveying, demonstrating, training, and promoting. Such process goals result from recent changes in the direction of community education which can be attributed to shifts in thinking about the nature of the community, of education, and of the relationship between the community and education.

Table 5-2 depicts the "conventional" model of community education which assumed a stable community upon which was imposed a community education program which was school-based and program-oriented. The community educator, in this model, was accountable to the school and was expected to exhibit qualities of charisma, loyalty, and dedication and to develop a high degree of human skill to facilitate his role of programming and public relations.

On the other hand, Table 5-3 illustrates the emerging model of community education and indicates future directions as reported by the majority of respondents in the national study of goals. The emerging model assumes an unstable community — one in which there is

TABLE 5-1

NATIONAL STUDY OF COMMUNITY EDUCATION GOALS

GOALS OF COMMUNITY EDUCATION
REPORTED AS PRIMARY
BY 50 PERCENT OR MORE OF RESPONDENTS

GOAL	PROCESS
Coordinates efforts of community agencies Provides effective communication Eliminates duplication among agencies Assists residents to secure educational services Provides forum for community problems	COORDI- NATING
Identifies community problems Surveys attitudes and interests Identifies required resources	SURVEYING
Demonstrates humanistic approach to education Demonstrates methods of social change Provides model for community living Demonstrates principles of educational leadership	DEMON- STRATING
Extends use of school facilities Increases multi-age and cross-cultural contacts Provides programs for senior citizens Provides teen-age enrichment and recreation Provides recreation programs Provides high school completion program Improves educational opportunity for minorities	PROGRAM- MING ED. OPPOR- TUNITY
Develops leadership among lay citizens	TRAINING
Increases participation in existing school program Promotes school as primary educational agency Improves public image of rhe school	PROMOTING THE SCHOOL

TABLE 5-2

NATIONAL STUDY OF COMMUNITY EDUCATION GOALS

THE CONVENTIONAL MODEL

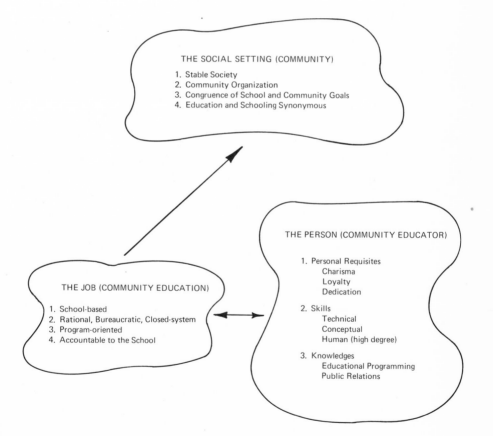

THE SOCIAL SETTING (COMMUNITY)

1. Stable Society
2. Community Organization
3. Congruence of School and Community Goals
4. Education and Schooling Synonymous

THE PERSON (COMMUNITY EDUCATOR)

1. Personal Requisites
   Charisma
   Loyalty
   Dedication

2. Skills
   Technical
   Conceptual
   Human (high degree)

3. Knowledges
   Educational Programming
   Public Relations

THE JOB (COMMUNITY EDUCATION)

1. School-based
2. Rational, Bureaucratic, Closed-system
3. Program-oriented
4. Accountable to the School

TABLE 5-3

NATIONAL STUDY OF COMMUNITY EDUCATION GOALS

THE EMERGING MODEL

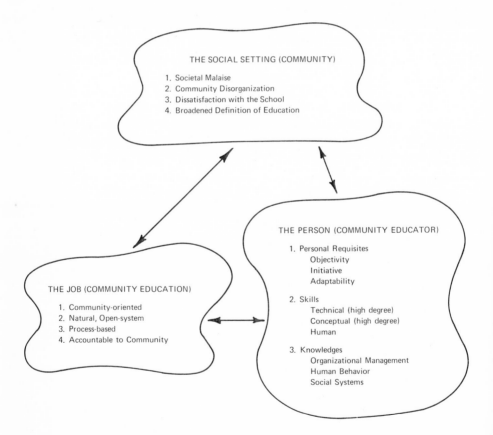

THE SOCIAL SETTING (COMMUNITY)

1. Societal Malaise
2. Community Disorganization
3. Dissatisfaction with the School
4. Broadened Definition of Education

THE PERSON (COMMUNITY EDUCATOR)

1. Personal Requisites
   Objectivity
   Initiative
   Adaptability

2. Skills
   Technical (high degree)
   Conceptual (high degree)
   Human

3. Knowledges
   Organizational Management
   Human Behavior
   Social Systems

THE JOB (COMMUNITY EDUCATION)

1. Community-oriented
2. Natural, Open-system
3. Process-based
4. Accountable to Community

considerable dissatisfaction, disorganization, and a general societal malaise. In such a setting, presumed to be representative of many communities today, the community education program is developed cooperatively with the community to assure the development of processes within a natural, open-system environment with reasonable guarantee of accountability to the community. The community educator in this setting must demonstrate personal requisites of objectivity, initiative, and adaptability and be the kind of person described by Melby (1972) as follows:

1. He is compassionate. He respects himself and others and feels involved with mankind.

2. He has a high estimate of human potential, believing all can learn and achieve, if they have adequate opportunity.

3. He is keenly aware of both the potential and the limitations of schools and other learning environments.

4. He is fully aware of the educational riches in the community and spends continuous effort in mobilizing them.

5. He is first of all a learner, a good listener, a constant reader, a seeker after educative experience.

6. He is accessible; his door is open. When people leave after a conference with him they are glad they came.

7. He is one of the first persons people think of when they are in trouble.

8. He is reluctant to take credit for accomplishments and slow to blame others for failures.

9. He can show confidence, optimism and enthusiasm even when most others have lost faith and confidence [p. 172].

In addition to the personal requisites above, the community educator must develop a high degree of technical and conceptual skill to permit him to analyze and manage the elements within the social system.

The implications of the emerging model of community education are clear; they indicate that the community education program of the future will be developed cooperatively among the community, the school, and other agencies with legitimate educational aims. The implications also indicate a guarantee of accountability to the community.

The community educator of the future will lead; he will release and channel energy within the community toward the accomplishment of community goals. He will initiate such leadership functions as coordinating, demonstrating, surveying, programming, training, and promoting — and in order to know when and how to use these functions, he will analyze a situation and recognize relationships among the relevant elements in the situation. That is, a successful leader uses conceptual ability. Furthermore, he uses skills of selection and implementation to get the job done — skills representing considerable sophistication in such technical aspects of group management as task and group maintenance.

Components of a Training Program

Of particular concern to those who train community educators are the components of a training program designed to develop the required leadership and management skills. Based upon the goals of community education identified in the national study of goals (see Tables 5-1, 5-2, and 5-3) and the skills implied in reaching those goals, the following components can be posited as necessary to the development of leadership and management skills in the field of community education:

1. *Conceptual skill.* Components which could be considered necessary to the development of conceptual skill are (a) organizational analysis, (b) leadership theory and model development, (c) behavioral analysis, (d) research, and (e) field experience and observation.

2. *Human skill.* Components which could be considered necessary to the development of human skill are (a) communications, theory and practice, (b) public relations, (c) group process participation and analysis, (d) social problem analysis, and (e) personality theory development.

3. *Technical skill.* Components which could be considered necessary to the development of technical skill are (a) organization management, (b) community organization, (c) financial management, (d) personnel management, (e) program development, (f) survey research, and (g) group leadership and analysis.

CONCERNING CURRENT TRAINING PROGRAMS

The community education concept has gained wide acceptance across the United States. A number of states have enacted legislation to provide funds for support of programs, and bills before both houses of the Congress would provide funds for the promotion of community education nationally. The Mott Foundation has established regional community education dissemination centers located in strategic colleges and universities across the country in an effort to assist communities in implementing the concept.

As a result of such efforts there is an increasing demand for trained leadership in the field of community education; and there is also increasing pressure upon colleges and universities to develop new training programs to meet this demand. Training programs leading to the masters degree in community education are provided in most of the institutions which serve as regional dissemination centers under the auspices of the Mott Foundation. Those institutions, however, cannot hope to meet the need for leaders trained at the masters degree level in the immediate future. Furthermore, the continued expansion of community education programs is creating a demand for leadership trained at the doctoral level. Few universities offer the doctorate with specialization in community education leadership. One notable exception is the consortium of seven Michigan universities operating under a grant from the Mott Foundation in Flint, Michigan. The Foundation provides stipends to qualified graduate students for a year's study in community education at either the masters or doctoral degree level at one of the seven universities. No doubt, there will be future demand for doctoral-level training programs in community education in addition to those provided by the Michigan institutions.

There is reason to believe that community education will be used increasingly as a viable means for providing educational services and, therefore, that demands for trained leadership will increase. However, despite what appears to be a developing agreement within the profession regarding the future role of the community educator, no such agreement is forthcoming regarding what constitutes satisfactory performance standards within the profession. Although the National Community School Education Association has addressed itself to this question from time to time, little progress appears to have been made.

At one extreme are those individuals within the profession who resist any attempt to specify performance standards for the community educator on the grounds that such efforts will minimize the human factor in performance. This group would certify anyone who could demonstrate a genuine desire to help people — regardless of his technical competence. Such a stance serves to substantiate the claim of many critics that community educators are a group of "good time Charlies" whose competence is limited to making good coffee and ingratiating themselves with the school clientele. At the other extreme are those who would base performance upon such statistical criteria as hours of credit and years of service — an unsatisfactory means of measuring effectiveness and one that has already been amply demonstrated as unsatisfactory by other professional groups.

It is probable that, ultimately, a plan for measuring performance against agreed-upon standards will be developed by the community education profession; and it is likely that such a plan will avoid overemphasis of the human factor and of the statistical factor. For example, it is possible that an individual's fitness to perform as a community educator might be determined by a system of carefully planned internships and laboratory exercises monitored and evaluated by experienced professionals trained for that purpose.

Until acceptable standards for satisfactory on-the-job performance of community educators are agreed upon, those interested in developing training programs would be well advised to (a) examine models with a view toward inferring the skills required of leaders working within the theoretical framework implied by the model; and (b) review training strategies currently used in the general field of educational leadership, recognizing that certain technical training requirements are, indeed, unique to the field of community education.

LEADERSHIP TRAINING PROGRAMS OF THE FUTURE

Since improvement upon past performance in the training of leaders for community education requires adaptation of the best in training strategies being used in community education and in related fields, any speculation regarding future efforts must consider the results of recently developed devices such as laboratory training, case method, and simulation. Many such training devices are already incorporated in existing programs. It will be helpful, therefore, to suggest some of the current training strategies which show promise for the training of educational leaders, generally, as the strategies which are likely to be used in training programs for future leaders in the field of community education. Strategies selected as being among those showing particular promise are: (a) provide experiences tailored to the background and needs of the individual student; (b) emphasize conceptual and technical skill training; (c) provide a variety of learning experiences involving a wide range of situational choices; (d) include field experiences; and (e) provide in-service training opportunities.

Experience Tailored to the Student

Leadership training programs will tend, more and more, to provide experiences tailored to the background and needs of the individual student. Since most candidates for advanced degrees have considerable experience before they begin graduate-level work, it is reasonable to assume that they already have highly developed skills in some areas and, therefore, should concentrate their efforts in areas where they have little or no expertise.

Two programs currently experimenting with individualized leadership training should provide direction in this area. The National Program for Educational Leadership with headquarters at Ohio State University utilizes interviews and a battery of tests to assist students in selecting new learning experiences which include reading, participation in National Training Laboratory (NTL) programs at Bethel, Maine, conferences with national scholars, and attendance at conferences of the American Management Association. And the Individualized Learning System for Administrators at New York University attempts to tailor a program to the individual student. Wynn (1972) describes the ILSA program as follows:

> Participation in the program is voluntary for both faculty and full-time students, either of whom may choose between the ILSA program and the more conventional instructional program. Students are encouraged to think carefully about their objectives and to approach content as a searcher or explorer with experienced guides (faculty) available to them. The main mechanism for achieving these skills is the student's individual plan for a year or semester, or even less, of his study. An orientation program acquaints him with the resources available in the university and the community. A conceptual-behavioral format is supplied for those who want it. When the plan is approved by the professor, the student proceeds to implement it in his own way and time.
>
> The plan indicates specifically how the student's work will be evaluated for marking purposes. The student is free to attend or not attend sessions of regular courses. In either case, course outlines and bibliographies are available to him. He may join with other students or faculty for one-time discussions or seminars. Special learning experiences, such as simulations of collective bargaining, seminars on research methodology, or sensitivity training, may be arranged. Field trips to metropolitan schools and agencies may be taken. Students frequently accompany faculty members to professional meetings and join them in field projects or research [p. 46].

Conceptual and Technical Skill

An emphasis upon conceptual and technical skill training can be expected to characterize leadership training programs of the future. Although human skills are considered of prime importance for successful performance by an educational leader, most graduate-level training programs will screen for human skills upon entry into the program and will, therefore, concentrate their efforts in the areas of conceptual and technical skill development.

Several strategies now in use show promise for the development of conceptual and technical skills. Among such strategies are those described by Wynn (1972). They include laboratory exercises, case method, simulation, and gaming. Usually such methods emphasize both technical and conceptual skill development through (a) bridging the gap between theory and practice; (b) providing practice in predicting consequences of decisions; (c) exercising the student's ability to think critically; (d) casting the student in an active decision-making role; (e) permitting analysis of variables in the leadership situation; and (f) critiquing the student's experience to permit analysis of behavior.

Variety of Learning Experiences

Leadership training will, in all likelihood, provide a variety of learning experiences involving a wide range of situational choices. One thing seems certain in the field of educational leadership — the decision to be made and the leadership style to be employed depends upon the situation in which leadership is being exercised. Hence, leadership training programs should provide opportunities for the student to select alternatives among a wide range of circumstances and to observe the consequences of the alternatives selected.

Field Experiences

Training programs for community education leaders will include field experiences. Unfortunately, the reality of educational leadership cannot be simulated on the university campus. Hence, if the student wishes to experience educational leadership as it is currently practiced in the community, he must spend part of his training time in the field.

The typical vehicle for providing field-oriented experiences has been the internship. An internship is intended to provide an opportunity to apply theory in a variety of practical situations under supervision of an experienced practitioner. Obviously, the quality of the internship experience depends upon the qualifications of those providing the supervision and the extent of opportunity for the intern to participate in an active leadership role. The possibilities for such participation are limited. At best, a given internship experience will provide a glimpse and a touch of the practical situation.

Opportunities for field experience, in addition to those provided by the internship, should be considered by individuals interested in developing doctoral-level community education leadership programs.

Three alternatives to the traditional internship suggested by Culbertson, and reported by Farquhar and Piele (1972), are:

1. A supervised internship experience supplemented by independent reading and periodic seminars. Near the end of the experience the student would prepare a paper describing the 'reading which he had completed during the last year of his study, the decisions and policy issues to which the knowledge acquired during his three years of study seemed most relevant and least relevant, and examples of the way decisions were shaped by the knowledge acquired.'

2. A team of graduate students (prospective administrators) and professors would select and define a major administrative or leadership problem in education, generate alternative solutions, logically evaluate the various solutions with the aid of personnel in a school district, and then assist these personnel in implementing and testing one of the solutions.

3. A team of prospective administrators would devote their final year of preparation to studying systems analysis and operations research concepts. The students would identify those concepts most relevant to decision-making in educational administration and then engage in field work in which they would apply selected techniques to actual decision problems in school districts. Finally, each student would prepare a paper in which he would report on his team's activities and results and present his ideas on the kinds of changes needed in school districts for better management planning and more effective use of operations research and systems analysis [pp. 36-37].

In-Service Training

A trend toward more regular provision of in-service training opportunities for community education leaders can be expected. If the slogan, lifelong learning, is appropriately applied to local participants in community education processes and programs, why should it not apply to the community educator himself? Regardless of the quality of his preservice training, the nature of the community educator's work, as does that of any other professional, requires that he update and expand his training periodically. Conferences, workshops, and seminars organized for the purpose of updating specific skills and knowledges are means of meeting the current training needs in the field. Here, as in preservice training programs, emphasis should be upon conceptual and technical skill areas, and programs should be tailored to meet the specific skill needs of the participants.

Selection of content for in-service training programs based upon input from the participants does not relieve the sponsoring agency from responsibility to provide appropriate resources from outside the group. Resource help from such centers of research and leadership as universities, state education agencies, and professional organizations will be required if in-service efforts are to result in substantive improvements among the participants.

The regional university centers are active in providing programs of in-service training planned specifically for community education leaders who are working in the regions of the centers. For example, the third major goal developed by the staff of the Western Michigan University Community School Development Center in 1973 was "Provide in-service educational opportunities for community educators, lay personnel, and students [as listed in Chapter Fifteen]." Classes and workshops held by this Center encourage study for college credit, and short-term programs and classes are held upon request throughout the region.

One of the key elements in the WMU Center's in-service program is an annual series of seminars for directors and other community education personnel – and for any other interested educational workers. The seminars are half-day meetings held each month from September through May. They focus on topics and issues central to the community education experience, particularly as such topics relate to leadership and administrative responsibilities. Each year the seminars deal with one topic on an extended basis, usually continuing work on the topic during three or four meetings. Other topics are usually completed in one session.

Extended work has developed around such topics as "The Environment in Education," "Gerontology and the Involvement of Older Americans," and "Writing Goals and Objectives." Subjects covered in one meeting, but sometimes repeated from year to year, include "Public Relations," "Special Programming Ideas," "Advisory

Councils," "Agency Coordination," "The Role of Community Colleges in Community Education," "The K-12 Implications of Community Education," "Funding Techniques," "Adult Education Recruiting and Teaching," "Recreation and Community Education," and "The Role of Superintendents and Principals in Community Education."

The format for the seminars varies from month to month and subject to subject. Sometimes the sessions focus upon resource people and their expertise. On other occasions the seminars are structured for sharing and exploring the experiences of the participants.

The seminars are jointly planned by various WMU departments, the regional community education center, and a committee of community education directors from the region. People who attend these seminars may elect to receive graduate credit by fulfilling specific requirements, and approximately one-fifth of the people so elect. Attendance in 1972-73 averaged more than 100 per month. These figures reflect a growing interest in the seminars — a growth which has caused the WMU center to split most of the seminars into two duplicated sessions, one in a morning and the other in an evening of the seminar week. During a year, only one or two of the meetings are held on the WMU campus; the other seven or eight are hosted on a rotating basis by community education directors in their own communities. This pattern tends to encourage the involvement of superintendents, principals, school board members, and other key local people in the seminars.

• • • • • • • • • • • • •

As a significant part of the history of efforts to improve the effectiveness of educational administrators, the CPEA project served to demonstrate the need for educational administrators to include study in the behavioral sciences as part of their training programs. Professionalization of the role of the educational administrator was improved, and a basis was provided for further improvement.

Educational administration can be separated into those behaviors involving leadership and those involving management. Leadership involves releasing and channeling energy within the organization toward the accomplishment of goals while management involves maintaining the organization. Those concerned with the training of educational leaders must develop programs which permit the development of both management and leadership skills.

The specific leadership and management skills required of the community educator are those resulting from the need to administer functions of "process" such as coordinating, demonstrating, surveying, programming, training, and promoting. The process emphasis in community education emanates from clarification in thinking regarding the nature of the community and the relationship of the institution of education to the community. An earlier community education model defined the role of the community educator as that of programming while the emerging model emphasizes his role as leader of the process of community education.

The implementation of the emerging community education model requires that the community educator develop the technical, conceptual, and human skills required in his role as leader and manager. The training program designed to insure development of these skills will need to include such components as organizational analysis, communication theory and practice, organizational management, community organization, personnel management, survey research, and group leadership.

There is likely to be an increasing need for community education leadership with consequent pressure upon colleges and universities to develop training programs at the masters and doctoral-degree levels. Hence, those interested in developing programs of training for community education leadership positions would be well advised (a) to examine emerging models and to give thoughtful attention to the necessary training components; and (b) to review current training strategies such as laboratory exercises, case studies, simulation, gaming, and internships which are applicable to the training of the educational leaders needed for the future.

The following chapter deals with the organizational and administrative structure for community education. The relationship between that structure and the leadership training programs discussed in this chapter is necessarily close. Leadership training prepares leaders to fill the positions within the organizational and administrative structure of a comprehensive community education program. Leadership training also prepares leaders to fill the positions within the organizational and administrative structure of each of the agencies which decides to cooperate as a component in a program of lifelong education for all the people of a community.

CHAPTER VI

ORGANIZATIONAL AND ADMINISTRATIVE STRUCTURE FOR COMMUNITY EDUCATION

ORGANIZATIONAL AND ADMINISTRATIVE STRUCTURE FOR COMMUNITY EDUCATION

GERALD C. MARTIN
AND
MAURICE F. SEAY

This chapter is not designed to describe the administration of individual educational agencies usually found in American communities. Furthermore, it does not try to describe the many organizational patterns of educational agencies because of the almost unlimited number of variables that would need to be considered. It does, however, contain some considerations that shed light upon the composition and responsibilities of the administrative teams and the decision-making bodies that plan and implement the community education concept.

The traditional organization of educational agencies, or "forces," is being modified rapidly. Clear-cut staff and line relationships become less clear-cut. These modifications are made as collective negotiations thrust administrators into new roles, as societal problems become curricular themes, as clarification of aims and objectives — with accompanying management and evaluation plans — are demanded by accountability-minded constituents. The impact of these new factors in educational administration is most noticeable, perhaps, in the public schools and in the public institutions of higher education, for they are indeed the largest of all the educational forces in a community.

The administrative structures of other institutional forces included in the comprehensive scope of community education are also in a state of unusual transition − YMCAs and YWCAs are merging into one organizational structure with new positions and new functions; scouting is reorganizing in order to serve variable populations; agriculture extension, shocked by the realization that its once highly successful adult education program no longer has the relevancy of earlier days, is reorganizing staff strength to achieve new goals more realistic for today's populations.

During this period of unusual transition a great variety of organizations can be expected to exist; the emerging models can be seen only dimly in the shadows. There is a continuing commitment to a decentralized system of administration and control which has marked the public schools and public institutions of higher education throughout American history. Other educational agencies vary considerably with respect to their administrative structure, but most of them claim to be flexible and at least partially under local control. This continuing flexibility is indeed fortunate for the growth of the community education concept. And the growth of this concept may prove to be the influence that retains for local communities control of their education in the face of increasing state and federal regulation.

The fact that American communities do not have standard organizational structures for their many educational forces places a great responsibility upon the local community. That fact also holds open a great opportunity. So long as the local-control policy continues to prevail and flexibility continues to be a dominant characteristic, communities have the opportunity to build viable educational organizations. Those communities which have succeeded in putting life into their comprehensive educational program have been doing it through some variation of the coordinating-cooperating process of community education. In those localities where the community education concept has not been introduced, or where it has failed in its purposes, the typical situation is likely to be some variation of the following: Schools and other educational forces working separately, defending their isolation, duplicating services and facilities, failing to recognize community needs, failing to fill serious gaps in the lifelong education of the people, and in their separate struggles to become larger and larger, wasting the resources of the community, both human and physical.

The choice presented to local groups of people in this period of transition seems to be (a) cooperative coordination of their community's educational forces into a comprehensive program of community education; or (b) wasteful, fruitless competition among their community's educational forces. It is a choice that will eventually be made by the people of each community, either by plan or by default. Those people who decide to use the community education process with its emphasis upon cooperative coordination will be thinking in terms of an appropriate organizational and administrative structure.

How to build an organizational and administrative structure that will facilitate lifelong learning for all the people of a community is a major problem facing lay and professional leaders in community education. The problem involves the many differing procedures being used today to implement the educational process for achieving a balance and a use of all institutional forces in the education of all of the people. The problem includes the fact that several differing viewpoints regarding the implications of the community education concept exist side by side today in the ranks of professional educators.

In order to describe possible solutions to this problem of how to build an organizational and administrative structure for community education, the authors of this chapter have (a) reviewed the literature noting the administrative structure of successful community schools and of effective adult education agencies such as the public library and agricultural extension; (b) studied the operation of community education programs that have been appraised as successful; (c) examined basic theory and principles of organization and human relations; and (d) gleaned insights from the general field of management by noting new developments in industry. As a result of these explorations, it is suggested that a balanced program of lifelong education, using the institutional forces of the community, can be facilitated by establishing an organizational structure which contains the following elements:

1. Procedures that facilitate and encourage the introduction of many features of community education in so-called regular programs of educational agencies or forces — thus creating a climate conducive to innovation and recognition of the community education concept.

2. Informal and cooperative action by staff members or other representatives of two or more educational forces — thus creating the beginnings of cooperative and coordinated relationships.

3. The use of consultative services to aid in selling ideas and in planning procedures — thus bringing in outside expertise to bear upon the problem of implementing the community education concept.

4. The infiltration of new and relevant educational activities involving two or more agencies by use of federal, state, and private philanthropic finance.

5. The provision within an established educational agency, usually the school, of a sound plan of finance and budget administration for those aspects of the community education program that must be initiated to provide the balance for lifelong education.

6. Official acknowledgement by boards of their acceptance of the community education concept, revealing understanding and approval of the concept.

7. The establishment of a position with a job description outlining responsibilities in the process of community education — which is perhaps the most effective of all these elements in administrative structure development. This position might be established in one educational agency (which would usually be the school) or in a specially established structure involving two or more agencies.

8. The development of advisory councils, which has proven to be the most effective way to get involvement of those for whom the program is planned.

Progress toward the implementation of the community education concept is made when two or more of these elements are introduced into the organizational and administrative structure. Real success, however, necessitates the inclusion of all eight of them. Each of these elements is discussed below.

Introducing Features of Community Education

When, for example, (a) a school has become concerned with the problem of environmental pollution and its curriculum has changed to reflect this concern; when (b) a public library has discovered senior citizens and has provided a lounge with special furniture and publications for this population, and when (c) the local units of public health have decided to emphasize preventative rather than remedial health, three agencies – the school, the library, and the public health units – are in a state of readiness for supporting a vigorous community education program. Their boards will understand the terminology, the philosophy, the implications for changes necessary for lifelong education. Their staffs, administrative and instructional, will welcome the opportunity to make their service more relevant to all the people of the community. A mere shift in emphasis in a traditional education program can be the beginning of a new attitude on the part of the various people involved: one which welcomes cooperative planning and coordination – and innovation.

Informal and Cooperative Action

The beginnings of a real community education program frequently result from the informal, cooperative efforts of the professional leaders of two or more educational forces providing services to a community. A typical example of such action is the cooperative plan for recreational activities during summer months worked out by a community school director and a city or area recreation director. This rather elementary plan reveals to the public, as well as to professional educators, the advantages of cooperative, coordinated programming. Locked playgrounds and gymnasiums are opened, staff duplication is eliminated, and additional employment is possible for nine-month professionals. But a more important result is the badly needed educational program which is made available to residents of the community through cooperation and coordination. From a simple beginning such as the opening of a playground, the more complex features of community education can be introduced. The necessary element for their introduction is the informal cooperation of professional leaders from several different educational forces in a community.

151

Using Consultative Services

As stated in Chapter Fifteen, a major function of the university centers for community education is the providing of consultant services to boards of local educational forces, to administrators, teachers, PTA's, and other lay groups interested in the community education concept. Such services can be secured also from university professors whose specialty is community education and from educational leaders who have successfully directed programs of community education. The aid given by consultants frequently involves planning, staffing, coordinating, and evaluating. A board of education in southwest Michigan secured through such services an in-depth review of its policies and its assignments to the local community education director. Many community education directors in Michigan have sought and received consultative aid in the preparation of proposals to the state and federal governmental agencies for financial assistance.

Infiltration by Financial Assistance

An old method of introducing change or of getting innovative ideas into practice is to secure from outside the agency financial assistance. The federal and state governments have during the past decade been primary sources for such assistance. As noted in various chapters of this publication, private foundations have aided many types of projects related to community education. And, although foundations have increased in large numbers during the past decades, their areas of assistance often go unnoticed because of their practice of limited publicity and restricted interests. In some communities private citizens and private industries have provided the funding for special features of community education. A large industry in a southwest Michigan city has provided funds for an assistant director of community education who is primarily responsible for working in behalf of minority groups.

Providing a Financial Base for Balance

No organizational structure for a community education program provides for that balance, included as a key promise in the definition of community education (see Chapter One), if the structure merely coordinates the activities of the established agencies in a community. Although such coordination is necessary to the development of a comprehensive, community-wide program and is extremely helpful to any educational program, filling the gaps in existing programs requires another step. These gaps represent educational activities needed in the lifelong education of the people of the community.

In a balanced program the gaps are identified and plans are made for filling them. Such planning usually requires special financing. In fact, before the gaps can be filled community education leadership must be provided. Employing a staff and setting up the basic facilities to support the leadership role is another part of the organizational structure that will require special financing. The amount of money needed is not large; small sums produce tremendous results.

Since implementation of the community education concept does require small sums of additional money, the number one question in every community wishing to start a program is, "How are we going to pay for it?" The trend toward more extensive programming adds to community concern that costs will rise as a program develops. Realistic planners seek answers to this question rather than making the mistake that is made too frequently by advocates of new endeavors – that funds for operation will somehow be available.

The facts are that no general statements can be made about the amount and availability of additional funds needed to introduce and develop a comprehensive community education operation. The actual amount needed and the source of such funds are entirely dependent on each local situation. There is, however, an estimate available as to the percentage of overall educational cost the increases may be expected to total when school systems assume the leadership role and finance the necessary new programming to "fill the gap." The following estimate is provided by Pappadakis (1971):

Obviously, the broad use of schools requires greater expenditure of funds than when facilities are used in the limited or traditional sense. When schools provide services on the extended day, week, and year basis, costs are increased. However, the increased cost for the broad use of school facilities is minimal. All research indicates that the additional net cost is six to eight percent greater when a school is operated on the extended basis. If all the schools in an entire district were converted into community schools, the increased cost would fluctuate between six and eight percent [p. 37].

153

No attempt is made in this discussion of finance to analyze the financial implications for the budgets of the many agencies that comprise the total education program of a community. It is assumed that shifting from traditional programs to those compatible with the community education concept does not involve significant increases in the financial burden.

Funding for the phase of community education involving special leadership and filling gaps usually occurs from a variety of sources which differ greatly in different communities: (a) The general fund of one or more agencies, (b) categorical provision of the local property tax, (c) categorical provision of the state appropriation, (d) federal grants for specific projects, and (e) activity fees paid by enrollees. Additional local funding is secured frequently from the Community Chest, Jaycees, industry, foundations, banks, service clubs, and village, city, township, and county governments.

The responsibility for securing adequate finances for special community education activities frequently falls on the shoulders of the community education director. Sometimes he raises money by writing funding proposals, soliciting local contributions, and carrying out special fund-raising activities.

The following sample of a typical first year budget for a small community shows a variety of funding sources; and it shows that large sums are not required. In this case the operation is funded entirely from funds other than the general fund of the educational agency, and thus the operation is limited in scope to its anticipated special revenues.

A Sample Budget for the Leadership and Special Activities Program of a Small, School-Centered Community Education Program

ANTICIPATED REVENUES

Student fees	$22,000.00
Foundation aid	3,000.00
State reimbursement:	
a portion of the director's salary	5,000.00
State aid for High School Completion: based on an estimated initial enrollment equivalent to	
30 full-time students	11,700.00
Adult Education Vocational Class:	
reimbursement	500.00

Total estimated revenues — $42,200.00

ANTICIPATED EXPENDITURES

Coordinator's salary	$15,500.00
Teacher salaries	18,000.00
Clerical salaries	1,000.00
Textbooks	4,000.00
Teaching supplies	800.00
Office supplies	500.00
Advertising and other expenses	1,000.00
In-service education:	
for teachers and director	1,000.00
Evaluation	300.00

Total estimated expenditures $42,100.00

Excess of revenues over expenditures 100.00

A few points to be considered when planning for the financing of a community education operation are described in the following list:

1. There are certain basic costs common to all community education operations. These costs would include (a) administrative expense such as director and assistant director salaries, clerical salaries, office supplies, and travel; (b) facility and maintenance costs such as office space, custodial services, heat, and lights; and (c) operational costs such as advertising. These basic costs must be financed adequately in order to provide a base of operation from which community support and other funding can be secured.

2. Program and activity development may occur in such a way that some projects will have a built-in plan of operation, their own source of funds, and complete provisions for staffing and supervision.

3. Programs should be initiated because of a need and not because of available money. The best program building occurs when two factors are present simultaneously: (a) a community need is expressed by the people and recognized by the appropriate educational agency; (b) finances for the programming required to meet that need are available.

155

Official Acknowledgement by Boards

Before outside sources will grant financial aid for community education programming, they often require the boards of the agencies which are to receive the funds to acknowledge officially their belief in and support of the community education concept. Such an acknowledgement not only puts the board on record, but in the process of making the acknowledgement the board usually acquires an understanding of the meaning of the concept and the implications of its programming and financing. A sample resolution adopted by a board of education reads:

The Board of Education endorses the community school education concept as a manner of serving the total educational needs of the local community. It shall be the policy of the Board to authorize the establishment of a community school program. This program will serve the educational and recreational needs of all age groups, preschool, youth, adults, and senior citizens. The community school programs will solicit the involvement of local government and organizations as well as neighboring communities in carrying forth programs. The community school program will be subject to the accounting procedures as well as other policies, rules, and regulations of the Board of Education [Policy Handbook, Board of Education, Paw Paw, Michigan, 1972-73].

Establishment of a Position

Leadership is a requisite for dissemination and implementation of any concept. Thus the growth of the community education concept has been most successful in localities where one or more positions related to a community education program have been defined and filed through the employment of trained personnel. The title of the position may not be too important; it varies from place to place. "Director of Community Education" is gradually replacing "Community School Director" where the programs are becoming more comprehensive and are involving a larger number of institutional forces. Other titles used are "Community Education Coordinator," "Community Education Agent," and "Director of Community Services."

Three combinations of responsibilities are shown in the following typical job descriptions of community education leadership positions in three different communities.

Job description No. 1. Duties of Community Education Director: The Community Education Director shall have full time administrative responsibility and be part of the school administrative team. He:

1. Programs, with the assistance of the school administration and other educators, all community activities relating to the school, including: (a) elementary, youth, and adult enrichment activities; (b) organization of school-related clubs, such as Teen Club, Women's Club, and Men's Club. (These examples are not intended to be all-inclusive nor are they meant to be restrictive.)

2. Promotes, publicizes, and interprets existing and planned programs to the educational staffs and the community.

3. Accepts responsibility for all activities of the school normally designated as community related.

4. Establishes rapport with lay leaders of the community (business, religious, and social).

5. Becomes familiar with the social and economic structure of the community and applies this knowledge to program development.

6. Establishes a community advisory council for the purpose of community program development and evaluation.

7. Assists in a constant evaluation of activities for the purpose of upgrading existing programs and implementing new ideas.

8. Establishes budget necessary for operation of the special educational activities not included in regular offerings of existing agencies.

9. Prepares and submits reports as required by the State Regional Coordinator's Office.

10. Establishes a summer enrichment and recreation program to meet the needs of the community.

11. Performs such other related duties and responsibilities as assigned by the school superintendent, or as appropriate.

Job description No. 2. Principal responsibilities of Community Education Director:

1. Adult education: He (a) determines what classes are required; (b) recruits the students for classes; (c) recruits and employs qualified instructors; (d) budgets anticipated funds; (e) schedules evening classes in cooperation with the building principal; (f) supervises evening classes and teachers; (g) counsels students; (h) evaluates individual teachers and programs; (i) communicates needs and accomplishments to the school superintendent and to the community.

2. Enrichment program: He (a) determines classes and programs that are needed and acceptable; (b) publicizes program offerings; (c) recruits sufficient enrollment to justify the activity; (d) budgets funds received; (e) supervises and evaluates the program; (f) communicates needs and accomplishments to the school superintendent and to the community.

3. Recreation program: He is responsible for this program which includes recreational activities for all age groups and is maintained throughout the year. The program includes the adult basketball league, recreational activities for school age children, and the community roller skating activity.

4. Summer program: He organizes, budgets, schedules, and supervises various summer-time recreational and enrichment programs for all age groups. Included in these activities are (a) summer camp for needy children; (b) instructional swimming (in cooperation with the YMCA); (c) swimming for fun; (d) Little League baseball; (e) roller skating; (f) gym

and field recreation; (g) instructional sports (tennis, badminton, etc.); (h) instructional classes (4-H photography, Kiddie Crafts).

5. Miscellaneous responsibilities: He must carry out other duties as delegated by the superintendent. These other duties include (a) matters dealing with public-relations; (b) attendance at pertinent meetings; (c) supervision of certain programs; (d) cooperation with the organization and administration of surveys.

Job description No. 3. Duties of the Community Education Director are:

1. Accountability objective. Under the direction of the Community Education Council, the responsibility of the director is to administer, coordinate, and supervise the adult basic educational program, adult high school completion program, community service, recreational, and enrichment programs. He is under the direction of and responsible to the superintendent of schools on all school-related matters.

   The director will have the responsibility of the community calendar and be responsible for coordinating the use of school facilities with day and evening programs. The director shall evaluate and assess existing community education program activities to determine their effectiveness and to make recommendations to the Community Education Council for future programs.

2. Nature of position. The community education director shall be responsible for the supervision and coordination of all adult education programs. This includes employing, assigning and discharging instructors with the help of the administrative assistant.

   The director shall observe classes to assess the effectiveness of all programs, and it will be his responsibility to see that there is a quality instructional program.

The community education director shall be responsible to prepare a budget and to submit the budget to the Community Education Council for its approval. After budget adoption, it is the responsibility of the director to see that the expenditures stay within the budgeted amounts. The director will be responsible for all state and federal reports, financial and otherwise.

The community education director shall determine the needed supplies and materials and see that they are ordered by the administrative assistant. The equipment and other large expenditures needed for programs must have the approval of the superintendent and the Community Education Council before they are ordered.

The community education director shall work closely with the principals and coordinate the use of all school facilities with the day programs. The principals have the responsibility of scheduling the facilities for the day program and submitting their schedule of needs of evening programs to the community education director.

The community education director has the responsibility to notify the respective custodians of the use of school facilities after the regular school day. It shall be the responsibility of the director to keep the principals and superintendent informed of the on-going programs and to make recommendations to the Community Education Council for the need of future programs.

The community education director shall have the responsibility for working with the recreation director and youth center director in implementing community recreational and youth center programs. The director of recreational programs and the youth center director will have the responsibility of the programs under the direction of the community education director.

The community education director shall assess the community as to the needs for programs. These programs will include social and community problems as well as enrichment and educational programs.

3.   Principal activities. The community education director shall
     (a) be responsible for adult basic educational programs, adult
     high school completion program, enrichment programs,
     community recreational and service programs, and other
     programs needed in the community and approved by the
     Community Education Council; (b) be responsible for the
     counseling of adults as to their individual needs to complete
     their education; (c) be responsible for employing and
     supervising instructors needed for the approved programs; (d)
     be responsible to see that the facilities and equipment are
     properly taken care of when being used by the community
     education program; (e) be responsible for coordinating the
     community education calendar between day programs as well
     as night programs; (f) be available to work with administra-
     tors of schools and other educational agencies in developing
     and coordinating total community education programs; (g)
     be knowledgeable about the trends in community education
     and be responsible to see that the school district takes
     advantage of any program that would be of value to the
     community; (h) be responsible for all reports and applica-
     tions; (i) be responsible for the ordering of supplies and
     materials for the community education programs; (j) work
     closely with the superintendent of schools in developing and
     coordinating the community education programs and submit-
     ting to the Community Education Council all programs for
     approval; (k) be responsible for other assigned duties.

The place of the community education director in the organizational and administrative structure where he is a staff member of a
school system was discussed by Martin in the November 1972 issue of
the *Phi Delta Kappen.* Martin stated that the experience of the Community School Development Center at Western Michigan University had
shown that the employment of a system-wide director (or coordinator)
was highly desirable [p. 187].

The position of system-wide director facilitates leadership in both
the initiation and the continuing administration of a community
education program in any type or size of community, whether it be in
an urban, suburban, or rural area. Illustrations of the introduction of a
specific community education program frequently overlook an important step when they show the program starting in one elementary

school and growing from there to encompass the entire school system and community. In almost all cases, before the program begins in the one elementary school, a community education leader has been functioning in some sort of system-wide administrative position. He has made sure that (a) he has won the support of the school system and the community for the community education concept; (b) he has coordinated the educational forces which will be involved in the introduction of the program; and (c) he has thought through, with the administrators of the agencies involved, the gradual, system-wide implementation of the community education concept.

Some of the advantages which can be gained from employing a coordinator-administrator at the beginning of the implementation of the community education concept are illustrated in the school-centered situation in which the school system employs a system-wide administrator to develop a program. Martin lists the advantages as follows:

1. The program in community education will be more closely attuned to the goals and objectives of the total educational system.

2. The coordinator for community education is involved more closely in the decision-making process within the school system and thus has the opportunity to establish greater relevance in programs, which will have maximum impact on the system and thus serve the people better.

3. A broader base for support for, understanding of, and involvement in community education will result.

4. The school system-wide approach in the initiation allows more flexibility in operational structure. A system may move toward employment of building directors (community education coordinators) servicing either elementary, middle, or secondary schools, individually or collectively. These directors can be professional educators, lay people, or even representatives of other community institutions. They can be employed part-time or full-time.

5. The system-wide approach allows more flexibility in meeting changing societal and cultural needs. It tends to unify people

rather than divide them. The elementary community school unit frequently is suspect when viewed by minority groups [1972, p. 187].

A majority of the community education programs which have been initiated in mid-twentieth century rural America and suburbia carry the imprint of their historical evolution from the community school. They are school-centered programs. They begin with the appointment of a system-wide "Community Education Director" or "Central Coordinator" of community education. A direct line relationship is established between the community education administrator and the central administration of the school. Usually the line relationship runs between the community education administrator and the superintendent of schools.

While the school-centered organizational model is found frequently, it is not the only model or, necessarily, a preferred model. A number of practical models have been developed to meet individual community needs. Figures 6-1, 6-2, and 6-3 show three typical models of organizational and administrative structure: one used in a small city in a suburban area, one developed as a cooperative plan involving three school systems, and one developed as a cooperative plan involving a school system and a city council.

Figure 6-1 shows a plan in which the Director of Community Education reports directly to the Superintendent of Schools. In Figure 6-2 the Community Education Coordinator reports to the three superintendents. In Figure 6-3 the Community Education Director reports to the Community Education Council formed by the Board of Education and the City Commission.

The applicability of the community education concept to any type of community is apparent from the examples of organizations shown in Figures 6-1, 6-2, and 6-3. The type of organization adopted to carry out the concept is developed as a result of process; its development is a function of present agency personnel and organization. The organization must fit the situation and be compatible with future goals and objectives. In Florida the organizational structure is aligned with the county school sytem. In a city in Ohio or Indiana it may be aligned with agencies outside the school system. In another

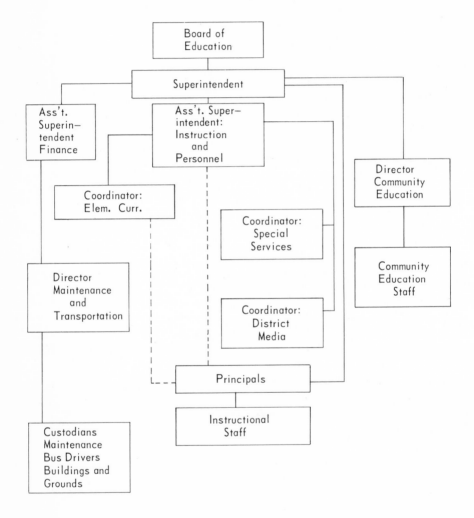

Figure 6–1. Community Education Organizational Chart:
A school–centered plan developed in a small city school in a suburban area with
system–wide leadership for a Director of Community Education.

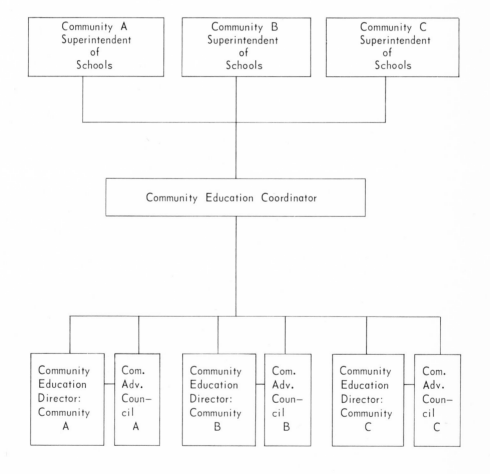

Figure 6-2. Community Education Organizational Chart:
A plan providing for cooperation and coordination among three small communities.

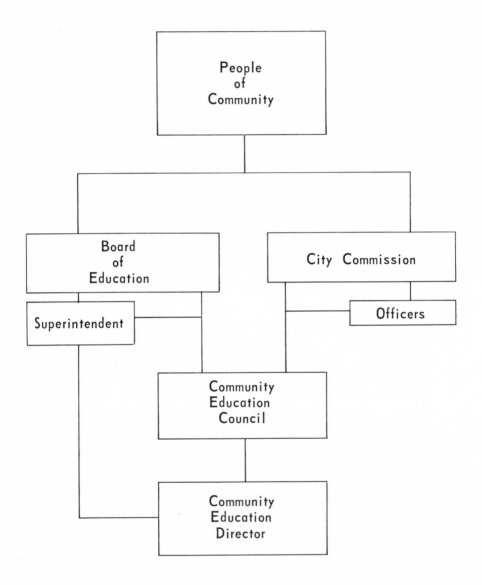

Figure 6-3.   Community Education Organizational Chart:
A cooperative plan involving a City Commission and a
Board of Education.

section of the country the intermediate school district may be the catalytic agent; or that function may be supplied through a community college. Flexibility is a valuable factor in adjusting the organization to the exact setting in which it must function.

One of the most important ingredients in a successful community education operation is the director, who is referred to in some organizations as coordinator or agent. This person's leadership style must be compatible with both his line and staff relationships, but the staff relationship can be expected to occupy a large part of his time.

The director is responsible for personnel under him. The staff relationship is not often shown in charts. However, this part of the director's responsibility is of primary importance. His operational working relationships, not only within a school but with other educational agencies and with other segments of the community test his leadership skills. While he carries out his direct responsibility for program initiation and supervision, he establishes and maintains working relationships with the individuals who assist and help at a cooperative level. In this leadership role, the director must lead by support and persuasion. His decisions must be in agreement with and, whenever possible, reflect fully the wishes and desires of others.

The agency itself has responsibilities for leadership by support and persuasion. In addition to the use of such skills on the part of the community education director, the educational agency, through its administrative ·personnel, must develop and use leadership skills that support the community education operation by providing opportunity for:

1. The input of a maximum number of representative individuals from all segments of society in all phases of the decision-making process.

2. The input of these individuals in policy development and policy implementation.

3. The development of a working relationship with these individuals which will enable them to feel a reasonable accountability and responsibility for their actions and relationships.

Leadership is, of course, a broad field for study — a study which is necessarily continuous for educational leaders. Further comment and suggestions on leadership will be found throughout this book, but particularly in Chapters Four, Five, and Seven.

Developing Advisory Councils

A basic principle of the community education concept, as discussed in Chapters One and Two, is that the educational activities are based upon the problems, needs, and interests of those for whom they are planned. A clear-cut implication of this principle is that in the organizational and administrative structure there will be provisions for official involvement of the people of the community served by the community education program.

Though sometimes difficult to fit into a neat organizational pattern, the citizens' lay advisory council and the coordinating council of agencies constitute vital links in the administration of a community education program. They give life to the basic principle that education is based on problems, needs, and interests of the people, and they bring balance into the community-wide program of educational opportunity for all.

The fact that lay participation and agency coordination do produce better educational programs can startle professionals. But the truth of that fact is being relearned in community after community today. Because the participation of lay people and the coordination of all the educational forces in the community are such essential components of the community education process, the next chapter provides a more detailed discussion of the representation and procedures used in advisory councils.

CHAPTER VII

ADVISORY COUNCILS IN COMMUNITY EDUCATION

ADVISORY COUNCILS IN COMMUNITY EDUCATION

STEVE R. PARSON
AND
MAURICE F. SEAY

Advisory councils put the community into community education. They provide a grass-roots level of participation in the process that achieves a balance and a use of all institutional forces in the education of all the people of a community.

People are not to be involved in advisory councils just for involvement's sake. Their participation in assessing needs, planning programs, and evaluating progress actually does produce better decisions. And better decisions result in better educational programs. The democratic principle? Yes. Belief in this principle is based on the long-tested knowledge that the people, given the essential facts and freedom to express their views, will make the best decisions in matters that affect their own welfare.

The state laws of this country place the responsibility for the operation of the public schools in the hands of elected school boards. Other educational agencies are usually governed by similar boards. The original intention of these laws was to provide a representative body of citizens who could decide basic questions of school policy from the community's point of view and according to the best interests of all the people. Through the years, however, the representation on school boards has changed. The boards are being charged with failure to represent the people they serve.

A nation-wide survey by Hottleman (1973) confirmed some of the charges. The survey found that many American schools whose constituencies were primarily the poor are governed primarily by upper-middle class men. Other findings included the facts that although 51.2 percent of the general population are women, only 20 percent of school board members are women; and while the average income in the communities surveyed was $11,694, the average income of board members was $22,682 (p. 51).

Most school board workers are conscientious public servants. Their lack of representativeness is no fault of theirs. The demands of the job and the peculiar functioning of the American political system simply do not provide a board that represents many of the interests in many communities. Thus other means of community involvement and participation must be realized. The community-wide educational advisory council is providing that representation for many communities today.

These councils are vital links in the organizational and administrative structure of community education — one of the eight elements discussed in the preceeding chapter. The councils take many forms, but most of them are either (a) made up of laymen representing the people of the community, or (b) made up of representatives of educational agencies in the community. In many communities more than one kind of council serves community education simultaneously.

Whatever the nature of an advisory council, the fact that it exists — that a group of community representatives have been called together — is meaningful. Olsen wrote in 1954 that the changing attitude among school people during the first half of the twentieth century had tended to follow three steps: "Keep out . . . . Come and see . . . . Let's plan together [p. 425]." When school people are ready to say to laymen, "Let's plan together," they have reached the stage of developing a school-community council with lay representation. And when the professional leadership of community agencies reached the stage of saying, "Let's plan together," the coordinating council was initiated.

Community Involvement through
Lay Representation

Since the school is frequently the catalytic agency in a community education program, discussion at this point is centered upon the school and its advisory structure. Many other educational agencies have similar councils.

A recent "Task Force for School-Community Development" of the Flint, Michigan, Community Schools developed the following definition of a school-community advisory council:

> A school-community advisory council is composed of representatives of those segments of the school-community . . . [residents and selected representatives of the school] who have a vested interest in the functioning of the schools and the quality of life in the community. The council should be recognized as a central component in the educational structure in each school in establishing and maintaining the linkages of communication among the important influences in . . . [a person's] environment that affect the ultimate outcome of his educational pursuits. . . . It is anticipated that this ensuing partnership will positively influence both the school and community . . . . The council can and should play an important role as an advisory group in the programs, policies, activities, and functions of the school. The council can also participate in the assessment of educational needs, the establishment of priorities, and advise on the resource needs of the school [*Guidelines for School-Community Advisory Councils*, Flint Community Schools. Unpublished interschool communication, 1973, p. 5].

The statement above indicates the purpose of a lay advisory council is, first of all, the establishment of adequate communication. Good communication between a community and its educational agencies makes possible a more active role for an advisory council. This role could well include advising on programs, policies, activities, and functions of the school or any other agency that includes an advisory council in its organizational and administrative structure. The assistance of the community, through its representatives on an advisory council, is particularly important in the assessment of educational needs, the establishment of priorities, and the tabulation of available resources and of those additional resources that should be made available. The planning of community education goals and objectives and the planning of community-wide problem-solving projects are also legitimate functions of a lay council.

Accurate representation of the population of the community is an important factor in the value of a lay council. The membership must be representative of the racial, ethnic, and socio-economic composition of the community served by the school. In some cases, it is necessary for a council to correct faulty representation through special action such as (a) a special general election; (b) a special election held within the population of the group not represented; or (c) a special committee formed for the express purpose of nominating or appointing representation for the overlooked group.

The plan for rotation of membership can produce any one of three conditions: effective, experienced membership; a frequent new, inexperienced membership; or a static membership with its point of view continued indefinitely. The first of these three conditions is the desired one, of course, and can be achieved with a small amount of thoughtful foresight and planning at the time of forming the council.

After planning to insure representation of racial, ethnic, and socio-economic differences in the community and a practical rotation of membership, the question of occupational and special-interest distribution of the council membership remains. This factor would include the matter of age representation.

The following list of criteria for council membership might apply to a school-community situation in which a lay council represents a school district or one school neighborhood:

1. Residents who are parents of children in school.

2. Residents who are not parents of children in school.

3. Residents who are active in school organizations such as PTA and booster clubs.

4. Residents who are active in neighborhood organizations such as service clubs and civic associations.

5. Residents who are students in school, young adults, middle-aged adults, and older adults.

6. The community education director.

7. Another one or two educational administrators whose presence at meetings would indicate the full support of the school organization behind the community education process and the council as part of that process.

8. A representative (or two) of the teachers.

9. A representative (or two) of the paraprofessionals on the school staff (and on other educational agency staffs when they are included in the comprehensive educational program of the community).

10. A representative (or two) of any other group active in the educational work of the neighborhood and school such as a particularly good friend of the young students who happens to be a custodian or a particularly valuable public-communications person who happens to be a secretary.

The role of the educational administrator as an active member of a lay council cannot be over-emphasized. If this involvement is lacking, the community education program may appear to be — and may actually be — an awkward appendage to the "regular" school program. Clark (1971) warns that community education leaders "must utilize representative community members in advisory and decision-making roles. Community education leaders who view advisory committees as merely 'on paper' or as 'rubber-stamping' units are missing the true meaning of community education [p. 9]."

Community Involvement through Agency Representation

An advisory council representing the agencies of the community is usually called a "coordinating council." The history of the development of the community education concept is also a history of the idea that the work of the various agencies of the community which have legitimate educational aims must be coordinated through some kind of "getting together." Olsen (1945) reported that the "first group to use the present term *coordinating council* was organized in Berkeley, California, in 1919 [p. 373]." By the time the "community school movement" was nationally recognized – during the forties and fifties – the use of coordinating councils was widespread.

In the seventies the necessity of involving the various educational agencies of a community in some kind of regular communication and cooperative planning of program is greater than ever before. That statement is not exaggerated. Never before has the American community sheltered, supported, and tried to use such an assortment of organized and staffed agencies with programs that include some kind of educational service for people. Many illustrations of this fact are given in Chapter Three. The possibilities of waste, competition, frustration, and confusion are limitless. Coercive centralization of planning might be one solution to the complexity. Voluntary coordination is a much better solution.

There are, of course, variations in the organization of coordinating councils, but the purposes and the representation are similar. The purposes of coordinating councils are quite specific. They include intentions:

1. To provide a vehicle for cooperation. Agencies, with certain educational aims, which send representatives to a coordinating council do so from mixed motives. The group will need to find a common purpose. Perhaps that purpose will be merely the general one suggested by Strang: "better persons in a better community [1953, p. 157]."

2. To bring about coordination of community educational services. A coordinating council does not provide services. It works only through its member organizations to bring about improved services.

3. To stimulate the acquisition of pertinent and accurate information on community educational needs and resources by member agencies and by the general public. This public communication function of a coordinating council is carried out through the member agencies.

4. To stimulate action on the part of all the agencies toward meeting community educational needs by balancing the

educational output of the various institutional forces of the community.

Excellent agency representation is achieved when all the agencies claiming educational goals — including civic organizations, social agencies, governmental units, public schools and church-related schools, industrial training departments, trade unions, professional associations, and the various training institutes that are operated for profit — send their representatives to sit down together at regular meetings. Initiative will have to be taken by one or two persons interested in community education, but once the council is organized, the council itself can take steps to improve community-wide representation.

The rotation of representation on a coordinating council is less important than on a lay council. The object of the representative structure on a coordinating council is to have the power structure of the agency firmly behind the words and actions of that agency's representative.

Frequently a coordinating council will include in its membership a few "citizens at large." Almost every community has a few individuals whose knowledge of the community and whose group-process skills make them invaluable members of planning, cooperating, coordinating bodies. Another type of member who would be valuable is the person representing a special interest in the outcome of the coordination of agency services. This person could be a member of a city planning council or of an area-wide planning organization.

A public school system frequently participates in a special relationship with the coordinating council in its community. In a small community, particularly, the school may have initiated the organization of the council and may have provided most of the early leadership. When the school is known as a "community school" the council based upon agency representation may (along with the council based upon lay representation) actually be a part of the organizational structure of the school. The relationship between the school representatives and the other agency representatives in such a situation is likely to require watchfulness on the part of the school representatives that they not feel, or seem to feel, aggressive, too knowledgeable, or in any way patronizing toward the representatives of other agencies.

177

Moon (1969) refers to a school-initiated council of agencies in the following list of principles emerging from the relationship between the various agencies:

1. Cooperation or interaction between agencies is vital to community education.

2. Communication is the heart of cooperation.

3. Organizations need adequate self-perceptions. Continuous evaluation must occur to be certain the self-perception is congruent with other-perception.

4. If possible, common concerns, and similarities between power and authority bases should be identified.

5. Each organization should emerge enhanced from a cooperative endeavor. Assurance must be given that preempting will not occur.

6. The school is the logical common vehicle. It may provide facilities, coordinate, facilitate, or initiate action [p. 63].

The 37th Yearbook of the American Association of School Administrators emphasizes the need in many school-community situations for the school administrator to play a particularly careful participative role: "The school administrator must be more than an interested bystander. ... Again and again, he must assume the initiative — although perhaps in subtle and sometimes unnoticeable ways — for community participation and progress in the solution of community problems [1959, p. 199]."

Procedures

All meetings of any advisory council should be open to the public. The meetings should be held on a regularly scheduled basis. The meeting dates should be publicized in advance so that interested persons, as well as all the council members, can arrange to attend.

The agenda. An agenda planned in advance for each meeting assists in making effective use of the time given to the meeting. A chairman might well multiply the number of hours to be used in the meeting by the average hourly wage earned by the members in their occupations — times the number of members. The total contribution in terms of dollars is usually an impressive figure. Each member of the group appreciates respect for his part of that contribution.

The items placed on the agenda may come from council members, individuals and agencies in the community, participants in programs, teachers, and administrative staff members of the various educational agencies in the community. The officers of the advisory council would, usually, seek the cooperative assistance of the community education director in the preparation of the agenda, but this is not necessary to the effectiveness of an advisory council in a comprehensive process of community education. The completed agenda should be distributed among council members prior to council meetings, preferably by mail several days before the meeting.

Minutes. The minutes taken at each meeting should also be distributed to members and to any other individuals who would like to be informed about council activities. The use of duplicated copies of the minutes, along with publicized, open meetings, can be quite effective in communicating the idea to every individual in the community that he is truly represented by the council.

Ad hoc committees. Advisory councils represent, in most cases, a large number of citizens. If the council members are to deal with the many issues that arise out of the job of developing, evaluating, studying, and developing further an effective community education program, they will need to distribute their efforts through the use of ad hoc committees.

The ad hoc committee is established to do a specific job. Examples of the kind of specific assignments which a lay council, advising on school-related matters, might hand to ad hoc committees are problems dealing with adult education programs, governmental relations, environmental improvement, curriculum evaluation, financial support, and improvement of school grounds. A lay council advising a comprehensive community education program could hand such ad hoc committees certain problems dealing with community use of a neighboring

179

community's civic center, the use of specialized talent in the community through special programs of the public health department, or the improved services needed from an underdeveloped city playground. Each committee is given a date when it will be expected to present its report to the council. Unless asked to do otherwise, the committee disbands automatically when its special job is finished.

The reports of an ad hoc committee should receive complete support from the council once the reports have been accepted by the council; and if the council represents various community agencies, the accepted findings of an ad hoc committee stand as the action of the council to be supported by each member agency. While such support would seem to be understood by all the parties involved, a controversial issue soon tests the firmness of that support. It is quite possible for communities to be divided, rather than coordinated, by unresolved disagreements within an advisory council.

The use of ad hoc committees provides an excellent opportunity for a council to involve additional members of the community. And if people are a part of the development of a program, they are more likely to communicate enthusiasm for the program to other people of the community and to provide the support necessary for the success of that program. Furthermore, programs developed through the involvement of many people will tend to be better programs because they will have evolved out of real needs actually known and felt by the people.

In-service training. Membership on a community education advisory council should be a learning experience. The regular meetings with other people of the community can qualify as a small learning experience, but the possibilities beyond that small beginning are exciting. Members can improve their understanding of leadership. They will be able to practice new skills as part of their council work. Members can learn about other communities and the outstanding, innovative councils which are beginning to deal with real community problems — difficult community problems — and are studying alternate ways of solving them. Accounts of helpful examples should be made available to members at the time of the regular meetings. Community education leaders have a responsibility for helping the members of advisory councils become more effective representatives of the community.

Clark (1971) suggests that community education leaders involve their lay council members in "visitations, workshops, and conferences enabling these leaders to gain from the ideas and experiences of others [p. 9]."

The leadership role. The leadership role in an advisory council involving lay representation is somewhat different from the leadership role in a coordinating council involving agency representation. In the first case members of the council, and hopefully the officers, come from many different kinds of backgrounds. A few of them will have had training in group leadership; a few others will have a natural flair for it; the majority will need to develop skills if they are to act as leaders in the council and in the part of the community they represent.

A coordinating council, on the other hand, usually draws a high proportion of its membership from the professional staffs of the agencies that are represented; there is no lack of leadership skill among them. Officers of the group may have to exercise all the group-process skills they can command in order to keep the work of the group focused upon the comprehensive educational goals of the total community. They will need to delegate much leadership responsibility to members of the council. They will need to make use of the leadership talents of other citizens of the community. And they will need to make sure that leadership roles, by prearranged plan or by election, are rotated widely enough and regularly enough that no agency can have a legitimate complaint in the matter.

Since the leadership role in the lay council involves one factor not usually considered in resource material on leadership, it will be mentioned here. It is simply the fact that an advisory council involving lay representation must function on the basis of lay leadership.

Allowing a lay advisory council to really function on the basis of lay leadership is a particularly difficult achievement for many community education leaders. There are many reasons for this situation. The strong motivation toward developing the resources of the community, which community educators must have, makes difficult a stand-by posture while others fumble with a job that needs to be done. Community educators study strategies of leadership; they practice the leadership role in almost every aspect of their work, talking and activating procedures all day and all evening, until they become, if they do not guard against the occupational hazard, non-stop "leaders." When that happens, they find it difficult to (a) listen, and (b) to act upon a group decision made under leadership other than their own. Difficult as such action may be, however, community educators must listen and they must act upon decisions of the group.

Biddle and Biddle (1965) offered a helpful perspective on the problem of how to use lay leadership in the following statement about "encouragers," as they aptly named professionals who have skills in developing lay leaders: "The encourager . . . hopes that the people may learn to exercise more control over change . . . and expects people, through their experiences with process, to discover many new ways. . . [p. 260]."

The encourager is, of course, a member of the group; in that capacity he can suggest innovations that will stimulate the expression of ideas by other members of the group, and he can suggest alternatives. The emphasis placed on the word "hope" in the encourager's attitude is a reminder that the community educator must put away all pretense, all tricks of manipulation, and accept fully the basic fact that lay leaders are able leaders. Minzey and LeTarte (1972) stated the idea in these words: "People should be done *with* and not *to* . . . [p. 45]."

Four "Don'ts" sum up the warning in the foregoing paragraphs:

1. Don't ask advice you know in advance you are not going to accept.

2. Don't use advisory councils to "rubber stamp" your own ideas.

3. Don't fail to explain why some advice given by an advisory council cannot be followed.

4. Don't underestimate the leadership potential of community members.

An Example of a Lay Council in a Rural "Community School" District

The Goldfield Community School District, located in rural Iowa, has conducted an unusually successful adult education program. The superintendent of the district attributes much of that success to the functioning of a community advisory council.

The Goldfield advisory council is made up of representatives of the surrounding community which includes both rural and small-town areas. The council members advise the community school on courses the community would like to see offered in the adult education program. They also assist in locating persons who are able to teach the courses.

After the classes are scheduled, the council members divide up the schedule and take several classes as their personal responsibility for promotion. Since the communications network in a rural community is highly developed, these council members are quite effective in a personal type of promotion, and the classes are well attended. The people on Goldfield's advisory council develop a real sense of pride in "their" program.

Example of Lay Council Involvement in a City

Community education would meet community problems by involving the people in using community resources to solve the problems. Advisory councils would bring about the involvement of the people. This is all very well in theory, as Nance and Snapp (1973) said in an article about Independence, Missouri, but too often serving on a community advisory council does not really involve people. Nance and Snapp believed that a major error exists in the ambiguity of the reasons for forming an advisory council. They said, "The objectives and task are usually not clear to all involved. There is also, in most instances, a misunderstanding about the degree of involvement of lay citizens [p. 12]."

City leaders in Independence challenged a Citizens Goals Committee on January 2, 1971, as follows: "We need a greater involvement of people in the affairs of the city. I [the mayor] feel that the Goals Committee can be the nucleus of a city-wide effort to make this a better place to live [p. 13]."

Earlier progress toward city improvement was studied, and a decision was made that the basic problem of city-wide deterioration was starting in neighborhoods. Citizens were no longer neighborly — and thereby society had lost one of the primary ways people had experienced social interaction. Of course, there were many complicated reasons why citizens were no longer neighborly, but those reasons would not solve the problem and revitalize the city. Nance and Snapp stated the forthright decision of Independence: "If neighborliness was a value which ought to be preserved for the sake of society, then a social structure ought to be devised suited to our times in which neighbors could be encouraged to be neighborly [p. 14]."

The plan for increased citizen involvement was built around the following organization:

1.   Neighborhood councils in every neighborhood.

2.   A Citizens Advisory Council composed of the presidents of Neighborhood Councils.

3.   Citizens Committees which were subcommittees of the Citizens Advisory Council were formed to function with the Fire Department, the Police Department, the Streets Department, and each of the other departments in the city organizational structure. Each Citizens Committee was made up of persons coming from every Neighborhood Council in the city.

4.   Citizens Workshops and Assemblies which met every month from October through May for purposes of communication between members of the Citizens Committees and the departments to which they were related. (Half of the Citizens Committees met each month on an alternating schedule.) A typical meeting was held in a public building, such as a neighborhood school. It started with a workshop: several small groups met in different rooms; departmental representatives shared information on their departments and citizens asked questions and shared information with the city councilmen who were present. A second hour was scheduled for the assembly; questions and information sharing continued in the larger group.

Each citizen committee gained an in-depth understanding of the individual departments of city government, learned to know their city councilmen, raised questions, shared ideas, and took valuable information back to their neighborhoods. The city departments, and city government as a whole, began to be responsive to citizen interest and participation.

Nance and Snapp concluded by pointing out three implications for community education:

1. The model provides a means of bringing together local government and other community service agencies and the people they are trying to serve.

2. The school has the opportunity to provide a medium where such communication and cooperation may flourish.

3. The delivery system is adequate to fulfill the program request based upon community-wide decision-making [p. 15].

• • • • • • • • • • • • •

Community advisory councils with lay representation are the lifeline of community education. They tie the agencies that provide educational services to the community which commissions those services, uses them, and pays the bill. They also enable educational agencies to be accountable to the people of the community because they provide two-way communication between the agencies and the people. To provide real communication, councils must be involved in (a) needs assessment, (b) policy formulation, (c) decision making, and (d) evaluation.

Coordinating councils, however, serve a different purpose. They bring together representatives of the various educational agencies in a community. Strengthening and balancing existing agency services through the coordinating process is one of the valuable contributions these councils make to community education.

Advisory councils of all kinds improve communication between the people and the educational professionals who work in the community. People need, however, a structure which enables them to deliver the participation and understanding that is asked of them. "Sitting on a council" is not enough. A major responsibility of community educators is to devise a structure that will fit the community setting and enable the advisory councils of that community to involve the people — actually and vitally — in the community education process.

The type of idealism surrounding the involvement of American people in community education can be found in other parts of the world. An English community educator, C. D. Poster (1971) expressed the conviction of many leaders that community education "depends for its success not upon theories or upon buildings, but upon people. Theories help; but the basic humanitarian concept upon which . . . [community education] depends for its success is more than a theory. It is an attempt to put into practice a principle that is shared by all men of good will, those of whatever religious persuasion or of none, who are prepared to accept the commandment 'Love Thy Neighbour [p. 116]'."

CHAPTER VIII

PROGRAMMING THE COMMUNITY
EDUCATION CONCEPT

PROGRAMMING THE COMMUNITY EDUCATION CONCEPT

GERALD C. MARTIN
AND
MAURICE F. SEAY

The organizational and administrative structure for community education, explained in Chapters Six and Seven, is established for three specific purposes:

1. To influence the existing programs of all educational agencies to the end that they are more and more based upon the community education concept that community education achieves a balance and a use of all institutional forces in the education of all of the people of a community.

2. To provide the means for cooperative planning, coordinating, and evaluating.

3. To add to programs of established agencies or to a cooperative operational plan involving two or more agencies those educational activities determined to be needed to fill gaps so that a balanced program is available for all people of a community.

Putting the Concept to Work in Established Agencies

The values and learning effectiveness of some of the various aspects of community education have been accepted and implemented in the established programs of many educational agencies for a long, long time. Some schools today, although not necessarily called "community schools," have in one or more of their teaching units characteristics that fit the concept of community education. Each of these schools:

1. Evolves some its purposes out of the interests and needs of the people.

2. Utilizes in some of its instructional programs a wide variety of natural, human, and institutional resources within the community and emphasizes solutions to problems of living as an important part of learning.

3. Practices and promotes democracy in many activities of school and community.

4. Builds the curriculum core for many grade levels around the major processes and problems of human living.

5. Exercises definite leadership for the planned and cooperative improvement of group living in the local community and in larger areas of the regional, state, and national communities.

6. Enlists children and adults in cooperative group projects of common interest and mutual concern.

7. Makes the school plant and its facilities available for use as a community center and as a demonstration of desirable operation and maintenance of property.

8. Provides for democratic participation of the teaching staff, the children, and other members of the community in the general administration of the total program.

9.   Has a satisfactory library service under the direction of a trained librarian, and makes the library available to adults as well as to young people.

10.   Participates in a coordinating council through which agencies of the community cooperate with the school in planning its educational program.

11.   Is staffed with teachers, some of whom have deep convictions as to the functions of the school in a program of community education, who are aware of their responsibility for the total growth of each child, and who improve themselves professionally through work conferences, Saturday classes, and summer workshops.

12.   Enriches the materials within the textbooks by bringing the children, youth, and adults in contact with the natural and social environment, and by providing special-purpose and school-made instructional materials based on the problems and resources of the community.

Thus, in some schools which are not known as "community schools" there are, actually, the beginnings of implementation of the community education concept. The same situation exists in other educational agencies as they, too, without community-wide leadership or coordination, incorporate into their isolated programs characteristics that fit the concept of community education.

These beginnings provide a ready point of departure for expansion of activities based upon the community education concept. From these beginnings − with appropriate organizational structure − a far-reaching program of community education can develop in a surprisingly short period of time.

On the other hand, some communities and the educational agencies within them have resisted change vigorously. The introduction of the community education concept can be expected to be more difficult in these communities. Here experience from attempts to be innovative shows that the promotion of the use of community resources as instructional materials is an effective way of introducing the community education concept. It is so obviously reasonable to begin a study involving pollution, for example, by observing local polluted areas and by asking public health staff members for information.

Irwin and Russell reflect and stimulate this interest in the use of community resources as part of the learning process. They open their book, appropriately entitled *The Community Is the Classroom,* with these sentences:

> Children are learning as they live. The natural learning environment is a rich one indeed, yet today many children are experiencing difficulty with a school curriculum which makes limited use of this valuable resource [1971, p. 3].

Clyde Campbell of Michigan State University urges that school representatives serve as catalytic agents for change. He is joined by many educators who may not be known as leaders of "community education," but who also see the necessity for change, for revitalization of learning in the classroom. These educational leaders serve as catalytic agents themselves when they work in community colleges, small liberal arts colleges, public school systems, and other centers for learning in local communities. They cause the members of their own school and community groups to see new possibilities, better solutions for old problems, better ways of using community resources.

George Eyster is demonstrating to an entire region better ways of using available resources to solve community problems. As director of the Appalachian Adult Education Center at Morehead State University in Kentucky, he is providing leadership for a number of projects directed toward improving the educational opportunity of adults in the region. At the time of this writing the Center is exploring and demonstrating possible uses of library services in local communities — thus helping libraries in Appalachia become more effective learning resources.

The problem-solving approach to learning, so characteristic of community education, is more and more becoming the approach of all educational agencies. The church and synagogue provide educational activities which deal with problems of drugs and sex; the Y offers training seminars to meet the problem of food preparation faced by senior citizens; the city commission appropriates funds for training out-of-school youth who face the problems of unemployment.

And so it is: Leaders of schools and other educational agencies often use the process of community education to solve community problems — whether or not they call such activities by the name "community education." They use the process because they have found that programs developed out of this process accomplish more effectively the traditional aims of education — transfer of skills and knowledge and the transmission of societal values. Thus, programs of agencies which reflect the characteristics of community education are more effective in educating the people of the community. Even agencies that are rigid or that are highly specialized may be infiltrated by being shown the obvious advantages of using some elements of community education. Appropriately, the organizational and administrative structure for community education which is described in Chapters Six and Seven names "influencing the educational forces of the community" as one of its three major purposes.

Cooperative Planning, Coordinating, and Evaluating

Throughout this book frequent reference is made to the waste and the gaps in lifelong learning that result from isolated operation of many educational agencies. In one suburban area a study showed that "small motor machines" was a short course offered at the same time by three adjacent agencies and that the enrollments combined would not be large for one course. No one of these agencies could afford to recruit by radio and newspaper advertisement; but in a nearby community a cooperative arrangement among training agencies made such public communication financially feasible and, in terms of recruitment, very effective.

Desirable as economy is, the most important reason for cooperative planning and coordination is not the avoidance of waste, but the assurance of improved educational programs — the assurance that learning by the people of a community can be a lifelong process and that a balanced program of learning experiences will be available to the people. No one agency — not even the school — can do the job of total education for the community. The public school, because of its vast resources, human and physical, can be a catalyst, and it can initiate and operate new programs needed to fill gaps. But the school must follow the policy of relinquishing an activity when some more appropriate community agency is ready to provide that activity. A carefully coordinated process can result in a balanced program of community education for all the people. Volunteer action by two or more leaders of agencies and advisory councils, as explained in Chapters Six and Seven, is a useful way of securing coordination.

Most educational agencies have been forced by their constituencies to face the demand that they be accountable and evaluated. This demand poses special questions for any educational process whose programs cannot be measured by a battery of true-false or multiple-answer questions. Community education leaders are asking: (a) For what is community education accountable? (b) To whom is community education accountable? (c) Accountability to what end? These questions and a sample accountability plan used for one program are included in Chapter Nine's discussion of the subject.

Balancing the Program: Filling the Gaps

Balancing the comprehensive program is a major responsibility of the organizational and administrative structure for community education. Because a balanced program meets the real — and current — educational needs of all the people, assessing needs is implicit in any operational plan for community education. The study of community needs reveals gaps that, in some instances, the agencies of a community will fill through their established procedures. Often, however, a special organizational and administrative structure will be necessary if the balanced program is to be achieved. This structure is explained in Chapter Six.

Of course, one hundred percent attainment is not realized in a lifelong education of all the people of a community. But this qualification of the ideal has not lowered the morale of the many community education directors who provide leadership in a dedicated effort to identify and fill gaps. Actually, the work devoted to filling gaps in the comprehensive community education program has, in many areas, become almost synonomous with the term "community education." Sometimes descriptions of "the community education program" are limited to a listing of special activities (usually for adults, youth, and children after school hours) made possible by a special organizational and administrative structure. These activities are of tremendous importance, but it must be remembered that they do not constitute the total community education program. Conceivably, a widespread confusion as to the relationship of (a) special activities designed to fill gaps with (b) the comprehensive community education program could lead to the development of an isolated program of adult and after-school education which would be a direct frustration of the community education process. Such confusion can be avoided easily by seeing programs of special activities as *part* of a community education program.

The organizational and administrative structure for community education has, built into its provision and purpose, guarantees that unity (coordination) shall be established and preserved. Since program is put into effect by organizational structure, such guarantees of community-wide coordination are valuable. Examples of actual programs show these guarantees to be operating in various ways. Several examples of programs are used illustratively throughout this book; therefore, the illustrations used here will be limited to (a) one program which emphasizes activities to fill recognized gaps in the comprehensive educational program of the community, and (b) three activities selected from another program for the purpose of emphasizing cooperative relationship with nonschool educational agencies of the community.

Three different types of structure are described in Chapter Six, and each type can activate an effective community education program. The most common organizational structure in community education is the one in which a director is administratively responsible to the superintendent of schools and is assisted in policy decision-making by lay and representative councils. One community, organized in this manner, was Orchard View, Muskegon, Michigan. The specific activities found to be needed in the year 1972-73 to balance this community's program for lifelong education were offered during a 12-month period to all residents of the community. The following list of the activities and descriptive statements is quoted from a "Fact Booklet" distributed in the community.

Adult completion. Adult completion provides a large variety of classes for individuals interested in gaining a high school diploma. This is an opportunity to take elective and required courses to earn credits toward graduation. The high school classes are ungraded so students are not classified as 9th, 10th, 11th, or 12th graders.

Who may attend? Any adults who are interested in receiving their high school diploma.

What will it cost? Classes are free for adults who have not finished high school.

How can I enroll? Call the Community School Office or mail the coupon below.

Adult basic education. The primary aim of the adult basic education program is to help improve your reading, writing, and arithmetic. This is for adults with less than an 8th grade education, for people who have completed or attended high school but want to refresh the basic skills, or to prepare one for high school completion courses; and it is all free.

English taught as a spoken language. Special classes will also be provided for foreign-speaking persons who wish to improve their English. These programs are entirely FREE. Both day and evening classes are offered.

Enrichment and recreation for adults. A wide variety of classes and activities are offered for your interest and enjoyment, such as:

Accounting	Family swim
Auto shop for men and women	Furniture refinishing
Basic bookkeeping	Golf
Basic snowmobile repair	Guitar
Cake decorating	Handbuilt pottery and sculpture
Candle making	Holiday decorations
Cashier sales training	Individualized painting
Ceramics	and drawing
Chess	Interior decoration
Conversational German	Jewelry making
Conversational Spanish	Knitting and crocheting
Creative writing	Modern math for adults
Dressmaking	Oil painting
Outboard motor repair	Slimnastics
Personal and basic typing	Small appliance repair
Poodle grooming	Speed reading
Problems in personal	Swimming
income tax	Tailoring
Psychology	Upholstering

Red Cross standard first aid	Welding
Self defense for women	Wig and Wiglets
Sewing (beginning)	Yoga

All enrichment classes have a fee, largely used to offset the cost of employing course instructors and activity supervisors. People over 65 may take one class free. In some classes we have family prices.

Senior citizens. The Gather Together Club held its first meeting in January, 1968, with eleven persons attending. Membership since has grown seven-fold with group activities broadening to well beyond the traditional card playing and bingo. The group, which meets twice monthly, participates in pool parties, picnics, bus excursions, and other events. Periodically, speakers address the group, or travelogue films are shown.

Membership qualifications — any person who thinks of himself as a "senior citizen." Meetings are held on the 2nd and 4th Monday of the month in the Home Economics room at 6:00 p.m. Besides special activities, each meeting has a potluck with each bringing a dish to pass. Membership fee: 25 cents annually.

The school system also provides senior citizens passes free to any school activities such as football, basketball, plays, and aquaette shows.

In addition to the evening senior citizens' Gather Together Club, we will attempt to organize a daytime drop-in center at each of the three elementary buildings. This may include games, handicrafts, or whatever the people involved would decide to do.

Men's League basketball. This year we will again sponsor a basketball league. The basketball league will begin Wednesday, November 29. The league will consist of six teams, running a ten game schedule with a possible week of tournaments.

Enrichment and recreation for youth. Enrichment programs in all elementary schools will provide four to five classes per week based on the wants and needs of each school. The program should include something in art, theater arts, physical education, as well as other programs not specifically included in regular day activities, such as "math for fun."

It is hoped the effort will allow students to increase skills and pursue special interests. These classes will be offered immediately after school. [This activity offers an excellent example of infiltrating change into the regular schedules of a traditional schooling program.]

Youth Recreation will also be offering Little League Basketball for 4th, 5th, and 6th grades. We will also be having an intra-mural basketball at the High School and an open gym night for middle and high school boys and girls during the winter months from November to April.

Family swim night for parents and children is on Wednesday. Cost is $1.00 per family up to seven members, or 35 cents per person. An adult must accompany the children.

We will be offering instructional swim for all ages.

Summer recreation. This year again we had our four play-grounds supervised by eight college students. There were a male and a female director at each center. It was their responsibility to conduct games and activities for youngsters 5 through 14 years of age to participate in during a six-week period.

Each week emphasized a special event that the children could look forward to. During the last week of the program, each playground presented a small trophy to the boy and girl who displayed the best citizenship throughout the summer.

We also plan to offer special programs during the summer for children and adults. There will be gymnastics, women's softball, men's softball, and tennis.

Preschool program. To a youngster going to school for the first time, a school building or a big yellow bus can be a frightening sight. The purposes of the preschool program are to acquaint parent and child with the school the kindergartener will attend in the fall and to bring about closer cooperation between home and school.

Each future kindergartener's home is visited and the parents are issued a personal invitation to participate in the program. Parent and child board the school bus together to ride around the district, and then they tour the elementary building.

In later sessions the children are placed with volunteer aides who teach rhythm games, tell stories, show movies, teach use of scissors, and conduct other activities. The parents meet separately in coffee sessions discussing problems pertinent to their situation. Past programs included meeting speech correctionists, diagnosticians, and guidance counselors. Parents also meet with the principal, kindergarten teachers, and reading teachers. At one of the sessions parents learn about the full program offered by community schools.

If you know of a youngster who will be a kindergartener in September, please call the elementary school office or the community school aide in your area.

Playschool for tots. This program combines play activities with planned learning experiences. It prepares preschoolers for kindergarten and encourages the children to express themselves, cooperate and share with others. It provides a program of games, arts and crafts, music rhythms, story telling, and finger plays.

Different themes are chosen each week with indoor and outdoor activities revolving around each theme. Some examples are barnyard week, health and safety week, and circus-carnival week.

Classes are held Monday through Thursday, two hours a day for six weeks during the summer with a minimum fee being charged.

Tutor program for elementary students. This program is offered to each elementary building as a special service to the youngsters in their home. There is no cost to this program.

The tutors will be capable, volunteer high school students. Games and special reading and learning materials are purchased through the Community Education Office. Tutors are offered upon request of parent, but if we have a shortage of tutors, actual placements will be based on educational needs.

Baby-sitting service. A baby-sitter training program is being organized with girls from the Middle and High Schools. The instruction will include entertaining children and handling emergency situations. Certificates will be given to the girls who complete the program. A directory of their names, addresses, and telephone numbers will be compiled and made available to residents upon request by telephone. Call the Community School Office.

Emergency mother program. The emergency mother plan is an effort to help children who become lost or hurt and to protect them from molesters. Each house in a group of selected homes in the community displays an easily distinguishable sign which identifies the house as an "Emergency Mother's home." Each emergency mother is supplied with a list of names such as the police or the school which she can call in different emergency situations. She is not expected to leave her property to assist; she has no legal status except that of a private citizen.

Block parents. Block parent committees have been set up in all of the elementary schools. The committees meet monthly to help evaluate and stimulate planning for the entire district. Their responsibilities have included taking a school census and providing their block areas with information on school activities.

The program described above, although school centered, is comprehensive; and it obviously fills gaps in the lifelong education of people of the community. Furthermore, and perhaps in a subtle manner, the so-called regular program of the school is being influenced by the organizational and administrative structure operative for community education.

Another Michigan community called upon the resources of several different educational agencies within easy driving distance of the central town of the community. As a result, its community education program was more community-centered than school-centered. Three activities which illustrate cooperative relationships with nonschool educational agencies are described below. The descriptive statements are taken from the 1973 annual report on "Community Education" made by the Paw Paw Public Schools to their Board of Education.

Swimming — Kalamazoo YMCA (fourth year). Swimming at the YMCA in nearby Kalamazoo is scheduled at a time when the "Y" is open and a segment of the student population is not in school. This year the 5th and 6th grade students were able to take advantage of the program. Forty students enrolled in the fall session and thirty-two students enrolled in the spring. The students are divided into ability levels at the start of the instruction period. Fee: $6.00.

Art — Western Michigan University (fourth year). Art is scheduled in the same manner as swimming. This year sixty-eight students are bussed to WMU on Tuesday afternoons. The students are divided into groups and assigned to students in a selected WMU class. This class is composed of students who will be art teachers. They need the experience of working with youngsters. Our students' interest in and appreciation for art are enhanced. All supplies and materials are furnished by WMU. No fee.

Explorer program (first year). The school cooperated with the Explorer Division of the Boy Scouts of America in the establishment of seven posts. One hundred and fifty students are participating in the program.

Programs: A Result of Process

Community education is defined as a concept implying or involving a process. The learning activities of a community education program become a function of that process. Programs result from that process. Minzey and LeTarte wrote:

Community Education is the over-arching conceptual base, while programs are the activities related to the solution of specific community needs. Thus, enrichment opportunities, recreation programs, cultural activities, avocational offerings, and political and civic programs are partial ways of resolving certain community problems [1972, p. 4].

A clear understanding of the relationship between process and program enables the community educator to use the process for the planning and building of community education programs that meet the specific needs of a certain community. He will be able to visualize the way in which the concept of community education results in program. He will be able to see why the process is essential.

Hickey and VanVoorhees (1969) expressed the relationship as follows:

> The most important aspect of community education is not program but process. It is the relationship between these two terms which is fundamental to the concept of community education. The ultimate goal of community education is to develop a process by which members of a community learn to work together to identify problems and to seek out solutions to these problems. It is through this process that an on-going procedure is established for working together on all community issues [p. 36].

Seay, in a discussion of the community education concept in the fifty-second Yearbook of the National Society for the Study of Education (1953), relates the emphasis upon community problems to the educative process:

> A community school . . . involves an educative process by which the resources of a community are related to the needs and interests of the people. A key phrase in this statement is 'an educative process' (p. 8). . . . The community school of today secures its impetus from man's new understanding of the power of education. Problems of people and of communities are being solved from day to day by appropriate use of community resources. The educative process is the force which relates the resources to the needs. The result from this unique relationship is the solution of problems [p. 1].

Process implies a social or educational atmosphere or environment in which there is opportunity for involvement of people in assessing needs, identifying problems, and proposing solutions. Process in community education is a happening and as such is unique to each situation!

Programs are developed by way of a specific community education process and are the logical results of a specific organizational and administrative structure. Programs should, therefore, evolve out of the community education process; they should not be imposed upon a community. Hickey and VanVoorhees (1969) expressed a similar thought when they wrote, "Programs are those overt activities which are designed to resolve the issues identified by the process. . . . Failure of community efforts are often the result of excessive emphasis on programs [p. 36]."

The value of the process of community education is lost if one community's education program is transferred and used in another community. For that reason, the categorization of programs and the examples used to illustrate these categorizations, whether listed in this chapter or in other chapters, should not be viewed as models to be transferred but rather as illustrative examples of the result of process.

• • • • • • • • • • • • •

The following observations relative to program development apply to community education activities irrespective of the type of organizational and administrative structures maintained.

1. The program is developed expressly to fit a "people need."

2. There has been involvement of not only the school and agency personnel in the planning and initiation of the program, but also those individuals most affected — the people who use the program to further their learning.

3. The program starts with a list of clearly stated goals and objectives and includes a plan of evaluation.

4. Individual and joint responsibilities of the school and other agency or agencies in carrying out these goals and objectives are clearly stated. Contracts should be negotiated when the situation warrants it.

5. Program goals, objectives, and school and agency responsibilities should be communicated to all citizens of the community. Any changes in either of the above also should be conveyed to the citizens. (Note that Chapter Ten carries

the title "Public Communication for Community Education.")

6. Adequate records should be kept from the onset to the development of a program and should continue to be kept throughout all of the operation.

7. The status and relationship of the school and other educational agencies should be evaluated regularly in addition to, and where applicable, in conjunction with, frequent evaluation of program goals and objectives.

8. Because programming is based upon the problems, needs, and interests of those for whom they are planned (as they are identified through the process of community education) there are great differences in the programs developed to meet the problems, needs, and interests of one community and those developed by another community. There are no program models to be transferred from one community to another.

9. Because the educational forces in communities vary, and because all of them are important in community education, there is no standard plan – no model – for agency participation.

10. When new educational activities are found to be needed, they are accepted as responsiblities of existing established agencies or they are planned and implemented by a special organizational and administrative structure which has been established either within one agency or within a cooperative arrangement involving two or more agencies.

11. The community education concept calling for a balance in lifelong education and a utilization of the resources of all educational agencies is a philosophical understanding, an ideal to be worked toward. Although a 100 percent level of attainment is never reached, the goal is a worthy one. The nearer American education can come toward it, the better will be the quality of life for the American people.

CHAPTER IX

**ACCOUNTABILITY AND EVALUATION
AS A BASIS FOR DECISION-MAKING**

ACCOUNTABILITY AND EVALUATION
AS A BASIS FOR DECISION-MAKING

GEORGE S. WOOD, Jr.
AND
MAURICE F. SEAY

In community education, as in any other kind of education, accountability and evaluation are useful tools for making successful decisions. They are means to an end. The ultimate "end" is an improved educational program accomplished through the process of better decision-making at every level and every stage of operation. Evaluation, spurred by the necessity to be accountable, provides the information for making decisions that are relevant to the elements and relationships in a given situation.

Accountability and evaluation should never be treated as ends in themselves. If seen as "ends," they become threatening to the very people whom they should assist, the people responsible for implementing and perpetuating the activities of community education — the decision-makers. Teaching to a test or limiting creative leadership by timorous adherence to the supposed expectations of certain groups is, of course, self-defeating. To be accountable is to be responsible for meeting adequately certain agreed-upon goals and objectives of performance. To evaluate is to gather information — and that information can be used to show the degree of accountability. This process of evaluating to show accountability leads to successful decisions, to program-development suitable for reaching the goals and objectives and suitable to the measurement of the achievement of those goals and objectives. Accountability and evaluation are part of any responsible management; they are necessary to any responsible decision-making.

Accountability and evaluation are obviously interrelated, meshed into the complicated process of goal and objective establishing and into the determining of whether, and if so to what extent, the objectives have been accomplished. As these two elements in the process of community education are discussed separately, their interdependence should be remembered.

ACCOUNTABILITY

The nineteen-seventies may well go down in the history of American education as the "decade of accountability." Not that the idea is new — the need to be responsible in the performance of duties is as old as civilization itself. But the widespread demands of public groups that educational practices be held accountable for their results are hardly compatible with an image of education as a separate, isolated institution. The new idea which accountability is bringing into the seventies is that accountable education cannot be separate from the community.

Time and energy are often wasted in arguing whether it is possible to measure what education tries to accomplish. The answer is clearly "yes." While it may not be possible to show proof that every planned educational outcome has been accomplished, enough can be measured to show whether major goals and objectives are being met and to guide decision-making toward the retention of old goals and the acceptance of new goals.

A more serious problem of accountability in the seventies — and in any other period of great social change — is the matter of differing societal value systems. When all special interest groups such as parents, churches, business organizations, educational agencies, and youth groups agree with each other as to the major goals of education, being accountable is a comparatively simple matter: educators work toward the agreed-upon goals, evaluate achievement, and show interested public groups what has been done and what needs to be done to continue achieving, or to achieve better, those goals. But when society does not agree on the goals — when some special interest groups want education to teach children how to make money in the business-industrial world, other groups want education to correct historical injustices to minorities, others want education to help individuals be fulfilled in a contemporary world, and still others want education to emphasize their version of "the old-fashioned virtues" — then accountability is difficult.

Serious questions regarding public agreement on the goals and objectives of education are, indeed, raised by the issue of accountability. Differing societal frames of reference resulting in differing value systems create a situation which can cause society's educational forces to isolate themselves. If confusion about moral standards and about criteria of success prevails in the community at large, an agency staff is tempted to set up program goals and objectives according to its own intra-institutional value system. Such isolation does not concern the community greatly if the agency involves only a small proportion of the people; but several educational agencies touch sizeable populations in a community. And every group of people in a community includes taxpayers, parents, and citizens interested in the educational development of people. When an educational agency sets up its own separate, isolated set of goals and objectives, those goals and objectives are likely to disappoint, or even to alarm, certain community groups whose members adhere to a different set of values. An isolated educational agency — one which has not worked out agreements with various groups in the community on the major purposes of education — can expect to have difficulty when groups that differ with the educational agency's values demand that the program be accountable for educational achievement according to their different systems of values.

Community demands for educational accountability are focusing the attention of educational leaders upon the importance of working with representatives of all the people in the early stages of setting educational goals and objectives. Leaders are recognizing that a comprehensive, community-wide concept of education is necessary to achieve community goals. They are recognizing the need for processes that involve community study and coordination, and that can bring about agreement on educational goals. To formulate details and strategies of the process, a special organizational and administrative structure must be established for each community or group of interrelated communities. This structure is described and illustrated in Chapters Six and Seven.

Because community education studies the values of various groups in the community, discovers their educational goals, and involves their representatives in the meetings where program goals and objectives are written, community education can be accountable. The techniques and steps used to demonstrate accountability are similar to those used by any other responsible institution: needs assessments, performance objectives, evaluation procedures, and contractual arrangements with built-in performance specifications. The community education process makes these techniques work because the program goals and objectives of community education are developed with the help of the community.

In Michigan, the State Board of Education is advocating an accountability system that includes these six steps (listed by Fisher, 1973, p. 14):

1. Development of goals.
2. Development of performance objectives.
3. Needs assessment.
4. Delivery system analysis.
5. Evaluation.
6. Recommendations.

To gain an understanding of the parameters of accountability, community education must explore the answers to two questions: For what is community education accountable? To whom is community education accountable?

For What Is Community Education Accountable?

Basically, community education is accountable for achieving its stated goals and objectives. In the enthusiasm of disseminating a concept, leaders sometimes become over confident and make claims for community education that cannot be fulfilled. If stated goals embody such claims, a coming to terms with reality is due.

Special kinds of accountability can result from the claims of the community education concept. The two following examples will illustrate the kind of agreements that develop between a community and the administrators of a community education program:

1. A community is promised that community education will increase the use of school facilities. The community employs a community education director, underwrites the costs of a community education program, and expects the promise to be fulfilled. The community quite reasonably demands proof that the school facilities are, in fact, being used more fully than before. After all, the community and the director of the program had agreed upon that goal.

2. Similarly, a community is promised that community education will identify community resources and apply them, by use of the educative process, to community problems, will coordinate community agencies which have legitimate educational aims, will involve people of all socio-economic groups in community educational planning, and will make education a lifelong possibility for the people of the community.

In each case the promise or claim was accepted as a program goal by the people of the community, and they believed that each promise was accepted as a program goal, complete with appropriate objectives, by the community education staff. The people provided their money to make possible a realization of the mutually accepted goal. In such cases community education is indeed obligated to show that the goal has been achieved or is on the way to being achieved. If certain changes have to be made in order to achieve the goal, then the staff is responsible for convincing the community of that need and winning the necessary approval.

Commitments to use the institutional forces of the community to provide a balanced educational program for all the people are far-reaching in their implications and involvements. When agreements are reached, all parties involved need to know the anticipated timing, costs, and major techniques to be used. The need for complex agreements — even for legally binding contracts in some cases — should surprise no one. Leaders who understand the community education concept know that this kind of education is not a single add-on service, but a basic educational process which is effective in meeting the educational needs of communities. Where the far-reaching implications are not immediately understood, however, by a majority of the groups which must cooperate, public communication will be an essential ally in establishing and maintaining goals and objectives that community citizens can support and educational programs can achieve. The role of communication in community education can hardly be over-estimated; it is discussed in Chapter Ten.

Objections to public demands for accountability which many instructors hold stem from a belief that much of what a teacher accomplishes cannot be adequately measured. Two reasons are cited: (a) certain kinds of learning do not result in action during the time period covered by the evaluation; and (b) some educational results, particularly in the subjective areas involving attitudes and values, cannot be recorded at all in behavioral terms. Since anxieties of this kind often cause grudging compliance with measurement procedures and less than cordial attitudes toward public groups that request accountability, the inhibiting belief calls for consideration.

The first assumption that evaluation procedures will miss certain kinds of learning may be quite accurate, but the emphasis placed upon it is out of proportion. The collecting of all relevant data in a social context is understood to be impossible. The key to effective measurement for accountability purposes is not whether *all* relevant data can be collected, but whether *sufficient* data can be collected for intelligent decision-making.

The second assumption is also an unnecessary anxiety. Educators regularly make informal deductions from the student behavior which results from learning in the affective domain. Robert F. Mager, in discussing educational objectives, wrote that people are often expected "to perform in ways that are not reflected in tasks or errors . . . . [Educators] are concerned with behavior because [they] have no other choice, no other route into the heart or mind of a person [1972, pp. 17-18]." Mager cites as examples students who are expected to want to go to school, citizens who are expected to take pride in their community and teachers who are expected to want all of their students to learn. Although measurement techniques being used in the area of the affective domain can be greatly improved, the area is not, and should not be, untouched by evaluation. If community education is to help people to be more community-minded, or is to contribute to stronger individual self-images, or is to restore the faith of the people in the educative process, then community educators must find ways to describe behavior patterns which will establish the fact that such results are achieved.

To Whom Is Community Education Accountable?

The positions held by the leaders of a community education program determine, in part and within the educational power structure, to whom the community education program is accountable. For example, a superintendent who is the chief community education administrator (as well as the chief school administrator — a double role which occurs, for example, in the Flint, Michigan, educational structure) has one kind of accountability mapping while a building director who works under the direction of a principal has a different kind. And different from each of these would be the accountability mapping of a coordinator who works, under a joint powers agreement, for both the city council and the school district.

But the question, "Accountable to whom?" has broader implications than the line relationships in an administrative pattern. Accountability factors are created by the community as a whole, the people in their on-going activities, an advisory council for community education, many local agencies, many local groups, the state and federal educational leadership — especially where state and federal funding is involved — and the vision of community education held by the immediate administrative officer of the community education program. These various contributors to accountability factors fall, roughly, into the following three categories which will be considered in greater detail: (a) the people of the local community, (b) state and federal funding agencies, and (c) the local organizational structure.

The people of the local community. Community education is a "people concept." The active involvement of "all the people in the community" is held as an idealized goal to be worked toward. The educational needs of all the people, regardless of their age or their socio-economic status, are to be met as adequately as possible. Their financial support of the educational program is to be respected by returning educational services worthy of their money. Thus community education accepts definite responsibilities to the people.

213

There are many ramifications in community education's accountability to the people. Public communication, as mentioned earlier, becomes an important tool in making accountability understandable to the community. Coping with societal differences in value judgements becomes an administrative — and at times, an instructional — responsibility. Problems of how to lead and at the same time be accountable have to be resolved.

Some accountability models have stressed the internal organizational functions of the community education staff and have given minimal attention to community process. The programs based upon goals written by the staff, alone, are likely to face accountability problems. Community process involving coordinating, demonstrating, surveying, training, and promoting leads to "community" in the development of goals.

State and federal funding agencies. The strongest accountability impact upon community education has come from state and federal funding sources. Most money grants from either level carry evaluation and reporting requirements. And, since most community education programs include special projects funded by state and federal agencies, these evaluation and reporting requirements touch most programs.

Possibly the phenomenon which will ultimately have the most profound effect upon accountability in community education is the increasing incidence of direct state aid to local communities for community education. Over a period of three years, from 1969 to 1972, first Michigan and then Utah, Florida and Minnesota appropriated money to reimburse local school districts for part of the community education director's salary. That funding led to comprehensive evaluation efforts in order to justify the existing appropriations and to provide bases for making state-level decisions about further funding.

The early evaluations were essentially collections of statistical data, but in 1972-73 Michigan added an accountability factor to its appropriation of one million dollars to be divided among 163 school districts with 261 directors eligible for state assistance. Local districts were required to submit performance objectives in the following areas as part of their funding applications:

1. Extending school services.

2. Providing in-service training for directors or coordinators.

3. Involving an advisory council and supportive agencies.

4. Coordinating efforts of community agencies.

5. Increasing participation in existing school programs through enhancement of skills and development of more positive attitude toward school.

Subsequently Michigan required year-end evaluation reports based on the same performance objectives. State officials indicated that these reports and other relevant program and participation data would be used as a basis for deciding the extent of future state funding. Other states developed similar accountability arrangements. Minnesota, for example, followed its original salary reimbursement funding for community education with a head tax by which local school districts could raise operating funds for the program. The state stipulated that the local program demonstrate the existence of an active advisory council.

Such state performance requirements become an important element in making local decisions and establishing local accountability factors. The community education administrator must coordinate the state expectations with those of the local community; he must develop a consistency of purpose which can be recognized by all the groups represented in the decision-making process.

Federal funding is sought by community educators in many different forms and some is received. An example of the accountability factors which accompany federal funding is shown in the following communication received by one of the regional university centers for community education. A congressional sub-committee wrote to the Center at Western Michigan University asking for "hard, documented evidence about accomplishments attributable to the community education approach [Center communication, August 3, 1973, p. 1]." The committee was preparing for hearings on a bill which would provide federal funds for community education. Nine items from a longer list are quoted as examples of the kind of evidence this particular sub-committee considered convincing:

1. Evidence that bonding issues, because of the implementation of a community education program, pass while in the past they failed.

2. Evidence of the attitudes of the community before and after the implementation of community education.

3. Evidence that community education is sound fiscal policy for business and for this reason they support community education with hard dollars.

4. Evidence that skills learned in community education programs lead to realized extra earning power.

5. Evidence that there is any real advantage to putting a program that already exists in the community within the community education context.

6. Evidence to show that as communities become more committed to their community education programs, the financial source for the community education programs is incorporated within the regular tax structure.

7. Evidence to show that community education claims concerning such things as drop-out rates, daily attendance of children, reading and math scores of children, facility utilization, PTA participation, vandalism, delinquency rates, etc., have data which support them.

8. Evidence to show that through community education, communities have avoided the necessity to build additional expensive facilities for various services.

9. Evidence to justify the appropriation of federal funds (and state funds) for community education at a time when there is so much pressure for federal funds for so many other programs [Selected from Center communication, 1973, pp. 1-3].

With the growth and maturing of community education as a basic educational concept, the time for overenthusiastic, unsubstantiated claims has passed. "Evidence" is asked by the congressional sub-committee in terms of the attitudes of the community, but also in terms of bonding issues, profits for business, extra earning power for citizens, support from the regular tax structure — evidence in terms of the values of a business-oriented society. This evidence is being requested by a segment of education's larger geographic community — the nation — which is being asked to help support local programs. Community educators know that they start with a local community and then they lead, they teach, they cooperate, they work with these various larger communities to develop and use all of the institutional forces in the education of all the people of the local community.

If communities and their educational institutions agree that one of their goals shall be an increase in the use of school facilities, then the resulting educational programs can be held accountable for achieving that goal. The congressional sub-committee simply asks for documented evidence that such achievement is occuring. Similarly, and by many other interested groups, community education is being held accountable for evident achievement in reaching such goals as identifying community resources and applying them to community problems; of coordinating community agencies; of involving people of all socio-economic groups in community-wide educational planning; of making learning a lifelong pursuit of the people.

State and federal offices of education have important and necessary roles to play in public education. The key to these roles is the need to provide equal and effective educational opportunities for all citizens. In the past, inequality of opportunity has been connected with a person's birthplace, place of residence, family socio-economic pattern — all factors interwoven with neighborhood mores which cause them to be extremely difficult for a local community to change. As Kerensky and Melby pointed out in 1971, "the share of school support carried by the state and federal government has been increasing slowly, but the trend is strong enough to suggest that there will be a time when the federal government will make sure that no American child will be denied his birthright for a good education [p. 111]."

It is one thing to call for more state and federal support of education; it is quite another to devise an effective plan for implementation that will satisfy everyone who is now involved in the support of education. Accountability is the name for that satisfaction for everyone. Certainly state and federal government are having increasing impact on community education; certainly that impact must be recognized and met in the decision-making that takes place in the local community.

217

The local organizational structure. The local organizational and administrative structure for carrying out the people's mandate that a balanced program of education be provided for all the people of the community is discussed in Chapter Six. There the prevailing pattern existing in the United States is described as one in which many agencies provide the learning activities that make up the total educational program of the community. Of these many agencies, the public school system is largest. Because of the school's size and dominant role in the traditional pattern of educational activities in a community, the school plays an important role in most local organizational and administrative structures of a coordinated, comprehensive plan for community education. As a catalyst, the school may be responsible for activating two important elements in any organizational and administrative structure for community education: (a) a lay council, and (b) a representative council. (See Chapter Seven.)

The use of lay and representative councils in the organizational and administrative structure of community education provides for accountability to the local community through two channels: (a) Lay participation provides the opportunity for accountability to informal groups of the general public; and (b) the council of agency representatives provides an organizational channel for accountability to the various institutional forces that compose a comprehensive program of community education.

Thus a comprehensive community education program is accountable to the special organizational and administrative structure established by the educational agencies of the community. Special activities which are designed to provide a balance in the comprehensive program of community education are often found within the organizational structure of the local school system. Accountability for such activities (i.e., high school completion, enrichment classes, and summer recreation) may be to the superintendent of schools and through him to the board of education. This accountability, however, should also be made to all of the other agencies involved and to the people of the community.

A Sample Accountability Plan in One Goal Area

The following accountability plan in one goal area was used by a community education director who was responsible for the special activities designed to provide a balance in the comprehensive program of community education. Since those special activities were set up within the structural organization of the public school, this accountability plan illustrates a common arrangement in which the community education director reports to advisory councils and to the superintendent of schools, and through him, to the board of education of a school district.

Goal: Provide educational opportunities to all age groups living within the boundaries of the public school district.

Objectives (in terms of the director's responsibilities):

1. To provide educational opportunities, the director will: (a) be directly responsible to promote the High School Completion and Adult Basic Education programs to the residents of the public school district (the community); (b) promote pre-school education programs and make all resources available to all district residents; (c) promote all college credit courses using the facilities of the public school as an extension center for all district residents; (d) provide and promote all leisure-time activities and after-school special-interest activities for all age groups in the district; (e) establish a citizens' advisory council comprised of district residents, the council's responsibility being to provide recommendations for program content in the leisure-time and special-interest areas.

2. To promote these educational opportunities, the director will: (a) prepare brochures to be mass-mailed to each district resident, explaining programs and providing registration information (to be mailed in January and August); (b) incorporate all activities into the "School Report" which is also mailed to every district resident; (c) use the newspapers, County News, and the Shoppers Guide to advertise all such programs; (d) ask the elementary students to take home fliers explaining the programs; (e) place posters and other visual devices in convenient business locations to promote specifically the High School Completion Program and the Adult Basic Education Programs; (f) hire a recruiter for a six-week period of time in the summer who will promote the High School Completion and Basic Education programs.

3. To assist the superintendent in evaluation procedures, the director will prepare a written report on program content twice each year, submitting the report to the superintendent and, when needed, to the Board of Education.

4. To evaluate the program, the director will use measuring devices that will check on the achievement of such expected results as: (a) increased enrollment in the High School Completion and Adult Basic Education program, increased number of diplomas granted, and increased number of adults improving their present reading level; (b) increased enrollment of pre-school age children in the community education program; (c) increased enrollment in college-credit classes; (d) increased enrollment in all leisure-time and special-interest programs for all age groups. Note that the long-range goals of these programs are to make them as useful as possible to all residents and to have as many residents as possible benefit from the programs.

5. To evaluate the program, the superintendent will: (a) receive and evaluate information periodically; (b) approve any policy statements and recommendations which he submits to the Board of Education for adoption; (c) incorporate information about the program in his annual report to the Board of Education.

EVALUATION

Evaluation is information-getting. Specific techniques used in evaluation must relate to the conditions of each evaluative task. In designing techniques or instruments for evaluation, it is necessary to identify clearly (a) what information is needed, (b) where it can be found, (c) what conditions determine its availability, and (d) what time and resources may be expended to get it. In some instances the needed information can be gleaned from informal conversations; in other cases a one-item telephone survey could provide the information. Sometimes it is necessary to use formal and complex reporting forms administered to the individuals of a particular group or to all the individuals in an area of activity. The object in good evaluation practices is to find an information-collection which will provide the desired data with the least possible expenditure of time, resources, and client cooperation.

Three stages are recognized in evaluation as it is commonly used in community education. The stages are (a) evaluation of the setting; (b) evaluation of action alternatives, and (c) evaluation of performance results. Each stage is discussed in the following sections; and under the heading, "Evaluation of Performance," a brief discussion of goals and objectives is included.

Evaluation Of The Setting

Adequate evaluation of the situation, or setting, at the beginning of a problem-solving process may be considerably more important than the performance evaluation made upon completion of the problem-solving. Setting evaluation seeks information about such basic matters as individual needs, problem areas, relevant attitudes, potential problem-solving resources, and human and organizational relationships. Anything that helps to map the setting and to prepare the way for making successful decisions and for taking successful action is part of the evaluation of the setting.

Voluntary input in the initial state of evaluation is provided by the cooperating agencies as their representatives contribute information at meetings. But much of the input is derived from the use of specific evaluation techniques. Some community education leaders use the technique of questioning advisory councils extensively. Paraprofessionals or part-time help may be employed to open lines of communication with citizens of the community through door-to-door visitation. In one community a representative citizen group was organized to learn community attitudes toward a proposed millage increase to be used in building a swimming pool to facilitate the summer recreation program. When a favorable attitude was found, the issue was put up for a vote, and the citizen group became a steering committee for selling the idea to the whole community.

The survey as an evaluative instrument. One community education coordinator and his staff surveyed the community every other year. The survey process involved citizens as volunteer survey takers — citizens who were, for example, PTA members, Jaycees, and adults in an evening sociology class. These surveys received an excellent response; and because the data were unusually representative of the entire community, they were used as an important basis for decision-making.

In another survey approximately 300 PTA mothers and fathers collected information from about 90 percent of the homes in the community — a city of 23,000 citizens. The surveyors, covering the community by elementary school districts, delivered the five-page instruments between the hours of 5 p.m. and 7 p.m. on one evening and returned during the same hours the following evening to pick up the instruments. These volunteers were trained by a member of the community education staff to be friendly and to encourage people to write out their answers to the questions. The returns were remarkably complete.

The questions in the five-page instrument asked people's opinions about such things as PTA, recreation, and the K-12 curriculum (for the benefit of the school board). One section gave people a chance to volunteer their services as teachers and committee members. Another offered 140 possible enrichment activities as a checklist and asked for time preferences as a help to scheduling. Still another section offered blanks for registering in adult high school completion courses and the "Older Citizens Club."

The survey discovered in that one canvass 72 new people interested in high school completion, 57 of whom enrolled in the program; 44 new people interested in teaching adult classes; 51 new prospects for the "Older Citizens Club"; and approximately 100 people who were interested in each of 29 different enrichment offerings. These 29 offerings materialized as classes. Another 57 offerings in which 50 or more people had expressed interest also materialized. A total of 965 citizens took the time to answer questions and write out suggestions for the volunteers who brought the survey to their doors.

Perhaps the most important result of these two surveys was the involvement of the large number of citizens who volunteered to help. The second survey, for example, provided the education program in that community with an experienced public communication person on every street. The educational setting was effectively researched, and the setting, itself, was improved for future interaction through the use of this one evaluation technique.

Expanding the area of the survey. Setting-evaluation can be as narrowly focused as on a single classroom or neighborhood or as widely focused as on an entire county. The scope of the evaluation would depend, of course, upon the scope of the particular problem being studied or of the action that is being contemplated.

An example of area-wide institutional cooperation illustrates an expansion in the territory covered by a community education survey. Ten community education directors and the community services department director of the community college in the area conducted jointly an informational survey of the educational services needed to make possible lifelong education. Problems of management which grew out of the complexity and bulkiness of the survey instrument were resolved through the cooperative efforts of the several directors. David Brophy (1973), one of the directors, distributed a report to his community soon after the survey was conducted. The report included the following statement:

> Many hours have been spent tabulating the responses to the open-end questions. . . . The College will tabulate the check-off class-interest responses. This information will be available in time for planning fall-term classes. . . . The Lakeview survey [the part relating to one of the ten communities] uncovered the names of 96 prospective teachers who have indicated an interest in teaching in our adult programs. These teachers have many talents to share. Their training and background vary from inexperienced teachers with no special certification to teachers with B.S., M.A., and Ph.D. degrees. These new prospective teachers, in support of our current talented staff, will provide new classes, new life, and new experiences for the community to share in the future [*Your Lakeview Schools,* p. 1].

Evaluation of Action Alternatives

Effective educational leadership is becoming increasingly identified as a process of dealing with a complex interaction of social systems requiring extensive analytical planning skills on the part of educational leaders. Stufflebeam (1971) called attention to the fact that education is subject to the interaction of two sets of forces: (a) the forces of the internal organization with their paticular intentions and relationships;

223

and (b) the forces of the external social, cultural, and technological pressures which seek to determine educational objectives. He suggested that "the operational task for the educational system is to devise strategies other than blind reaction for responding to these two forces. Evaluation assists in the creation and implementation of these strategies [p. 28]."

In evaluating for the purpose of securing information upon which to consider, and perhaps to decide between, action alternatives, an attempt is made to secure the information which will describe precisely what a given situation is, what values and forces are at work, and what the alternatives are. Given that information, the responsibility for analyzing it and using it wisely falls upon some group of educational leaders.

A model for accountability and evaluation is shown in Figure 9-1.

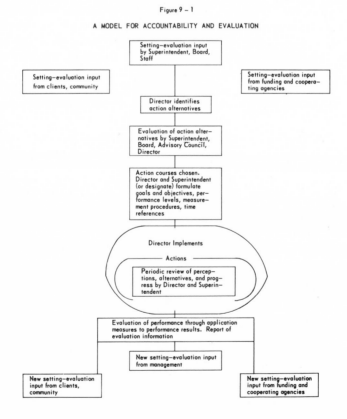

Figure 9 – 1

A MODEL FOR ACCOUNTABILITY AND EVALUATION

The evaluation of action alternatives, as shown in Figure 9-1, usually involves the chief organizational officers and governing board, the community education leader, and often the advisory council. Input from specialists and other individuals may be added; and certain setting-evaluation techniques may be repeated for clearer definition of the alternatives in context. The central action, however, is an in-depth discussion by the chief decision-makers. The key elements here are (a) a careful, objective weighing of the alternate possibilities and (b) a willingness to spend time and resources to seek additional evaluative information when the situation calls for it.

Evaluation of Performance

Performance evaluation is the most generally recognized form of evaluation. Community education leaders are usually concerned with two sources of demand for the results of performance evaluation: local institutional management and funding agencies located outside the community. Two types of evaluation are needed to supply the information desired by these two sources of demand; they are discussed separately.

Evaluation for local management. Performance evaluation to meet the purposes of local management should, of course, follow the procedures implied or identified in specific objectives that are written in advance to apply to a specified time period. Since specific objectives, and the more general goals from which they derive, are particularly important to this type of evaluation, a more careful consideration of them is appropriate.

Goals and objectives. In writing goals and objectives it is necessary to have clearly in mind the difference between them and their relationships to each other. A *goal* is the broad, intended result of a combination of specific related actions. An *objective* is the intended result of each of these specific actions.

For evaluation purposes, objectives should be written in measurable, behavioral terms and should include specific references to completion time, measurement procedure, and one or more criteria for success — which should be spelled out in terms of an acceptable level of performance. An evaluation of the progress made toward meeting the total group of objectives is the basis for evaluating the progress made toward meeting the goal. It is important, then, that the objectives listed under any goal represent truly the means by which success in reaching the goal is to be established.

The following example of a goal with five objectives will illustrate the relationship between the two:

Goal: To improve the enrichment segment of the community education program.

Objectives:

1. Four new classes or activities will be added to the existing list of twenty by the end of the academic year.

2. A survey of community enrichment interests will be completed during the first six months of the contract year.

3. Citizen participation will increase by ten percent in at least five of the existing activities.

4. Overall citizen participation in enrichment will increase by at least three percent.

5. Enrichment participants will demonstrate a 3.00 level of approval in a random sampling of clients in June using the Enrichment Attitude Scale.

Although there could be differences of opinion about the choice of objectives, there is little doubt that the findings of an evaluation of these objectives would indicate something about the progress being made in improving the enrichment program.

Objectives fall into two categories: (a) input or process objectives which indicate what the program director and staff intended to do; and (b) output or product objectives which indicate the responses that are expected from the clients. The first two objectives in the example above are input objectives; the last three are output objectives. The input and output objectives can be incorporated into one series of objectives, as they are in the example, or they can be identified in separate sections.

There are some advantages to incorporating both kinds of objectives in an accountability format. People are justifiably interested in the results of a program; good intentions and directed energy are of little value if they fail to produce results. On the other hand, the mere fact of a lack of success in producing results at any given point does not tell the whole story. On continuing problems information about the process itself, what was done, how well planned the action was, and indications of success in the future may be more significant than the degree of success at the time of evaluation. Such factors of input are particularly important when judgments are being made about the competence of personnel and about the redefinition of a problem situation.

Evaluation for funding agencies. Performance evaluation for funding agencies usually calls for specific information fitted into predetermined categories. Frequently the information required is of a complex and statistical nature.

State departments of education usually administer procedures of state funding for education. The following list of purposes was set up in 1972 as a guideline for state evaluation of funding results by the program services administrator of the Florida Department of Education:

1. Obtain data which will be needed to report to our State Board of Education and the Legislature primarily to maintain philosophical and financial support at the state level.

2. Develop an instrument which will encourage local districts to think about basic community education concepts.

3. Involve the "grass-roots" in developing an evaluation system.

4. Make the state evaluation as useful as possbile for local school people for program analysis and reporting to their own decision-makers.

Reporting forms vary. Forms for statistical performance data from state departments in Florida, Michigan, and Minnesota are similar in the kinds of information they request. These forms usually require certain participation statistics by age group and by activity type, statistics on the use of buildings and other facilities, a specific account of advisory council involvement, data on interaction with community agencies, a statistical description of the community education staff and volunteers, and in Florida's case, a review of the operational budget. Michigan requests, in addition to the items listed above, the inclusion in each local evaluation report of the following: (a) a brief description of the program, (b) the objectives of the program as stated in your approved application or approved amendment thereof, (c) a description of evaluation procedures, (d) a description of the analysis of the data with respect to each objective, and (e) implications of the evaluation for program development.

State department officials explain that they need all of the requested information in order to present a complete set of facts about community education to the state and federal officials and legislators who make the decisions about allocating funds for community education. The argument that extensive evaluation is a key to sound decision-making is a valid one.

On the other hand, educators in the community see at close range the educational goals which are the purpose of the funding and of the resultant evaluation reports. Sometimes local administrators are able to incorporate evaluation procedures used to secure special information for funding agencies into the data-gathering procedures used for local operational purposes, but often such two-fold use of one procedure is not possible. To expedite the pursuit of educational goals, any unnecessary proliferation of fact-finding and paper work should be avoided. Regular review of evaluation forms, simplification where possible, and elimination where possible are indeed in the best interest of the entire educational enterprise.

DECISION-MAKING

In considering the action alternatives discussed in an earlier section of this chapter, evaluation was emphasized as necessary for securing the information needed by the chief organizational officers when they meet to analyze the possible actions and perhaps to agree upon following certain actions. The decision-making process includes this consideration of action alternatives, but it goes further.

Community education leaders make major decisions in collaboration with their governing boards and advisory councils, perhaps with other agency and lay representation, frequently with representatives of the instructional staff and the student body, and often with specialists called in to provide technical or other specialized information. Careful preparations are made for such meetings. Usually the preparations, the work of the sessions, the implementation, and the beginning of new development will follow these steps:

1. Evaluate the community setting or problem situation.

2. Identify major educational goals.

3. Identify possible actions.

4. Evaluate the possible actions.

5. Decide which of these actions to implement.

6. Formulate specific goals and objectives.

7. Implement the selected actions.

8. Hold progress reviews.

9. Evaluate the results of the actions.

10. Evaluate the new setting.

With the evaluation of the new setting the entire procedure begins again. This spiraling characteristic of decision-making is shown in Figure 9-2 which appeared in a Michigan State University study published in 1968. The statement, quoted as a caption to Figure 9-2, is taken from the original study which emphasized the importance of a feedback system to both evaluation and program development:

A systematic approach to decision-making is also an effective procedure for insuring communication among all parties concerned in the planning, implementation, and accountability of the community education process. A two-way pattern of communication is established between individuals who must agree frequently on matters of policy

FIGURE 9-2

Evaluation and Program Development

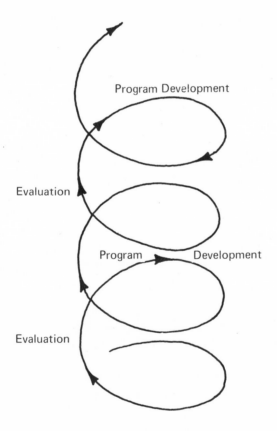

Program Development

Evaluation

Program Development

Evaluation

Evaluation leads to constructive program development.
. . . A highly refined feedback system contributes to both
evaluation and program development [Vol. 1, Sec. 2, pp. 58-59].

and implementation. This is a situation which would be true, for example, between a director of community education and the director of the local public library.

At the same time a multi-directional pattern of communication is established among the heads of the many cooperating educational agencies, among representatives of various population groups in the community, and even across generational gaps and socio-economic barriers. The principles outlined in Chapter Ten for effective public communication and in Chapter Five for effective communication between leaders and the group apply to the communication necessary for decision-making.

● ● ● ● ● ● ● ● ● ● ● ● ●

Whatever procedures are used in reaching decisions, the necessity of using evaluation as a tool remains basic. Careful and systematic use of evaluation prepares for realistic and convincing accountability to management, state and federal funding agencies, and to the people of the local community — and of the larger communities, as well. Such confident accountability is a wholesome, strengthening influence upon the process of community education.

CHAPTER X

**PUBLIC COMMUNICATION
FOR COMMUNITY EDUCATION**

PUBLIC COMMUNICATION
FOR COMMUNITY EDUCATION

KENNETH F. SIMON
AND
MAURICE F. SEAY

In the United States, educators have long been interested in the effects of public communication. Horace Mann conducted a study in 1838 to ascertain changes in public opinion which were brought about by the publication of his annual report. The study of public communication received much emphasis from 1912 through 1920. However, research in educational communication was not pursued to any great degree until the period following World War II.

Rapidly increasing enrollment in schools, new educational activities including adult education, and new pressures and relationships evolving from urbanization in the post World War II period were major factors influencing educational leaders to seek facts that would enable them to develop more effective communication programs. Improved communication is recognized as essential in order to obtain sufficient public understanding and support for adequate community educational programs.

Because community education continues to be a major objective of cultural, economic, and political planning in the United States, and because the process continues to become more complex, community education leaders need information and direction for developing effective public communications programs.

PUBLIC COMMUNICATIONS OR PUBLIC RELATIONS

Public communication is an accurate description of public agency efforts toward citizen participation, feedback, understanding, and support. The quick-profit motive is absent. Many public relations programs, although synonymous with public communication in the minds of many educators, tend to be somewhat limited in feedback functions. They also tend to overutilize one-way communication devices to attain quick acceptance of short-term goals.

When the term, "public communication" is used rather than the term "public relations," it becomes clear that the communication process is used to achieve the goals of public understanding and support.

COMMUNICATION PROCESS

The basic nature of communication has been defined by Schramm. He suggests that communication is "an effort to establish a commonness with another person or group by sharing information, ideas, or attitudes [1955, p. 3]." A similar definition by Albig suggests that "underlying all social processes and all societal forms is the transfer of meaning between individuals. Social life can exist only when meaningful symbols are transferred from individual to individual. Group activities of any sort are impossible without a means of sharing experiences. In the terminology of the social studies, the process of transmitting meaningful symbols between individuals is designed communication [1956, p. 33]."

The definitions of both Schramm and Albig imply much similarity between the processes of communication and learning. Indeed, much learning is a result of communication. Without communication, higher levels of learning would be impossible.

Communication in its simple and most direct form takes place between two people. Fitzgerald states:

> When one man takes another by the arm and says something, the communication which goes on is about as direct as communication can ever be. The speaker may be unclear, the auditor befuddled. The effort may fail. But this may be true under other circumstances. All things equal, the spoken words that pass directly from man to man seem to communicate best. They certainly produce more action [1950, p. 154].

But it is not possible to meet the demands of our complex culture by limiting communication to the person-to-person verbal-symbolic method. There is need for leaders in community education to communicate indirectly with large numbers. Likewise, in an organized interdependent society, groups must communicate with other groups. Extensive use of mass-media is now necessary and promises to become more essential in the future as patterns of urbanization become more complex, and as the demands for community education increase. Recent technical developments have increased the potential amount of communication to a degree not imagined one hundred years ago.

Means of communication are generally constructed to depict either or both of two forms of communication: one-way and two-way. Two-way communication is likely to have greater effect than one-way communication. Feedback utilization is the element that adds effect and power to the two-way process. Two-way communication efficiency is an essential element of genuinely representative government. Lasswell states:

> There is a vital two-way connection between government and public opinion in a democracy. Democratic government acts upon public opinion and public opinion acts openly and continually upon government. The open interplay of opinion and policy is the distinguishing mark of popular rule [1941, p. 83].

The channels of information should be maintained in an open and honest manner. "In the absence of information, the public would be expected to have little competence for rational decisions and to fall easy prey to emotional symbols [Hyman and Sheatsley, 1950, p. 12]."

Fear of the unknown is a factor that impedes some communication (Fitzgerald, 1950, p. 217). This condition is not a reason for educational communicators to reduce the introduction of new and unfamiliar material. Instead it indicates the importance of using frames of reference known to receivers when unfamiliar material is introduced.

Effective communication of useful messages is perceived by receivers as a service. When honest services are rendered, the communicator increases public goodwill and knowledge about education. Effective communication services give pleasure to receivers, they promise reward; and because they are useful and constructive, they make it possible to communicate the new and unfamiliar material with a minimum of resistance. Schramm (1955) conceptualizes some services and returns of the communication process:

1. Communication helps us watch the horizon.

2. Communication helps correlate our response to the challenges and opportunities which appear on the horizon and reach consensus on social actions to be taken.

3. Communication helps us transmit the culture of our society to new members of the society.

4. Communication helps entertain us.

5. Communication helps sell goods for us [p. 33].

Communication processes may be intricate and involved. A communicator may become so personally involved in communication mechanics that the major purposes of educational communication are overlooked or obscured. Kyte (1952) lists three major purposes of school-public communication:

1. The sound improvement of the educational program for all learners.

2. The maintenance of an adequate educational organization.

3. The educationally efficient operation of the organization. [And he adds that] an educational communication program

should serve by keeping the public intelligently informed regarding the educational program and school conditions, and apprising the school officials and employees of community conditions and people's attitude toward the educational program [p. 427].

A basic principle in the communication process is to take the initiative and to keep it. McCloskey (1959) explains, "This principle is the action corollary of the communication principle of primacy, which is that people tend to maintain their first concept of an event or issue, and that the first message they accept is likely to have the most influence on their opinion [p. 103]."

Research reveals that direct experience through constructive participation in the educational program creates effective communication. The principle of involvement increases public support and understanding of education. Increased understanding obtained through constructive participation associates the products of personal efforts with the purposes of a program and contributes to consent and support.

Seven Public Communication Principles

Research indicates the importance of seven public communication principles: (a) taking and keeping the initiative, (b) providing realistic frames of reference to introduce new and unfamiliar material, (c) giving useful services, (d) involving people by encouraging direct and constructive experiences in the program, (e) having the purposes of the program firmly implanted as a basis for action, (f) keeping the communication program continuous, and (g) being thorough and truthful in all communication effort.

Taking and keeping the inititive. Professional public communicators emphasize the importance of the ongoing aspects of communication. The communicator needs to be thoroughly acquainted with the calendar of events. All staff activities including planning sessions, workshops, regular classes, informational meetings, inter-agency activities, and professional association gatherings need to be monitored and analyzed for useful feedback and potential news items. Each activity of a community education program has an interest to a specific audience

239

and that interest needs to be stimulated constantly by such things as news articles, announcements, reports and personal observations.

Providing realistic frames of reference to introduce new and unfamiliar material. It is normal that unfamiliarity and potential change produce considerable negativism and fear at first exposure. New material and potential change should be introduced using familiar frames of reference. They should hold potential for solving identified problems. Frames of reference refer to what the receiver knows at the time new material is presented or change is suggested. It is the communicator's responsibility to be aware of the knowledge level of the audience or receiver. Awareness is achieved by the skillful use of polls, surveys, and other devices of feedback. Knowledge levels should become expanded by well planned and implemented communication programs.

Giving useful services. This principle, although seemingly obvious, is often ignored. Planners of community education programs can become so personally involved that the program purposes and the needs of citizens are overlooked. It is the task of the communicator to analyze feedback and monitor output so that program planners have access to accurate information that helps them to meet real needs with useful services. Communicators need to monitor and analyze the public information services in the same manner. A well planned program with poorly planned publicity and feedback activities gives few useful services.

Useful communication services include accurate calendars and announcements to users offered well in advance of the coming events: providing administrators and community leaders with brief, accurate, easily read information about new programs and program plans; publishing results of surveys and polls; and having accessible accurate program information available by telephone service. Such services give pleasure to receivers, they promise reward; and because they are useful and constructive, they make it possible to communicate new and unfamiliar material with a minimum of resistance.

Involving people by encouraging direct and constructive experiences. Community educators usually recognize this principle immediately. It is the basis of their program.

Direct experience through constructive participation in the educational program creates effective communication. The principle of involvement increases public support and understanding of community education. Increased understanding obtained through constructive participation associates the products of personal efforts with the purposes of a program and contributes to consent and support.

Communication techniques to achieve constructive experiences for people include the use of advisory councils and ad hoc special purpose committees. (See Chapter Seven on advisory councils.) Participation in such groups provides honest first-hand feedback to the communicator. This information is essential for planning new programs, assessing existing programs, and maintaining continued support of users.

Having the purposes of the program firmly implanted as a basis for action. Community education is quite specific. Yet, it is possible to confuse personal motives, assume responsibilities of existing but ineffective agencies, and get involved in a myriad of fringe activities that take time, are of questionable use, and do not contribute to stated program purposes. The public communication plan, each of its goals, objectives, and acts should be directly related to stated community education purposes and should be constantly monitored by feedback devices to provide assurance that the program purposes are being served.

Keeping the communication program continuous. Too much public communication is haphazard. Poor planning, fuzzy community education goals, and misdirected communication efforts make it impossible to achieve continuity. But with a well planned program, clear goals, and a basic understanding of the complex process of communication, continuity can be achieved. A well planned, continuous communication program includes such things as an annual report that *appears annually*, weekly news releases that are *released weekly*, advisory council meeting minutes that are published immediately and consistently, workshop evaluation reports that are analyzed and summarized *before* the next workshop is planned, and monthly newsletters that are published *monthly*!

Being thorough and truthful in all communication efforts. History is filled with gloomy examples of leaders who lied or misused the facts to meet personal needs. The ranks of unemployed educators, and the

241

rosters of some jails, include those who succumbed to the false allure of expediency and by-passed the truth in their public communication efforts.

The democratic theory of government is based on the premise that citizens have a right to accurate information about public services. Communicators and leaders of community education programs are obligated to facilitate that right by providing truthful information.

Responsibilities for Public Communication

Responsibility for the operation of community education programs includes planning, organizing, and executing an effective public communication program. The democratic theory of government is based on the premise that citizens have a right to information about public services. Even private educational agencies have the responsibility of reporting to their constituencies.

Research indicates that an informed public is more likely to support adequate educational programs. Public support depends upon information and favorable attitudes. Authorities indicate that the public has an active interest in education.

There is evidence that public interest in community education is now more active than at any other time in the past century. Legislation before Congress now would create, with federal and state support, community education programs on a nation-wide basis. Community educators have the vast communication technology and media such as television, radio, news printing processes, economical sound reproduction and film at their command. These techniques of public communication combined with an active public interest give community education professionals an unprecedented opportunity to generate widespread support for expanded programs.

There has been a great deal of public misunderstanding about community education. Too much educational communication is propaganda of desperation. Considerable evidence indicates that this is due, in part, to inadequate or misdirected communication effort, to haphazard communication planning, and to too little understanding of the complexities of public communication responsibilities.

A synthesis of school-public communication research reveals a surprising amount of agreement among the authorities about the importance of certain communication responsibilities. Itemized references to responsibilities and guidelines for planning are quoted from seven different sources as a demonstration of their basic similarity of position.

According to Cutlip and Center (1952), a good public communication program includes the following responsibilities for the educational leader:

1. Facilitating and evaluating a free flow of opinions, attitudes, ideas, and reactions *from all persons,* however far removed or remotely affected, concerned with the acts and policies of an organization.

2. Bringing these attitudes, opinions, ideas, and reactions to bear on the policies and programs of an organization to enable it to chart a course that will serve the mutual interests of all concerned.

3. Explaining and dramatizing the chosen course to all those who may be affected and whose support is essential to the success of the organization served by the practitioner [p. 85].

Kyte (1952) listed seven public communication responsibilities:

1. Conducting a continuous survey of all significant phases of the school and its community and making critical analysis of the data thus obtained.

2. Determining the possible means to be utilized in administering and directing a public-relations program.

3. Considering the possible agents to participate in planning and executing the public relations program.

4. Organizing the personnel and agencies into a workable program.

5. Training the agents as efficient, constructive operators of the program.

6. Putting the program into operation and maintaining its efficiency.

7. Appraising the results in terms of defensible sound purposes [p. 427].

Cutlip and Center (1952, pp. 394-397) conceived public communication program responsibilities to be the following five:

1. Deciding upon the goals to be attained and the underlying philosophy upon which the program should be based.

2. Diagnosing community needs and problems.

3. Planning a program related to community needs.

4. Setting up an efficient working organization.

5. Evaluating the program and its various activities.

The Wilmington, Delaware public school system emphasized public communication when it defined part of the responsibilities of its communications director in this manner:

1. Establish a plan of public information and interpretation of the work of the schools.

2. Determine standards for the evaluation of public relations needs and methods.

3. Serve as an agent for requests made of school personnel to fill speaking engagements.

4. Provide assistance to all schools and staff members in preparing material to be used for public information purposes.

5. Establish routine for reporting of newsworthy activities by parent-teacher, principal, teacher, student body, and other school organizations.

6. Develop plans for the stimulation of the staff to make community contacts, publish articles, address professional groups, and engage in similar activities.

7. Develop means of communication between the central office and the schools, committees, and working groups, and between the schools and the public [from an unpublished-job-description handbook].

Morphet, Johns, and Reller (1959) listed eleven community relations guidelines:

1. Multidirectional communication is essential and must be both the basis of the program and one of its purposes.

2. A policy statement regarding school-community relations should be adopted by the board of education making clear the purposes of the program and the role of the school personnel.

3. The program must be planned.

4. An effective program can only be designed with some clearly defined goals in mind.

5. Reporting is an essential element of the total program and needs to be developed in an effective manner with reference to the variety of groups to be reached.

6. Involvement of many citizens is desirable.

7. A wide variety of media should be employed.

8. The significance of the individual school in school-community relations should be recognized.

9. The central office should take responsibility for a few system-wide school-community relations activities and should concentrate its energies on the development of a staff for more effective participation in the work.

10. Responsibility for coordination and leadership in school-community relations should be fixed upon some one person.

11. Evaluation of the program and of its various aspects is of vital importance [p. 135].

Bernays (1955) gave the following eight responsibilities for the engineering of public consent:

1. Define your objectives.

2. Research your publics.

3. Modify your objectives to reach goals that research shows are attainable.

4. Decide on your strategy.

5. Set up your themes, symbols, and appeals.

6. Blueprint an effective organization to carry on activity.

7. Chart your plan for both timing and tactics.

8. Carry out your tactics [p. 9].

McCloskey (1960) recommended seven steps to effective communication planning:

1. Establish a sound public communication policy.

2. Determine what educational services and developments benefit pupils.

3. Obtain facts about what citizens do and do not know and believe about educational values and needs.

4. Decide what facts and ideas will best enable citizens to understand the benefits children obtain from good schools and what improvements will increase these benefits.

5. Make full use of effective teacher-pupil planning techniques to generate understanding and appreciation.

6. Relate cost and tax facts more closely to opportunity for boys and girls to achieve.

7. Decide who is going to perform specific communication tasks at particular times [pp. 15-17].

The process of achieving the purposes, attaining the objectives, and obtaining the desired results of a public information program involves the communicator in a maze of socio-psychological phenomena. Phenomena such as controversy, public attitude, and public opinion appear repeatedly as important factors in the communication process.

Controversy can be constructive and is not to be avoided; it can stimulate fact finding and feedback. Controversy can reveal personal opinions and attitudes. It can be used effectively for educational purposes if its function is recognized by the communicator. "The danger is not so much that the schools will be subject to controversy as that, because we do not recognize the function of controversy, we will permit it to focus public attention on trivialities instead of major issues and problems about which we should encourage public discussion [McCloskey, 1959, p. 125]." It is important to the public information transmission process to stimulate feedback and to create, through true understanding, an educational program that has the consent and support of pupils and patrons. McCloskey emphasized this need by saying that the purpose of public understanding is to provide "a means of enabling individuals and groups of citizens to perceive schooling in the framework of their needs and aspirations [1959, p. 29]."

Educational leaders know that they have clear-cut responsibilities to provide public information; they recognize the importance of public information in the success of their program. However, the leaders themselves say that they have not met this need. An example of this admission appeared in a report issued at the 1958 San Francisco

247

meeting of the American Association of School Administrators: "Many citizens do not understand or support the basic goals and philosophy of universal education because the educators have not met their responsibility in interpreting education to the public."

Educators who recognize the importance of public information are, at times, naive about its technology. According to Schramm [1955, p. 8], communication has three basic elements: source, message, and destination. He warned of the danger in assuming "any simple and direct relationship between a message and its effect [p. 18]" without knowing all the other elements in the process. Informing the public requires technical proficiency in communication, a fact which means that the community education director or some specialist on his staff should become a technically proficient advisor, analyst, and advocate of the public communications program.

It follows that community education leaders are obligated to inform the public with honest, affirmative, and well planned communication programs. They should identify instructional needs through community-wide evaluation. Then they should formulate public communication policy to help citizens understand and support those needs, and to participate in the community education programs which are developed to meet those needs.

BASIC FUNCTIONS AND ACTS
OF PUBLIC COMMUNICATION

Research, such as that referred to in preceding sections of this chapter, has identified typical functions and acts of the communications process. Well-designed public communication programs utilize these functions and acts to form a basis of operation. *Functions* of communication are defined as those processes necessary to create and maintain a public communication program; *acts* of communication are the actions necessary to implement a communication function. There are four major communication functions; numerous acts implement each function.

248

The following list of the four major functions includes the acts which implement each function.

1. *Planning,* implemented by the acts of (a) examining, (b) appraising, and (c) organizing.

2. *Encoding,* implemented by the acts of (a) defining and (b) developing.

3. *Transmission,* implemented by many acts involved in conveying a message to a destination.

4. *Feedback evaluation,* implemented by the acts of (a) stimulation, (b) reconstruction, (c) analysis, and (d) interpretation.

The descriptions which follow deal with each of the foregoing items. Community educators are familiar with many of the acts; however, seeing them in relationship to specific functions clarifies the procedures of public communication which are used regularly in the community education process.

Function of Planning

Planning is based on concepts of communication strategy. It establishes the direction for carrying through the communication policy. Planning involves identification of beneficial services, public communication goals, identification of facts that need to be communicated, facts and ideas most likely to contribute most to understanding and public action.

The function is implemented by the following acts:

Act of examining. Examining is the investigation of the existing state of public receptivity to useful messages. It includes obtaining information about the present state of public awareness, interest, and attitudes with respect to essential educational services and developments. It also includes the tasks of taking polls, interviewing people, and considering people's opinions in order to identify areas of concern and misunderstanding.

Act of appraising. Appraising is the process of evaluating facts that bear on an existing situation and determination of their implications. It includes determination of correct timing to take advantage of current conditions, establishing priorities, and making future projections.

Act of organizing. Organizing is the process of defining and allocating communication responsibilities of the staff in public presentations.

Function of Encoding

Encoding is the phrasing of messages. It is the process of making messages understandable by their receivers. It involves the use of recognizable and acceptable frames of reference and consideration of what facts and ideas will best enable the citizens to understand the benefits obtained from community education programs.

The function of encoding is implemented by the following acts:

Act of defining. Defining is the act of determining audience readiness to receive and accept messages. It involves the process of determining audience motives and frames of reference. Purposeful involvement of community leaders in the defining process assists the communicator to encode so that an audience can understand a message easily and accurately.

Act of developing. Developing is the act of increasing the effectiveness of encoding messages by rewriting, redefining, and reorganizing. Research reveals that success or failure for the communication program may rest upon the skill with which fact sheets, reports, and mass media materials are encoded.

Function of Transmission

This is the process or processes by which a source conveys a message to a destination. A message may be transmitted by means of a letter, newspaper, conversation, radio, television, film, book, magazine or by symbolic behavior. Common message transmission media are individuals, groups, and mass media. Skillful transmission of messages is an effective element of the communication process. It is essential for conveyance of information and for solving problems of public inerita, criticism, and controversy. Effective message transmission, if appropriate, creates a positive public image for the community education program.

Acts that contact people directly or through mass media initiate the function of transmission. Initiating and maintaining working relations with mass media professionals, and working person-to-person, person-to-group, and group-to-person are acts that implement the function of transmission.

Function of Feedback Evaluation

This is the process of getting information about which messages are decoded as the communicator intended and which are not. Feedback includes physical reactions such as smiles, frowns, and gestures as well as formal, written, and spoken replies to a message. Feedback is an essential feature of two-way communication.

The function of feedback evaluation is implemented by the following acts:

Act of stimulation. Stimulation of feedback acts to motivate community members to express opinions and attitudes about educational programs. Some surveys and polls can be designed to stimulate the expression of these opinions and attitudes.

Act of reconstruction. Reconstruction is the act of utilizing the feedback material. Effective utilization of the feedback information involves revision of fact sheets, reports, and mass media materials. Discussion guides, rescheduled meetings, and new speeches are redesigned to resolve the inadequacies and misunderstandings identified by feedback reconstruction acts.

Act of analysis. By statistical and qualitative analysis of the data received from polls, surveys, and conversations, communicators can ascertain the nature of existing opinions and attitudes. Tests for validity, significance, and accuracy can be made; and, effectively used, this information can help give direction and meaning to the communication program.

Act of interpretation. Interpretation is the process of explaining the results of statistical and qualitative analysis. Appraising the levels of public understanding, defining the nature of criticism, and clarifying the reasons for public misunderstanding are important elements of interpretation. Messages can be more effectively re-encoded and retransmitted if results of analysis are carefully interpreted.

A skillfully planned community education public communication program that adheres to the basic functions of communication and employs well trained writers, editors, media specialists, speakers, and planners will enhance community education program development, increase citizen participation and support, expand public knowledge and improve public understanding of education.

DEVELOPING A PUBLIC COMMUNICATION PROGRAM

With the public communication principle and responsibilities firmly understood and the basic functions of communication well in mind, major goals and objectives for a community education public communication program should be determined. To accomplish this, a problem solving activity is used by staff members. Once the major problems are identified, plausible programs with specific goals, objectives and actions can be planned and implemented.

A simplified problem statement with a suggested program for a community education public communication program could look like this:

Problem

Community education activities need to result in educational services, training processes and new curriculum materials specifically designed to meet the educational needs of the resident citizens — all ages. Problem statements should be kept brief but inclusive. Services would include such items as instruction, information, and development, but need not be listed in their entirety in the statement. Training processes would include designation of agencies offering educational activities and methods of organization and presentation such as special seminars and workshops that deviate from the ordinary and that can be lumped in a generic term in the problem statement.

Two groups of persons need to be made aware of the community education program and its work: (a) potential users, i.e., all citizens of a given community; and (b) those who influence decisions directly related to community education, i.e., state departments of education, colleges and universities, congressmen, professional associations, local service organizations, advisory councils, school boards, and other educational agencies. These two groups need to be aware of available services, to see samples of the completed curriculum material and to know how the services and materials may be obtained and utilized in training programs. Personnel conducting community education programs need to receive public communication support services.

Goal. The goal is to plan and implement a public communications program that: (a) facilitates utilization of community education services, training processes, and new curriculum materials; and (b) provides public communication support services to personnel conducting community education programs.

Objectives. Four objectives are (a) provide a continuous flow of information about community education services, training programs and new curriculum materials to selected audiences; (b) design and produce printed materials and a variety of audio-visual presentations about community education services, training programs, and curriculum materials — presentations that will appeal to the interests of specific audiences; (c) implement a planned program of demonstrations and visitations using printed materials, audio-visual presentations and person-to-person meetings that will inform specific audiences about community education services, training programs and curriculum materials; and (d) implement a planned program of feedback evaluation and use of data received from polls, surveys, opinionnaires, and conversations — used to revise and reconstruct program and public communication activities.

Actions: The Program

To achieve the objectives listed above, specific actions should be undertaken. These actions, combined in a pattern appropriate to a specific population, form the working program for communicating with that population. Figure 10-1 indicates the various communication channels which could be involved in such a program and suggests the media which might be used in developing two-way flows of communication.

Figure 10-1
COMMUNITY EDUCATION PUBLIC COMMUNICATION PROGRAM
Communication Channels and Two—Way Flows

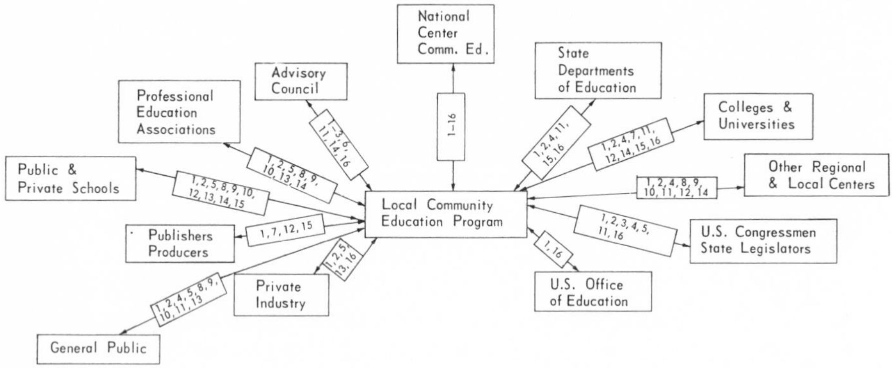

MEDIA

1. Newsletters
2. Fact Sheets — Brochures
3. Annual Report
4. Polls, Surveys, Ques—
   tionnaires, Results
   and Participation
5. News Releases
6. Advisory Council Minutes
7. Monographs
8. Tape — Slide Presentations
9. Films
10. Audio Tapes
11. Special Reports
12. Training Materials
13. Speakers
14. Conferences
15. New Curriculum Materials
16. Proposals (New Programs)

The figure lists many different kinds of media in use as part of a community education public communication program; arabic numerals are used as keys (in blocks) to indicate which media are utilized. Most of those media are described in the paragraphs which follow. The first paragraph, however, suggests a device not shown on the chart: a logo.

Develop a logo. A problem of communication is to get the attention of audiences. The attention getting device called a "logo" is often used. It is an easily recognized symbol that can be used on all printed matter, film titles, and advertisements. It should be attractive, distinctive, simple and have some meaning related to the purposes of the agency.

Publish a newsletter. Newsletters need to be planned with certain audiences in mind; and they should be designed to fit specific needs of those audiences. Newsletters are often expected to do too much. They can become cumbersome, irrelevant, unattractive, and confusing. Newsletters should contain short news items that are current, and they should include only basic facts about programs and the people those programs serve. Staff publicity for political purposes and long, opinionated articles are not appropriate for newsletters. A regular publication schedule is important. Inclusion of feedback devices to determine reader reaction and to maintain the current addresses of readers is necessary.

Provide news releases. Regular news releases to the mass media agencies should be an important part of each public communication plan. Carefully selected material of importance to general audiences should be released. Dramatic or sensational accomplishments and announcements should be released through open news conferences with time allowed for questions from the media representatives. Written releases should contain basic facts. Expect them to be edited. Keep a file of all releases and the resulting articles for feedback analysis purposes.

Publish an annual report. Annual reports should be attractive, truthful, simple, and annual. They should contain easily read and charted basic information about yearly objectives, fiscal developments, program accomplishments, problems, personnel and policy changes, and plans for next year. Fiscal information should be summarized. Audiences should have the opportunity to obtain more detailed information about fiscal details and any other contents of the report.

Use surveys, polls, and questionnaires. Well designed feedback devices give useful information about services. Wasted effort can be avoided if trained professionals are used to help design these devices and to help plan the treatment of resulting data. Poorly designed surveys, polls, and questionnaires usually result in useless information.

Produce an audio-visual presentation. Modern technology enables public agencies to produce high quality information programs at relatively low cost. A short, well written and well displayed presentation about each major program should be produced. Tape-slide presentations, films, audio tapes, filmstrips, transparencies, charts, and speeches can be prepared in advance and made available to certain audiences. These presentations can be updated easily and can provide enough variety to be extremely useful. Care in matching the media, subject, and audiences is essential. Keeping the presentation concise and relevant requires skill.

Publish fact sheets. A fact sheet is a single printed page that explains briefly the essentials of each major program. A series of fact sheets in an attractive folder has many advantages for public communication. A well-written fact sheet provides basic information about a specific subject. This means that superfluous information is never disseminated — only the sheets that apply to a specific audience need are provided. Each sheet is complete in itself and can be revised as the need arises. Fact sheets can be assembled as a complete packet of information, or any combination of specific information can be made available. As a basis for news releases and news conferences, fact sheets are indispensable. They can be quickly produced and attractively designed; they are useful and easily transported; they are also valuable for documentation purposes.

Provide brochures. Brochures are most effective in convincing people that something is good or useful, in urging them to take specific action. Brochures contain a grabber to attract the reader's attention and are designed to keep his interest throughout the entire message. Some facts are used, but the action objective is more important than the information given. Feedback devices are usually built in to assure the documentation of action.

Publish monographs. Monographs are somewhat lengthy, well documented publications about a single subject or issue. They appeal to the audiences that request more information than can be given in fact sheets, newsletters, or brief reports. Monographs give evidence of professional research, analysis, and concern. They provide documentation of initial thinking and a means for its dissemination.

Write special reports. Newsletter stories, minutes of meetings, and speeches often create a need for more detailed, referenced information. This need is met by the use of special reports. Feedback analysis is used to determine subjects for and extent of need for special reports. Researchers are sometimes employed to produce reports. Special reports are disseminated to those who request them or those whose work would benefit from the information contained therein.

Organize a speaker's bureau. Staff members, advisory committee members, and other interested people can be organized and trained to provide audiences with informational programs. Prepared speeches, audio-visual presentations, and printed information should be available for bureau members. Feedback is essential for re-encoding materials. A dependable system to enable users to obtain programs should be developed. A fact sheet or brochure about the service should be distributed.

Train staff in the art of holding conferences. Advance publicity, ease of registration, efficient transportation arrangements, good housing and food, stated purposes, attractive program material, feedback opportunities, follow-up provisions and reasonable costs are essential to successful conferences. Conference arrangements are usually delegated to public communications people. Close working relationships between conference planners and conference organizers are essential. Skillfully planned and conducted conferences increase public understanding and support. Some local and national professional organizations offer workshops and training in the art of conducting conferences. Community education communicators need these skills.

● ● ● ● ● ● ● ● ● ● ● ● ●

The community education leader who has become familiar with the principles of public communication and, in cooperation with his staff, has developed a public communication program which fits the particular setting is to be congratulated. After becoming that knowledgeable in the field of communication, he will hardly need to be reminded that the process of communicating with the public is a continuous one. A community is a growing, changing body of people; community education is a growing and developing process. The maintenance of an established understanding between these two interdependent entities is somewhat like maintaining a warm friendship: honesty, attention to feedback, and a constant sharing of experiences are essential to the maintenance of warm public communication.

CHAPTER XI

COUNSELING IN COMMUNITY EDUCATION

COUNSELING IN COMMUNITY EDUCATION

WILLIAM D. MARTINSON
AND
MAURICE F. SEAY

Little attention has been directed to the vital role of counseling within community education. For some unexplained reasons, the various programs that have been discussed in the literature seem to avoid mention of the specific term "counseling." Perhaps the early emphasis in community education on the program or project within traditional educational settings tended to focus on in-class instruction. Or perhaps community educators, fearful of invading the professional domain of the helping professions, deliberately circumvented areas of controversy. While these and many other related factors may have been involved, community education has tended to ignore counseling. However, community education can not abdicate responsibility for the education of the total person. Fully functional counseling services, as dispersed as they may be in society, need to be considered a vital part of a complete community education package.

A COMMUNITY COUNSELING CONCEPT

Somewhat paradoxically, although community education counseling has not been written about to any great extent, isolated practices in the field abound. One need only reflect on the services of agencies such as child guidance clinics, family consultation centers, planned parenthood and the various manpower development agencies to recognize that a considerable amount of effort, although uncoordinated, is being directed toward providing counseling within the community. Since such services do in fact exist, what is their role and function within community education? What is the role of counseling, generally, within community education?

A Human Resources Development Laboratory

To understand fully the role, function, and potential impact of community education counseling, as differentiated from mental health services of the community, one must develop an appreciation for the philosophy of developmental counseling. When viewed within a broad educational scheme, developmental counseling is a growth process which involves the total environment as a learning laboratory. Individuals have, at various stages of their lives, characteristic patterns of growth or developmental tasks which require the acquisition of new knowledge, new skills, insights or patterns of behavior in order to make necessary changes for effective adjustment. These individuals are in constant interaction with their environment and are influenced by various stimuli in the community. They learn from these exposures and experiences. The community, therefore, becomes a laboratory for growth – a human resources development laboratory. The extent to which the community has a positive influence on the lives of its citizens, is, in part, a function of the quality of community education.

Assuming the posture that the nature of man is such that each individual has the desire to develop into a fully effective member of society, opportunities for such development must be made available. If individuals are deprived of growth opportunities or encumbered by real or imagined obstacles, they are restricted from normal development. Unfortunately, many people need assistance in identifying and utilizing nontraditional learning resources.

From a general knowledge and understanding of behavioral psychology and individual development, it is apparent that individuals cannot be expected to grow in the same directions or at the same rate, nor are the specific needs of all individuals the same. In addition, the needs of the individual are not uniform throughout his life span. Each of us should readily recognize that these differences in individuals suggest variations in individual learning styles. Long recognized, but all too infrequently practiced, differentiated delivery systems or instructional methods are necessary to accommodate such individual needs.

In a speech in the fall of 1972, delivered to a conference of adult educators in Minnesota, Congressman Albert Quie captured, in part, the essence of community education when he talked about the three "L's" in education: Life Long Learning. His remarks were obviously directed toward adult educators and, therefore, he talked about the process of continuing education — couched in terms of "continuous education." Expanding upon his emphasis, but still within his intent, he talked about a process involving all individuals from birth to death. Congressman Quie was aware, as a layman, of a general concept of community education. Within this generalized context of community education the concept of community counseling should be developed.

In considering the problems of educating for "Life Long Learning," one must recognize that mere exposure to learning opportunities does not ensure acquisition of knowledge or the learning of a new skill. Individuals are inclined to absorb those kinds of things necessary for immediate use; and frequently they are unable to store and subsequently retrieve knowledge necessary for solving later problems when those problems arise. Acceptance of this fact certainly suggests the need for a continuous education process, one which involves the frequent replication of services to meet recurring or emerging needs. Within this framework of education, a community counseling service should strive to individualize learning opportunities in order to provide personalized relevancy.

When viewed within the context of a developmental counseling service in community education, many of the service programs could be viewed as fore runners for a good mental health program. Developmental counseling attempts to eliminate the causes of serious problems. It is not intended to emphasize the remedial aspects of a community mental health program, but instead, assists people to develop skills necessary to cope with problems in their environment. By helping individuals to become aware of their strengths and weaknesses, counselors can prepare people to make better decisions. The preventive aspect — the educative process — tends to differentiate the community education counseling program from remedial mental health services. Obviously, there will be some overlap and possible conflict between such a counseling program and a community mental health program, but skillful coordination and communication should enable both to serve the community through their differentiated services.

Developmental counseling is concerned with the various stages of transition in a person's life which enunciate the need for problem-solving and decision-making skills. The developmental counselor, in turn, recognizes the need for accurate informational input and a breadth of life experiences in such processes. It is to the end of assisting in providing the informational input and the life experiences that the community education counselor must be alert. Frequently, the task of the counselor is one of packaging or coordinating the somewhat fragmentary resources into meaningful and relevant learning experiences. Further, the counselor must be available to assist individuals in using these resources in problem-solving and decision-making.

Community educators can do much to improve the services of counseling programs — and other helping professions within the community — by (a) communicating information to citizens about such services; (b) matching services to needs; (c) helping citizens to help other citizens; (d) promoting cooperative attitudes throughout the community; and (e) generally coordinating in the broadest possible sense, the helping services within the community. Those topics are discussed further in a later section of this chapter.

The Need for Counseling

Counseling, whether in the formal or informal setting, is a professional activity arising as a result of several factors related to specialization. A few words of explanation at this point may help the reader understand why counseling services came into being and why the need for counseling persists.

Several generations ago life was much simpler than it is today. In the days of our forefathers life went on something like this: An individual was born into a family residing in a relatively small town or rural area. As he grew, he found the resources near at hand for learning to meet most of his developmental tasks. The local school provided the instruction necessary for his transition to adult life within the community. Geographical mobility was relatively limited, and the affairs of the local community greatly overshadowed state, national or international events. Apprenticeships and on-the-job training provided sufficient preparation for entry into most occupations. A general college education was all that was required in many top-level positions while preparation for professions was usually directed toward a general practice.

As technology expanded, however, and as knowledge mushroomed, an individual discovered that he could not be a "jack of all trades." Modern transportation surrounded him with a nation on the move; therefore, an individual left his local community to find employment in other communities, states, or even in other nations of the world. The developmental transitions of this individual on the move were no longer simple. The increase in technology and knowledge created a need for a specialist who could help this individual meet his developmental tasks.

Technological advances tended to force all individuals to specialize — to focus their learning on narrow fields of knowledge at the expense of a broad general education. As people learned more and more about less and less, they ceased to try to have the knowledge or the time to fill the counselor role for their family, friends, or employees; therefore, a new profession emerged. The counselor became the specialist who could help in this area.

A second factor related to the development of counseling centers about a related kind of specialization. The behavioral sciences have developed a new field of understanding in the dynamics of behavior and the problems of adjustment. This broader base of understanding has given greater insight into problems of communication and the complexities of problem-solving and decision-making. The new found knowledge has direct application in counseling, both individual and group. Through formalized education programs and supervised counseling experiences, individuals are prepared to aid others in solving problems and meeting needs. Only as these strategies and practices are brought into play in professional practice, however, can individuals be assisted.

Only as counselors are made accessible to the community can a community education program of counseling become effective.

Counselors, be they professional or paraprofessional, recognize that counseling is based on an understanding of the dynamics of human behavior and communication process. If counselors are to provide for the developmental needs of people as they progress through life stages and transitions, a knowledge of how people develop and adjust is essential. Further, the counselor needs to know about the multitude of resources within the community that can be used to provide growth experiences. The counselor needs to be familiar with different learning styles of his various clients, and he must develop effective communication channels to help them in incorporating new learning into their behaviors. Obviously, counselor preparation is an ongoing, continuous process, and the levels of counselor effectiveness may well be a correlate of education and experience.

Levels of Counseling

Most professional counselors recognize that counseling is a unique blend of a science and an art. While no amount of practical interpersonal experience will substitute for scientific knowledge of the psychology of human behavior, the ability to relate effectively with selected individuals appears to be a characteristic of numerous "unschooled" individuals. This human relationship skill is frequently found in social service oriented people. Although such persons could undoubtedly improve their effectiveness with increased formal education, many do function well in a paraprofessional capacity. Within the limits of their abilities, and with the recognition of their limitations, paraprofessionals can render valuable service.

During the early years of the profession, counseling was considered primarily a one-to-one relationship wherein a counselor assisted a client in the resolution of a problem. However, during the past decade, most counselors have supported the practice of group counseling and guidance. Furthermore, most counselors now recognize differentiated levels of counseling and recognize the contributions of a wide variety of helping professions.

This chapter takes the position that differentiated counseling services do exist and are appropriate within the community. The professional counselor, fully trained and qualified in an area of specialty, is prepared to engage in individual and group counseling practices designed to provide a therapeutic treatment or growth experience for clients. A paraprofessional counselor, skilled in communication and understanding, as well as referral techniques, is prepared to deliver informational and instructional programs within his capabilities and is prepared to refer clients to experts when the problems are beyond his level of competence. The nonprofessional in the counseling service is frequently a volunteer worker who functions primarily as a "listening ear" and a disseminator of information. This person, usually without specialized training or a degree, is sympathetic to the particular needs of a segment of society and relates well with the members of that group. Whether with ghetto youth or members of the "Golden Age" society, the nonprofessional can fill a much needed function.

The use of the term "counseling" to describe a wide range of activities tends to cause some confusion about the role of the professional counselor. Counselors working in educational agencies are considered to be specialists who assist students in resolving educational, vocational and personal-social problems of adjustment. Society in general, however, does not have a commonality of understanding of the counselor role. Much to the chagrin of professional counselors, the term "counseling" is used by the general public to refer to a great variety of services.

Examples of the confusion that exists in the use of the term "counselor" are numerous in the "help wanted" sections of city newspapers. One metropolitan Sunday paper listed, under the general employment classification, such jobs as cosmetic counselor, insurance counselor, budget counselor, preneed memorial counselor, and travel counselor. In spite of the use of descriptive adjectives, the precise nature of the counseling function remains rather obscure. Under the rubric of "professional help wanted," were such occupations as marriage and premarriage counselor, employment counselor, drug counselor, vocational rehabilitation counselor, psychiatric counselor, and mental health counselor. The adjectives used here convey a better understanding of counseling than did those used under the heading, "general employment," but the specific nature of counseling remains vague. To many persons, apparently, counseling services range from the bizarre and spectacular to highly professional therapeutic services. Palmistry, phrenology, graphic analysis, tea leaf reading, hypnotism, and advanced psychotherapy are all cast in the same mold. Perhaps counseling actually is that which is perceived by the consumer. However, the problems of role definition and function continue to plague the counseling profession, and extensive efforts are being made to communicate more effectively with the profession's various publics.

Counselors would admit readily the existence of several levels of counseling. Much counseling is carried on by the nontrained and the paraprofessional as well as by the professional counselor. Counseling is also performed informally by a wide range of other individuals. The levels of counseling should be differentiated by the ability of the counselor to deliver the services; such ability is usually associated with specific education and training in the helping professions.

No community education coordinator or director is going to be expected to be the "watch dog" of professional counseling in the community. However, community educators may find it helpful to become familiar with the professional standards for various levels of counseling. More specifically, they may want to develop a kind of resources inventory which describes the "typical" practices of various agencies.

THE COMMUNITY EDUCATOR AS A COORDINATOR

Considering the paucity of personnel and physical resources of most community education programs, such programs should not be expected to deliver counseling services only through the deployment of community education personnel. Rather, the counseling function within community education must emphasize coordination. Without negating the personal counseling role of the staff members of an education program, the larger role to be fulfilled is that of coordinating the counseling services of the community. More succinctly, one of the major objectives of an effective community education counseling program is to make available to each member of the community, through effective public and personal communication, those counseling services which do exist for the express purpose of serving citizens.

Service agencies within the community are not competing for clients or case-load. Service agencies are those agencies that are primarily concerned with educational, vocational, and personal social problems of citizens. Their first objective is to meet the needs of their constituents. The juvenile home, the drug education center, the youth employment bureau, and many other service agencies are all attempting to serve the special needs of a specific segment of society. Unfortunately, the pressures of daily work and the vested interests of many groups often hamper effective inter-agency and agency-citizen communication. Frequently, a community education coordinator will be able to observe duplication of efforts, redundancy of service delivery, or more frequently, an inadequacy in providing for the needs of the community. Perhaps more commonly, the coordinator will find a breakdown in communications which results in uninformed citizens who fail to utilize the services available.

Individuals under stress, experiencing anxiety or confusion, frequently become somewhat diffuse in their activities; they may then be unable to identify or to know how to approach the helping services. While no community education program has the capability of reaching every citizen of a community, the program has the potential to serve in a "multiplier" fashion by informing citizens who are participants in community education activities about the helping resources available and by asking those persons to communicate with their friends and neighbors.

The community education coordinator has a responsibility for promoting a community atmosphere, a cooperative spirit among citizens and agencies, which will use facilities and resources to assure the maximum development of each citizen's potential. To serve effectively in this capacity, the educator must, formally and informally, determine the existing status of community services and then proceed to identify the specific needs of counseling services. Without intending to expound on the methods and procedures of community need surveys, the following general admonition may be in order: Because individuals are frequently unaware of their own developmental needs, and equally important, because they are frequently reticent to communicate those needs, the survey methodology utilized must be sufficiently sensitive to reflect the subtle and nonobvious needs of the citizens.

A "fingers on the pulse" approach through the use of key sensitive informants at the grass-roots level may be highly effective. After surveying the needs and services of the community, the needs must then be cross matched with the explicated services of the various counseling agencies of the community. The stated objectives of these agencies are frequently unfulfilled and, therefore, the community education coordinator must arrange to discuss in a nonthreatening manner with representatives of the various agencies, the unmet and projected needs. Such an approach is not easy; and, at best, it is fraught with political overtones. The community education coordinator has no direct power or sanctions which he can bring to bear on these agencies, and he must rely, therefore, on personal influence and political acumen to bring about change.

The coordinating function of the community education director is, obviously, not a simple task. He starts his job of coordinating community counseling services with the knowledge that developmental counseling is a continuous process. But he sees that just as today's college students are obtaining their educations on a drop in, drop out basis, so are community citizens receiving their developmental counseling as drop in, drop out clients. The transient nature of every community's population suggests that many of today's immigrants may well be tomorrow's emmigrants. This mobility phenomenon (one of five families will move each year) means that new citizens will constantly need an introduction to counseling services. To complicate further, the continuous or permanent needs of residents are apt to change as their immediate environment changes. The opening of a new industry or the shutting down of a plant, the passage of new social legislation, the shift from urban or suburban to rural living — all of these changes may be indications of new needs for counseling. The community educator must be alert to the changing nature of his community and its effect upon citizens.

The implementation of human developmental processes within a community depends upon informed citizens who are aware of the goals — of the direction of change — in the community where they live. One of the tasks of the community education coordinator, therefore, is to interpret the community to its citizens. The community educator may well serve as a barometer of change for the community, projecting the kinds of problems such change might bring to the community. As individuals become more aware of the growth directions of the community, they tend to become more actively involved as participants in the community and to direct their efforts in developing themselves toward meeting the challenges of change.

Decentralization-Outreach Delivery System

During the early development of formalized counseling services, administrators founded central offices or centers for the delivery of their services. The general idea, perhaps patterned after the medical professional, was that individuals who were experiencing development or adjustment difficulties would find their way to the practitioner most easily through a centralized system. However, several factors have suggested that such a delivery system may be inappropriate.

First, the consumers of developmental counseling services may not experience sufficient discomfort or displeasure with their condition that they will aggressively seek out help. Rather, they will tend to ignore their frustrations or maladjustments in the hope that the condition will pass. Frequently, time alone does provide some relief, but the relief is at the expense of personal fulfillment and growth. Subsequently, the individual will encounter other situations of conflict or opportunity and be ill prepared to cope. A nearby, easily available counseling service would encourage use.

A second factor which enters into the inappropriateness of a central office system centers around the stigma often attached to seeking help. To admit a personal inadequacy tends to be viewed as a sign of weakness. Thus an individual feels that going to a central, easily identified center or clinic to search out professional help is akin to a confession of weakness. However, he feels that he can accept help which comes to him — or even to a familiar setting in his local community. The various "outreach" programs are designed to reach the public at the point of action. Such types of delivery systems have been well received and rewarded. The counselor has no specialized office furniture nor extensive equipment to transport and, therefore, no physical restrictions to an outreach approach. Many of the community counseling services are reflecting a belief that decentralization will reach more of the people who need them.

Outreach, or decentralized counseling services, that may be found in many communities include a variety of specialized types of counseling. Family service centers, for example, will frequently be found in neighborhood settings where specific needs can be met. Similarly, service agencies for poverty programs will locate their personnel in "store front" offices in the ghetto or in substandard housing areas. Drug abuse counselors will attempt to locate at the scene of the problems. Additional efforts need to be made to provide "on the spot" assistance for those individuals who are uninformed or otherwise reluctant to seek out professional help. As decentralized services grow and develop, the task of the coordinator of such services becomes a critical necessity.

Accountability by the Community Educator
Who Is a Counseling Coordinator

In his efforts to serve as a coordinator of a decentralized counseling service, the community educator must be responsive to his public responsibility. Publicly funded projects are always subject to fiscal review. A concerned community will expect to be informed not only about the scope of service, but about the costs of such services.

This trend toward accountability in various kinds of education must be viewed quite carefully by a counseling coordinator. Not only are the ultimate effects of counseling difficult to ascertain at any given time, but also the individual nature of most counseling makes accountability a difficult process. For many years, educators have been caught in a ground swell of mass production wherein effectiveness has been determined by large numbers. In counseling, however, such a concept has little validity. The counselor realizes that his services cannot be packaged to meet the "common needs" of all residents, but must be formulated to meet individual needs. Therefore, the community educator, in assessing the worth and value of counseling must keep in mind the nature of the helping relationship.

The counseling coordinator must attempt to identify the specific objectives and the target populations of the various counseling services he is coordinating. He must also attempt to evaluate the effectiveness of the counseling programs at frequent intervals. While adherence to the ethics of confidentiality must be maintained, records of the nature of problems presented by citizens and of the services provided to those citizens should be available. The coordinator will be required to interpret the worth of this part of community education in terms of the development of human potential, the relief of human suffering, and the prevention of more serious disability. Chapter Nine, "Accountability and Evaluation as a Basis for Decision-Making," relates these topics to the total community education program of a community.

COUNSELING AND THE GROUP PROCESS FUNCTION IN COMMUNITY EDUCATION

The multifaceted roles that must be carried out in community education require many staff members of the enterprise to have the background of educational generalists. To expect such generalists to be professional counselors is quite unrealistic; but to expect familiarity with the concepts of counseling is not unreasonable. In fact, the president of the National Community School Education Association stated (1972) that the community educator must be "a student of human behavior." He inferred a need on the part of the community educator for group process skills. There can be little doubt that interpersonal skills, if not some specific counseling skills, are necessary for the effective community education administrator.

While it is hardly necessary to suggest that a graduate degree in counseling be considered a requisite background for a community educator, much of a counselor's preparation does seem essential to successful leadership in community education. Certainly, counseling techniques, appraisal methods, career development knowledge and group counseling skills are all necessary for the community educator. Everette Nance (1972) commenting on counseling, stated "the community education coordinator is called upon to do individual and group counseling . . . . Adults frequently come to the coordinator with problems relating to employment, finance, home or community adjustment [p. 53]." Although Nance does not spell out the desired educational background of the coordinator, his statement of functions suggests a strong background in counseling.

If the community educator is to (a) provide at least minimal individual counseling, (b) conduct various kinds of growth groups and

273

task-oriented groups, (c) refer individuals to appropriate counseling services, and (d) provide coordination of community services, then he needs both knowledge about and skills in basic counseling. Ideally, the community educator will be qualified, by virtue of specific preparation, to do both individual and group counseling. Although the coordinator, because of other administrative duties, may not be engaged in extensive counseling practice, he should be knowledgeable about counseling as a general background for his various responsibilities. Should the community education director not have a counseling background, certainly someone on his administrative staff should have such expertise. The counseling function in community education begins with the central staff.

Opportunities for individual counseling abound, and the need for counseling-coordinator skills are obvious. Frequently, the community educator will need to refer members of the community to professional services. His knowledge of the resources of the community is indispensable and his referral techniques must be practiced. In other words, the need for specific skills in group process cannot be ignored by any community educator. The assumption that a community education coordinator will possess such group process skills is implicit in the definition of his title.

One of the great challenges to community education is that of marshaling the resources of a community in the manner that will produce the greatest benefit for the most people. The coordinator must be able to help groups of people define their problems. He must then assist these citizens in their search for solutions to the problems, securing any needed assistance from other qualified people in the community. He must be a person, sensitive to the needs of others, capable of listening with understanding, and skilled in promoting sound interpersonal relationships; as such, he can be invaluable to the community. Understanding of and skill in using task group and developmental group processes should be part of the coordinator's preparation.

An example of one type of request brought to the community educator led to a 1972 conference in Lansing, Michigan. At the request of the United Indian Tribes of America, a conference was called to discuss methods of improving the life styles of many groups of Indians. Tribal leaders, community education program directors and trainers, and counselor-educators discussed methods of identifying, isolating, and resolving community problems in various reservation areas. Central to the effectiveness of meeting such needs was the skillful use of group processes. As a result of the planning conference, a contract was negotiated to provide group leadership and counseling skills to leaders of the reservation population.

People need assistance in gaining the necessary insights to enable them to see what changes could be of benefit in helping them achieve their goals. Task group forces could prove invaluable in meeting community needs. Not only should the community educator be skilled in group process, but he should also be able to teach others such skills.

The group process centers around a group of concerned citizens who are organized to accomplish specific tasks. A skilled leader will help the members to listen, to understand the various meanings being expressed, and to focus on the specific tasks. The leader helps to involve all members of the group and teaches members to respect the rights of others. Members will learn the different facilitative roles in group process and will be instructed in several leadership styles. As a core of group leaders becomes prepared, these leaders can help concerned groups meet community needs.

SOME TYPICAL COMMUNITY COUNSELING PROGRAMS

Not too many years ago, the "purist" in counseling would have seen counseling as an individual, one to one relationship conducted in a traditional private office within a counseling center. Today, however, most counselors embrace the concept of the helping professions serving in a multitude of settings to bring assistance to both individuals and groups. Therefore, the idea of the community as a laboratory for human development should be readily accepted.

Actually the programs of many service agencies in a community can be considered in the broadest sense, as counseling programs. The programs that are presented in the following descriptions are merely illustrative of the many services that are operating in many communities; and, while the descriptions are brief and necessarily incomplete, they should stimulate thought about the potential in every community for a well-coordinated community counseling service.

Family Consultation Center. As an agency sponsored by the United Fund, or a similar community effort, a family consultation center provides professional counseling services to members of the community. Such a center, usually staffed with a paid professional staff, assists individuals and frequently entire families in resolving personal and interpersonal problems in adjustment. Most centers offer services on a voluntary basis; i.e., without individuals being "sentenced" by the center to seek assistance. Fees are frequently charged on the basis of ability to pay. These centers are usually well organized and have well formulated statements of purpose, objectives and procedures. These centers, which are usually centrally operated, rely heavily upon referrals from other agencies.

Rehabilitation Services. Nearly every community offers its citizens, either through local agencies or thorough referrals to state organizations, services for the rehabilitation of individuals. These services are concerned with the restoration of clients to productive work roles, and they usually involve individual counseling and educational and vocational training. The State Vocational Rehabilitation program offers a free service to citizens with various kinds of handicaps that limit their effectiveness. Similarly, state, regional, and local societies or agencies provide counseling and rehabilitation services for the blind, for crippled children, and for specific disease victims. Most services are free of cost or based on the client's ability to pay.

Drug and Alcohol Abuse Program. Within the past decade many communities, responding to the needs of both youth and adults, have developed counseling services to provide assistance to drug and alcohol victims. The services range from providing information to complete hospitalization. Obviously, the range of skills to be found in these programs is broad. Many of the information programs are staffed with volunteer workers with little or minimal counselor training. Others, funded by community funds, may employ highly specialized professional workers.

Perhaps one of the best known programs, on a national level, is Alcoholics Anonymous. This organization, offering assistance through individual and group counseling, relies heavily on volunteer unskilled or paraprofessional personnel. Various other related organizations have been patterned after this successful model and provide services for youth and spouses of alcoholics.

Drug abuse programs may take the form of drug information centers, drug crisis houses, half way houses or full treatment centers. Levels of counseling range from ex-addict volunteers to specially trained addiction therapists.

Planned Parenthood Associations. Many communities offer, under various titles, services related to family planning. "Birthright," "Women's Center," "Unwed Mothers' Program," "Alternative to Abortion," and "Plan Your Family" are examples of services related to planned parenthood. These programs, frequently funded by the community, often use trained specialists on a part-time, voluntary basis as consultants for a corps of volunteer workers. Church groups and other civic minded organizations may sponsor these services.

Community Centers. Although organized to fulfill a host of community needs, many community centers offer specific counseling services. One such center familiar to the authors offers programs of assistance to the elderly, to the unemployed, the under-educated, the problem drinker, the indigent and many other classifications of people. Staffed with a combination of professional, paraprofessional and volunteer workers, these centers attempt to provide counseling and other assistance at the "grass roots" level.

YMCA-YWCA. These associations are a source of dedicated community service. Although YWCA and YMCA programs are not labeled as typical counseling programs, nearly all of them are concerned with human potential development; many of the directors have, for many years, been drawn from the counselor ranks. The recreation programs, the arts and crafts centers, the women's opportunities programs, and other semiformal or formal education programs are concerned with the development of human potential and the resolution of adjustment difficulties. A review of the yearly calendar of a local YM-YWCA is education about local services.

277

Religious Organization Sponsored Services. Many churches and religious organizations provide a wide range of counseling and guidance programs. While some services may be offered to members only, others are available without consideration of creed — or race or color. The services include a wide range of counseling assistance from working with youth in vocational guidance to financial planning for senior citizens. Although some unskilled volunteer help may be used, many such agencies employ specialized professionals.

Court Related Services. Nearly every community provides counseling programs for individuals who have been brought before the court of law. The county court system provides rehabilitation services for juveniles as well as adults, and assistance and supervision is provided for persons released from various kinds of correctional institutions. Probation and parole officers frequently have backgrounds in counseling.

The court may be responsible for conducting special group or individual counseling programs for nonsentenced first offenders. Other court functions may include providing for a juvenile home, coordinating a court volunteer program, and providing for drug and alcohol addiction therapy. Specific services of the court vary from locality to locality; a services directory should be consulted for accurate information.

Obviously, this listing does not cover all of the many community counseling services available, but it does suggest the wide range of programs that exist. A directory of agencies and programs in Kalamazoo County, Michigan, contains over thirty-seven pages plus an additional six pages listing state and federal agencies. Without question, "people" services consume tremendous community effort.

A major and much needed contribution which can be made by the community educator is that of coordinating community efforts toward delivering the various counseling services. Through a series of meetings of representatives of agencies concerned with categorical problems, the community educator may assist in clarifying goals, identifying specific services, and identifying areas of duplication of efforts and of inadequacies in meeting community needs. Since the diversity of service-sponsoring organizations is so great, inter-agency communication is frequently inadequate. A coordinating effort should be welcomed. As the coordination of services is improved, a systematic effort to communicate the scope and nature of all services to the citizens of the community should be made. Perhaps such a follow-up could be a coordinated agency project.

COMMUNITY EDUCATION COUNSELING –
A LOOK AHEAD

If the past is prologue, the future role of community education counseling is indeed challenging. The relative position of counseling within community education is analogous to infancy in the human life cycle: community education counseling has emerged as a new helping profession and is now reaching out to find its full role. While many of the functions discussed in this chapter will continue to be important, societal changes in the future will dictate new directions for counseling. As advances in technology and expansion of knowledge created circumstances in the past that fostered the emergence of counseling, future pressures of an increasingly complex society will produce new needs and demands for services.

Predicting the precise nature of society in the next quarter of a century is, of course, an impossible task; however, some projections based on current trends are possible. The following counseling needs appear to be a plausible outgrowth from the trends visible today.

Some kind of "war on poverty" will be in all probability a continuous battle for years to come. Although the programs will use many attention-getting titles and slogans, and each of them will be new and exciting, they will be introduced to combat the same problems known today: ignorance, communicable diseases, mental illnesses, and unemployment. Within such community action programs, various educational components can be anticipated which will have direct implications for counseling. The community educator, knowledgeable about legislation and the direction or intended direction of societal change, should stimulate the development of counseling services, supported by state or federal appropriations, to assist citizens in becoming prepared for social change. In the future, community education will be increasingly aware of the fact that knowledge about self, about alternative courses of action, and about possible consequences of action is an ingredient of sound decision-making. The process of helping the people of a community acquire that kind of knowledge is essentially the concern of counseling.

A second projection is related to the role of work in the lives of people. The initial years of the decade of the 70's have reverberated with the rumbles of "blue collar blues," labor sabotage, and general dissatisfaction with the indignity of production-line labor. In a quest for the "good life," the not so common "common" man has struck for better working conditions, shorter working hours, and early retirement. From past successes, a prediction of continued gains in shorter hours and early pensions seems reasonable, but the gains will not be made without paying a price. While the gains appear to be distinct worker benefits, early and possibly premature indications suggest that several adjustment problems are concommitant outgrowths of labor's gains. As the working hours decrease, the leisure hours increase, and frequently they hang heavily on those who are unprepared to utilize leisure time. Similarly, early retirement may produce a population ill-prepared to meet the common problems of reduced income and increased leisure time.

The implications of changing work patterns for community education are easy to discern. The probable need for increased counseling services seems obvious. Not only must community educators provide individual growth and enrichment through educational programs for citizens; but they must also provide counseling services to help individuals take advantage of such growth opportunities. The employee with the short work week may need assistance in developing avocational interests or in discovering that education may be more than vocational training. The early retiree may need to be guided into activities which will help fulfill the normal human need to be productive and to give service.

The shortened work week, early retirement, and the accompanying boredom for the nonfulfilled person will produce a population searching for relief from the tedious daily routine. Problems of drug usage and escape through alcohol will become more prevalent. Interpersonal conflicts will probably become more acute, and daily personal adjustment may be more difficult to maintain. The community education counseling program will need to develop new strategies for reaching people who need assistance in managing their lives.

Counseling skills pertinent to promoting good interpersonal relations will be mandatory for some members of the community education staff.

As society experiences shifts in working conditions and further growth in technological sophistication, increasing numbers of workers will need to be retrained to keep pace with labor needs. As machines are programmed to perform the unskilled and semi-skilled tasks in production, many workers will need re-tooling to keep pace with change. Assistance in helping workers to gain a better understanding of their strengths and weaknesses and the projected opportunities for employment can be given by counselors within the community education program.

Lastly, but certainly not exhausting the many possible future counseling needs, a recent societal concern for the value orientation and social responsibility of its citizenry speaks to the need for greater understanding of the "whys" of behavior. Counseling programs, either individual or of a group nature, may be needed to assist individuals in grappling with some basic philosophical issues related to values and morality. Racial friction, sexual morality, governmental ethics and honesty, human freedom and dignity — whatever the issue, counselors may have a vital role to play in assisting education as it tries to help members of our society learn to cope with issues — to help them learn to solve their societal problems.

● ● ● ● ● ● ● ● ● ● ● ● ●

The community education program is faced with unprecendented challenges. Community education must call upon the skills of counseling to help it meet the challenges. And community counseling must call upon the coordinative assistance of the community educator. This professional partnership in community service can hope to meet the challenge of providing for the human relations needs of citizens. This partnership can hope to make meaningful contributions to the formation of an environment wherein individuals are provided growth opportunities for the fullest development of human potential.

CHAPTER XII

ART IN COMMUNITY EDUCATION

ART IN COMMUNITY EDUCATION

RUTH H. SEAY
AND
MAURICE F. SEAY

> Esthetic perceiving and creating and esthetic peak experi-
> ences are seen to be a central aspect of human life and of
> psychology and education rather than a peripheral one.

— Maslow (1962, p. 45)

Community education has a special stake in the current surge of
interest in the arts. Directors of community education programs,
administrators of educational agencies, curriculum specialists, teachers, and citizens — in other words, all people who determine the kind
of education available to the men, women, youth, and children of the
United States — take note: the arts are receiving increasing attention
from the American people. The arts are being seen again as a way of
fulfilling the potential of individuals and of distinguishing our civilization. The arts are being seriously considered for a place in the center
ring of the American way of life. The arts can be most effective in
our way of life when they are coordinated in a comprehensive
community education program.

THE SIGNS

No longer do educators have cause for complaint about a frontier influence in American culture that leads to popular disdain of the arts. Nor does the national obsession with business and technology exercise the undisputed hold upon our culture that it did a decade ago. During the sixties people of all ages watched youth groups express their passionate disapproval of that obsession; and even though gaps in understanding distressed everyone, people began to think new thoughts and ask new questions. The multiple tragedies of an ill-advised war, crime in the streets, crime in government, homicide by automobile, and destruction of the natural environment stunned the American people. Meanwhile, as they listened to a din of commentary and contention, many of them looked at their social institutions for the first time. And many people thought about their own lives more seriously than ever before.

Some of that thought led to action. Minority groups and women raised their voices above the general tumult to claim what they believed to be their rights to more fulfilling lives. Retired men and women grew more numerous in the population and began to demand a better kind of life. Middle-aged citizens, whose increasing burden of responsibility for longer-living parents coincided with the growing wants of their children, accepted the burden of new taxes to provide welfare for the unrelated poor, security for their own old age, and proliferating largess for all. They were too busy making economic and emotional ends meet to raise an organized voice in protest, but they, too, wondered about their own rights to "fulfillment."

As people realized their dissatisfaction with the fruits of technology, they looked to educational agencies to help them learn how to build more satisfying lives. They sought help quietly. Mothers went to city art centers when their younger children entered school. Fathers studied the "Great Books" in evening discussion groups. Grandparents enrolled in craft classes in "Senior-Citizen" centers. And parents encouraged their children to learn more than they themselves had taken time to learn about literature, music, theater, the dance, and the visual arts. Few people knew how to put into words the lacks they were beginning to feel. They sought help even though they could not tell a news reporter or a television feature writer what they were seeking.

Those people who looked at contemporary culture from the perspective of history reiterated lessons handed down through 6000 years. Historians Arnold Toynbee and the Durants called attention frequently to the fact that the arts of a civilization are what live after that civilization is gone. History reminded each generation that a civilization is distinguished only by its art.

The signs were posted. The meaning was clear to those who could read them; but these signs were small, quiet ones, and comparatively few leaders in the expansive post-World War II period were able to see quiet signs. That small number included many of the pioneers in community education. After they saw the signs, they sought help in reading them.

Pioneers in Reading Signs

Several pioneers among psychologists and educational philosophers offered suggestions for reading and following the signs. For example, Carl Rogers, as he conducted scientific inquiries into human behavior in the late forties and early fifties, discovered significant information about the human personality. His work with client-centered therapy led him to conclude that the human organism "... has one basic tendency and striving – to actualize, maintain, and enhance the experiencing organism. Rather than many needs and motives, it seems entirely possible that all organic and psychological needs may be described as partial aspects of this one fundamental need [1951, pp. 487-488]." And in an earlier paper he wrote, "I find that the urge for a greater degree of independence, the desire for a self-determined integration, the tendency to strive, even through much pain, toward a socialized maturity, is as strong as – no, is stronger than – the desire for comfortable dependence.... the balance seems invariably in the direction of the painful but ultimately rewarding path of self-actualization or growth [1948, p. 218]."

Educational psychologist, Jerome Bruner, wrote in 1962, "In our time, the requirements of technology ... and the rise of idelogies ... subordinate the individual to the defined aims of a society. ... At the same time ... man's understanding of himself and of his world – both the natural and social world – has deepened to a degree that warrants calling our age an intellectually golden one. The

287

need is now to employ our deeper understanding not only for the enrichment of society but also for the enrichment of the individual [p. 116]."

In educational practice, curriculum design may or may not reflect the findings of research, but one 1971 publication would indicate that curriculum revision is in progress and that humanistic points of view figure prominently in the educational philosophy of curriculum specialists. *The Curriculum: Retrospect and Prospect* carried in its preface the statement, "The school . . . is not as effective an instrument for individual fulfillment and social change as most would like . . . [McClure, p. vii]."

The various chapters of this publication, a yearbook of the National Society for the Study of Education, contained many indications of the thought which curriculum workers had been giving to human potential and to the education needed to develop it. For example, Robert M. McClure, speaking of educational events to come, mentioned, "the development of new techniques in interpersonal relations, intergroup relations, and ultimately in intrapersonal relations, [pp. 47-48]."

In the same yearbook, Charles E. Brown, dealing with emerging priorities for the "continuing" aspect of community education, emphasized the need for greater aesthetic understanding. He suggested several possibilities that continuing education could use in filling the void in people's lives caused by increased leisure hours, and concluded, "Chief among these in my judgment is the development of a higher capacity to enjoy and create beauty [p. 260.]"

Bruce R. Joyce, also writing in *The Curriculum: Retrospect and Prospect,* described the likely future which could be expected to develop out of the progressive bureaucratization which had already taken place in the curriculum field. Then he offered "a humanistic alternative . . . which can help people make contact with each other in new and stronger ways and can help individuals create lives which are unique, uniquely fulfilling and socially productive, even transcendentally cooperative [pp. 311-312]."

The emphasis is clear. Pioneering psychologists and educational philosophers read the signs of the sixties — and of several decades before the sixties — to mean that people must be encouraged to develop as self-actualizing, growing individuals. As educational practices proceed along their course of inevitable change, educational leadership should make sure that the change is in the direction of humanistic modes of education. This emphasis is noted in Chapter Five on leadership training.

Community education has an opportunity — and a necessity — to choose the directions in which it will develop. One of the major choices which will be made, either by active intent or by passive default, is that between progressive bureaucratization and a new humanism. The humanistic alternative offers community education one of its greatest challenges.

Connecting Links

Connecting links between the research and writings of university-based theorists and front-line practitioners have always been too few and too late, but in spite of that flaw, the connecting links do serve to put theory into practice. One of these links, destined to be used widely, is the *Curriculum Handbook for School Executives,* published in 1973 by the American Association of School Administrators. The *Curriculum Handbook* was planned for the administrator who is "besieged with information, claims, and counterclaims about new curricular concepts in every conceivable subject [p. iii]."

The Association asked 14 national organizations to co-sponsor the preparation of the chapters which were to identify, for the use of educational administrators, emerging curriculum concepts in specific subject areas. While this overview of "surfacing curriculum developments" is school-centered and somewhat feeble in its approach to the future, it provides a window through which a community educator can see viewpoints representative of national organizations such as the National Council for the Social Studies, National Science Teachers Association, National Council of Teachers of English, American Association for Health, Physical Education and Recreation, and the National Art Education Association.

The chapters of the *Curriculum Handbook* reveal at least a few references to humanistic values. For example, social studies educators were reported to be debating whether a value-centered or a value-free approach is most appropriate. This ideological polarization in the field of social studies was described as being "complicated by the desire on the part of most social studies educators to help students develop humanistic and democratic values [p. 346]."

Writers dealing with subjects which traditionally include areas of the arts were unanimous in recognizing a current interest in greater emphasis on the humanities. In the field of English language arts, a proper balance of skills and content was considered a likely path to student success in using language effectively and toward finding in literature a "storehouse of human understanding [p. 104]." Physical education should lead to realization by every student of his "individual movement potential" through the learning media of sport, dance, and gymnastic movement forms (p. 268). Music education should "establish for every student a sound and permanent relationship with music, . . . A comprehensive music program should . . . demonstrate the joy that music can bring [pp. 241, 247]."

Educators in the visual arts have, from the evidence in this *Curriculum Handbook,* seized rather firmly upon the curricular trend toward a new humanism. John Mahlmann and Stanley Madeja wrote that one of the most encouraging sights to art teachers has been the vocabulary of education in recent years, exemplified by such phrases as "qualify of life." The authors commented on the fact that quality of life seemed to be interpreted by educators recently as meaning more than physical needs and comforts − as referring to the kinds of values that are nurtured by art education. "Perception, sensitivity, critical awareness, and creative problem-solving abilities − all items high on the priority list of any art educator − are beginning to receive increasing emphasis as we strive for true quality and appreciation of life in an increasingly complex environment [p. 34]."

Connecting links include, also, the two *Handbooks* of the American Educational Research Association. Robert M. W. Travers, editor of the *Second Handbook of Research on Teaching* (1973), called attention to the immense change which had taken place in the behavioral sciences during the decade between 1963 and 1973: change, some of which "has occurred so gradually that those who have been participating in it have hardly been aware that they have been moving slowly, but inexorably, into a world of new techniques, new ideas and new research endeavors [p. v]."

Elliot W. Eisner reviews, in Chapter 37 of the Travers *Handbook*, the research of the 1963-1973 decade in the field of teaching the visual arts; and he accounts for the limited field of significant studies by citing several problems characteristic of all educational research. One of these, the rapid change in the educational values of educators, has led, for example, to a shift in the purposes of art education from the major goal of developing creativity to the major goal of developing "visual sensitivity and the understanding of art as a human contribution to man's cultural experience [1973, pp. 1198-1199]."

Other writers on the subject of art education have, in the past, often taken an ambivalent stance. They have asked whether art is, or is not, a discipline and if there are fundamental concepts which should be taught in the same way that the concepts of mathematics are taught. They have frequently looked at art education as something visual and manipulative that goes on only in an elementary or secondary school classroom. In 1941 the National Society for the Study of Education produced a yearbook entitled *Art in American Life and Education* which influenced the thinking of many educators. The yearbook grew out of the experimental work of the thirties when, for example, the Owatonna (Minnesota) Art Education Project attempted to infuse a typical American community with the idea that art was a way of life. Another yearbook, *Art education* (1965), surveyed developments after 1940 and called upon teachers and administrators in art education to recognize the liberating function of art; to see that art can free people to conceive of other problems and solutions; to know that art experience is wider than the studio, the gallery, and the art classroom [adapted from pp. 226-227].

These examples of connecting links — a "handbook" on developments in curriculum co-sponsored by a national organization of school administrators, "handbooks" reporting educational research sponsored by a national association for the promotion of educational research, and the yearbooks of a society organized "to carry on the investigation of educational problems, to publish the results of same, and to promote their discussion [NSSE constitution, Art. II, published in each yearbook.]" — these examples illustrate the kind of

291

literature that is informing teachers and administrators of the findings of research, innovative projects, and the thinking of certain leaders in specific fields. Graduate study, in-service education, and professional conferences provide other links. The growing conviction in our society that American education must be made more effective in the transmission of humaneness (as well as the transmission of a technology for supporting physical life) is shared today by many teachers and administrators.

BUT WHY ART?

The study of art is recommended as a central aspect of education because art in its many forms — the performing arts, the visual arts, literature — can open up human minds to new insights into truth. Art can help to meet a critical need that the American people are recognizing — a need for new perception of the human condition.

When people take off some of their cultural blindfolds they can find themselves free to work out new solutions to some very stagnant social problems. They also have a fresh opportunity to work out some believable, usable systems of human values. The human condition today requires development of the capacity of people to respond accurately to current reality. And the study of art helps people develop this capacity.

If people are to feel, as well as comprehend intellectually, the full meaning of reality, they will have to learn more effective use of a part of their mental equipment that traditional schooling has belittled. Purely verbal thinking — the kind of abstract, analytical thinking that has been used almost exclusively in the traditional schooling process — has enabled people to master certain kinds of knowledge, but it has left them handicapped in handling intuitive and aesthetic kinds of understanding.

Psychologically healthy people, according to Abraham H. Maslow (1962, pp. 44-48), are able to use their pre-verbal primary processes; they are able to dip into the unconscious and the preconscious instead of always repressing or controlling them. Thus they release their creative powers; they use all their capacities. A healthy integration of the conscious, the preconscious, and the unconscious enables people to enjoy living. They can be whimsical and humorous; they can laugh and love and enjoy the everyday emotional experiences of living. Maslow speaks of such integration as making possible the "peak experience." Peak experiences are integrative of the splits within the person, as well as of splits between persons and between a person and the world. Striving is replaced by a sense of being. Time disappears. "Peak experiences are moves toward health," Maslow explains, "and are themselves momentary healths. These experiences are life-validating, i.e., they make life worthwhile [p. 45]."

Members of the National Committee on Art Education planned three of their annual conferences around the question, "Why art?" Three educators were asked to answer. Each spoke to his audience from the depths of his own special understanding of art. Irwin Edman, addressing the 1950 NCAE conference while he was a professor of philosophy at Columbia University, submitted the hypothesis that the arts, adequately taught, were perhaps the most central and important means of education. Because the arts teach, not by argument or demonstration but by presentation and disclosure, they are an education in fulfillment. He described the hypnotizing of man's mind by the geometric view of reality while man's imagination has been left empty and frustrated. What "men have felt to be real . . . the visible shapes and colors of existence . . . the acute intimacies of fear and hope, of happiness and misery in confrontation of the soul with the world . . . have been explained away in terms of a physical mathematical explanation [pp. 36, 40]."

The director of the Orthogenic School at the University of Chicago, Bruno Bettelheim, addressed the NCAE conference in 1962. He warned that art is not the outpouring of the unconscious, but rather the disciplined molding and working over of such outpourings. It is interesting to note that John Dewey (1934) expressed similar disapproval of certain acts of so-called self-expression masquerading as art. He wrote, " . . . to express is to stay by, to carry forward in development, to work out to completion. . . . What is sometimes called an act of self-expression is only a spewing forth [p. 62]."

Bettelheim explained that the unconscious is not to be repressed — as it is in much school experience — but it is to be used as a natural resource which can enrich the total personality. A student of art needs to listen carefully and try to understand what is moving man from inside, and then to make disciplined efforts to express his understanding in external form, both to help himself to understand better and to let others see his understanding. In his study of art a student can try "to bring order and comprehension to the chaos that reigns within him . . . to grow into a free person struggling with and expressing his vision of himself and of life [p. 59]."

George D. Stoddard, Chancellor of New York University at the time he addressed the NCAE conference (1963), said, "The aim of education is life fulfillment through learning and the creative process. . . if life is to be worth living, it must be so in terms of a constant search for truth, beauty and humanity. . . . Art is a form of truth, and truth of many sorts is revealed in and through art [pp. 7, 17]."

Art has many unique attributes. The creations of artists, accumulated through thousands of years, enrich human civilization. The original insights of contemporary artists teach people about themselves and their own time. Individual experiences in aesthetic perceiving and creating help people to develop capacities that they neglect in other schooling. And it is these very capacities for knowing by intuition, feeling, and recognition which are needed if people are to improve the general quality of life for themselves and for those they love.

Community educators must recognize the unique values of art. Those who experience these values personally know that they are of central significance in the lifelong mental and emotional growth of human beings. Those who have not developed such personal understanding must believe the evidence.

ART IN COMMUNITY EDUCATION

Education to improve the quality of life is already a familiar goal to community educators. They are well aware of working for social improvement through helping individual people grow. And they have known art education to be a strong ally when they design programs to implement that goal.

Any examination of actual community education programs involving art must be prefaced with a brief reminder of the dichotomy prevalent in the usage of the term "community education." The comprehensive concept of community education views the process as one that achieves a balance and a use of all institutional forces in the education of all the people of a community. More traditional understanding of the term "community education," however, refers only to special programs that supplement or "enrich" the educational programs available through the public schools and other local agencies. This dichotomy of usage leads, therefore, to the following subheadings under "Art in Community Education": (a) Art in Certain Enrichment Programs; and (b) Other Art in Community Education.

Art in Certain Enrichment Programs

In the informal structure of a familiar type of community education program which uses the facilities of the public schools, enrichment classes are usually planned to meet a specific need recognized by a class-size group of individuals. In each program certain classes become favorites with large groups of people in the community and are offered regularly while other classes are offered from time to time on a trial basis. Such procedures guarantee a close relationship between instruction and the conscious awareness of specific lacks on the part of people in the community. In other words, enrichment programs are relevant. That relevancy is a basic factor in their educational value.

Significantly, enrichment programs contain a high proportion of art-related classes. A director of one community education program, speaking from his experience in administering classes involving approximately 3600 people each year, said that participants in the art activities accounted for about one-third of the total enrollment in all community education enrichment classes.

An example of the kind of art instruction which has characterized many community education enrichment programs is shown in Tables 12-1 and 12-2. The directors of several programs in Michigan were asked to list their 1972-73 program activities in the "expressive arts" and to estimate the number of people who participated in each activity. The term, expressive arts, was defined as any creative activity which offered opportunities for self-expression.

Table 12-1. MOST FREQUENT ART-RELATED ACTIVITIES
IN SAMPLE OF ENRICHMENT PROGRAMS

The following art-related activities were taught in 3 or more of
the 14 Michigan community education enrichment programs
reporting in the 1972-73 questionnaire.

Activity	Number of programs offering the activity	Estimate of the total number of people participating
Cake decorating	9	250
Ceramics, including clay sculpture	10	268
Dance, square dancing for couples, round dancing for couples, creative dance including ballet, tap, and acrobatic	6	949
Decoupage	7	128
Drawing	8	196
Flower arranging	5	117
Guitar: beginning and advanced, elementary, teen, and adult	10	428
Macrame	4	79
Painting: oils and acrylics	12	341
Photography	6	129
Sewing	3	190

Table 12-2.   LESS FREQUENT ART-RELATED ACTIVITIES
IN SAMPLE OF ENRICHMENT PROGRAMS

The following art-related activities were taught in fewer than
3 of the 14 Michigan community education enrichment programs
reporting in the 1972-73 questionnaire.

Activity	Number of programs offering the activity	Estimate of the total number of people participating
Antiques	1	30
Baton lessons	2	96
Bridge	1	90
Candle making	1	15
Chess	1	20
Community chorous	2	42
Community orchestra	1	20
Creative writing	1	12
Crocheting	2	50
Drum and bagpipe	1	20
Film study	1	20
Furniture refinishing	1	40
Gourmet cooking	2	84
Hairpin lace	1	10
Holiday decorations	1	24
Knitting	2	115
Landscaping	1	20
Lifestyle workshop	1	9
Needlepoint	1	35
Power boating	1	60
Puppet theater	1	30
Quilting	1	12
Spinning	1	12
Swedish embroidery	1	8
Theater, summer youth	1	20
Weaving	1	35
Wood carving	1	30
Yoga	1	30

The art-related activities listed in Tables 12-1 and 12-2 indicate a strong preference for active, skill-related classes. While some appreciation was undoubtedly gained as an incidental reward by students learning to draw or to play the guitar, classes named "Art Appreciation," "Music Appreciation," and "Know Your Bible as Literature" drew few registrants. A director explained, "If they take Art Appreciation, it is likely to be for college credit, not for 'enrichment'."

Some people question the extent of the value of this type of enrichment activity. Much depends, of course, on the teaching and learning that occurs in a class — and the truth of the matter is that adults, youth, and children learn more effectively when they enjoy their learning activities. Perhaps it is sufficient to say that, although improvement undoubtedly needs to be made, the "enrichment programs" of community education are relevant to certain needs of many people of a community. The classes are flexible in their use of available resources to meet current needs. And, significantly for the student of art in education, these rudimentary educational efforts have drawn upon the unique attributes of art in a direct effort to meet the great contemporary need in America for a better quality of living.

Other Art in Community Education

The entire art curriculum of formal schooling is part of the art instruction offered to the people of a community in the comprehensive process of community education. The school's art curriculum includes the scheduled art classes and the nonclass activities of preschool, elementary, and high school art plus any courses or nonclass activities that may be available in the community from institutions of higher education.

Paralleling the art program of the schools and the art-related "enrichment" activities of many community education programs are other community-wide educational opportunities in art. This art education is provided by agencies with legitimate educational purposes, with their own facilities (in most cases), and with their own budgets (in most cases) underwritten (in whole or in part) by the seqment of the community which patronizes them. These agencies include art institutes and museums, theater groups, dance groups, community choirs and church choirs, community orchestras, writers' groups, college art programs, the art departments of libraries, a variety of craft associations, and many other miscellaneous art-related activities.

United arts councils Many cities organize some of their activities in the arts into a community united arts council. Thus fund drives can be unified into one effort, comprehensive program listings can be distributed among the citizens, and the total cultural impact upon the community can be planned cooperatively by area-wide representatives. Newspapers usually present, at least once a week, the local possibilities in this area of community education. Two examples of the kind of presentation made to two different urban communities are illustrative of the view the public receives of this group of programs.

The June 24, 1973 Sunday edition of the *Courier-Journal & Times* of Louisville, Kentucky, in a 20-page section entitled "Lively Arts," listed the following sub-headings: art, motion pictures, records, the stage and summer theater, television, and travel. Features dealt with a "Festival of American Folklife" which was about to open in Washington, D.C.; a "Poke Sallet Festival" to be held in Harlan, Kentucky; revivals of old movie music to be released in new recordings; performances on various stages in the region including 16 summer theaters; and reviews with illustrations of special showings of prints, paintings, and sculpture which were appearing at six different art galleries and museums, four in the region of Louisville, one in New York, and one in San Francisco.

On the same day a 16-page section of *The Pittsburgh Press,* also entitled "Lively Arts," listed the following sub-headings: theaters, "prestige" events, books-music, food, and puzzle. Feature articles dealt with a new motion picture opening in the city, sets in production for the civic light opera, location problems remembered by the director of an awards-winning motion picture, and a description of international stars appearing with the Pittsburgh Symphony Orchestra in its summer season. The section also carried, however, seven full-page grocery advertisements.

299

College and church art programs. Community colleges offer residents of many areas a wide range of programs and exhibits by local and visiting artists as well as more formal opportunities for study in the various aesthetic fields. An interesting accommodation to community needs was made by one college which rescheduled 134 courses, of which 11 were in the visual and performing arts, during the hours from 9:00 to 11:00 a.m. and from 1:00 to 3:00 p.m. for the benefit of housewives, mothers, second- and third-shift employees and others who found those hours to be their free time. The 11 art classes included art for elementary teachers, beginning photography, speech, acting, theater directing, and set construction. This college cooperated with several "community education centers" in its service area by offering college institutional credit for adults who enrolled in enrichment and self-development courses offered by the local centers.

Churches often provide community education in music through their choirs and special youth programs. The art of the dance and the theater contribute to the more modern church programs, and the visual arts and crafts are encouraged by special exhibits, fairs, and bazaars — usually organized as money-raising projects by women's auxiliary groups. Churches which employ highly trained organists and choir directors frequently provide the community with two sources of music education: the music heard in church services and the organ, piano, and voice lessons that the expert organists and choir directors offer for modest fees.

Libraries. The comprehension of art that can be gained from reading can hardly be overstated. A wealth of art-related periodicals, handsome art books, and miscellaneous pamphlets can be found in the larger public libraries and in some art-center libraries. Books can be borrowed through interlibrary loan services if they are not found in the library of the community itself.

The lending of prints of masterpieces and the original work of local painters, sculptors, and craftsmen is a library service that is becoming increasingly popular with the public. Many libraries lend sound recordings and photographic slides, and these libraries often provide the electronic equipment necessary to the use of technology's reproductions of art.

A more traditional service is the lending of the works of literary artists. The vast treasure produced by the poets, playwrights, historians, novelists, and other writers during all of civilized history sits quietly on library shelves waiting to be rediscovered by each generation of readers.

Rural involvement in the arts. The Agricultural Extension Service has encouraged interest in many kinds of "housewife crafts." Members of Extension Clubs learn from state and federal bulletins and from demonstrations by agents of the Service to make useful and decorative items. For example, many handsome pine-cone wreaths can be found on the walls of tastefully decorated farm homes as a result of the work of this agency.

Rural families often get together for cultural expeditions, sometimes through the Extension Club or the neighborhood church, and sometimes independently of any agency. The expeditions may lead across several states to see, perhaps, the country-music recording industry centered in Nashville, Tennessee, or to hear an afternoon performance of the Chicago Symphony Orchestra and to see a touring Broadway production during the evening.

The variety of organized art instruction offered by schools and other community agencies has been indicated briefly. In this uncoordinated area, instruction is duplicated, educational opportunities exist unknown to many people who long for such opportunities; worthy programs languish for lack of support and use, and other programs struggle to cope with multitudes of patrons. Improvement in the use of these community resources in art depends primarily upon coordination. Improvement in the quality of these community resources in art also depends primarily upon community-wide coordination. The leadership of community education should be giving thought to this immediate need for coordination of the institutionalized art resources of the community.

Still other areas of art activity are part of the community art scene. Among these are the handicrafts and folk arts, the popular arts, business and government participation in art, and traditional presentations. In the sense that people are constantly learning from the social and cultural environment in which they live, each of these areas is part of the total community education in art.

Handicrafts and Other Folk Art

Handicrafts occupy a special place in American culture. Delight in crafting beautiful utilitarian objects, pride in their use, devotion to the idea that creation of fine handicraft somehow inspires and ennobles a society — these emotions accompanied our pioneer ancestors as they came from Europe, and the same emotions moved west with our forefathers in covered wagons. Favorite handicrafted heirlooms have been handed down through American families for about a dozen generations. Museums display with increasing care the coverlets and quilts, silver, treen, and blown glass of the eighteenth and nineteenth centuries. Collectors search estate sales and grand-mothers' attics for choice items.

Community education uses indigenous interest in handicraft as a learning resource. Beautiful antiques are studied as lessons in design; they are drawn and painted; they are arranged as objects of interest in interior decoration. New utilitarian objects are crafted as part of lessons in the use of various categories of tools. Collections are visited. The fine points of the art of collecting are studied. Teachers recognize the easy rapport their students feel with handicrafts.

Some teachers see learning possibilities in exploring the con-temporary world of handicrafts. Their students may find individual craftsmen in their own communities producing unexpected treasures. Other craftsmen work in manufacturing plants where they function as industrial designers. Craftsmanship, in many instances, involves the kind of creative action usually associated with the "fine arts." When a craft activity goes beyond mere technical mastery of process, it qualifies as an art experience.

Students may also explore regional groups of artist-craftsmen. Many of these individuals participate in handicraft organizations such as the Southern Highland Handicraft Guild which serves a large area in the southern Appalachian region. Travellers in the middle South have come to know this guild as the sponsor of the Craftsmen's Fairs held each year at Gatlinburg, Tennessee, or Asheville, North Carolina. Here craftsmen from six to eight states exhibit and sell their products. But the work of the Guild is year-round. It assists craft centers "by pooling knowledge and resources, and providing help in designing, producing, and marketing craft work [Stevens, 1962, p. 282]."

The entire country has been enjoying a vigorous revival of interest in all of its folk arts. Each region has its own folk art, whether the art receives public attention or not, and its roots go deep into the cultural heritage of the people. Even though the people of our different regions may be separated by different ways of thinking, speaking, and living, they can reach back and forth to each other across the cultural barriers by means of their poems, songs, and dances; their weavings and wood carvings; their homemade toys and games. Community education must not overlook the humanizing values inherent in this rich cultural resource. American handicrafts and other folk arts almost beg to be used by community educators.

The Popular Arts

A distinguished New York patron of the fine arts, August Heckscher, has identified another contemporary realm of art: the popular arts. They are part of community education in a most incidental, unplanned manner, but they must be understood by those who plan programs in community education. The popular arts parallel and, to some extent, replace the folk arts in our increasingly urban society. Heckscher wrote a chapter in the report of President Eisenhower's Commission on National Goals (1960) in which he explained that the popular arts are the result of conditions in American life which have brought about a vast homogeneity among most of the people and a highly organized mass market to meet the demands of a developing technology. People today, regardless of income, buy their supplies in this mass market. They go into a "supermarket" and buy clothing at one counter, books on the left, toothpaste down the aisle, and tape recordings on the right — with "original oil paintings" on the wall by the metal shelving. People begin to think of art as something to be bought in the same way they would buy any other commodity — and to be judged on the basis of the same qualities: novelty, eye-appeal, enhancement of status and comfort.

This popular culture has its limitations, of course, but it also has merits that should not be overlooked. Products adapted to machine production and keyed to the desires of the mass market can possess as genuine a value as folk art. Modern industrial design has developed from popular fashion and taste rather than from the individual tastes of craftsmen. Many early movies are being studied now as examples of popular art at its best. Heckscher concluded that the very "rootlessness and restlessness of American life, its changefulness and diversity, may shape a culture admittedly different from anything known before, yet like folk art in being popular without being degraded [p. 132]."

Business and Governmental Participation in Art

Along with the revival in regional folk art and the evolvement of popular art are the newspaper headlines that tell of record sums being paid for works of American "fine art." United States collectors have seen investments in contemporary art succeed as a hedge against inflation. Museums have expanded their modern collections and thus have exposed larger numbers of Americans to new styles — which has encouraged further collecting of contemporary art. Young men and women buy confidently according to eclectic tastes, paying a few dollars for a poster or a print or investing several hundred dollars in an unusual oil or acrylic painting.

Increasing public interest in art has led to an unexpected partnership between business and art. Department stores feature art exhibits to help sell new fall showings of clothing — and at the same time give publicity to promising painters and sculptors in the community. Utility companies here and there offer purchase prizes through community art centers to reward — and stimulate — local artists. A New York bank offers to match depositor donations to the New York Public Library. A major oil company supports a 20-week series, shown on the television network of the Public Broadcasting System, which brings world artists in music and dance to home audiences. A brewing company underwrites New York Philharmonic concerts in New York and Milwaukee parks. Influential sectors of the business community have decided that their own best interests are tied to a healthy cultural environment.

The United States government, in 1965, established a subsidy for art through the National Endowment for the Arts and its sister agency, the National Endowment for the Humanities. In eight form of matching grants to specific community art projects had

304

increased from approximately 40 cents a year per United States citizen to 80 cents — as compared with Great Britian's allocation of about $1.15, Canada's of $1.40, and Germany's of $2.00 per citizen. A major purpose of the federal program was to open up the arts to less affluent Americans.

Traditional Presentations

While American business and government show new interest in the art scene, traditional modes of presentation draw untraditional audiences. For example, an exhibition of Renoir paintings at the Chicago Art Institute could be seen in 1973 only by standing in long lines at the gate and, upon admittance, milling with a crowd through the exhibit. Young people were there, and so were the elderly, the middle-aged, and children with their parents. Such patronage would seem to indicate that people are, indeed, seeking community education in art. And it must be remembered that there are, in addition to this one particularly popular exhibition, symphony concerts, theatrical productions, recitals, readings, and gallery showings every day and every night in each of our largest cities. Hundreds of thousands of individuals know the personal rewards of participating in the creative masterpieces of music, literature, painting, and sculpture. These are the people who have learned to hear and see with knowledge and understanding; they have learned to sense the artist's meaning, to feel his feeling, to grasp his unique vision.

The varied programs in each community are scattered geographically. They are individualistic programs in the sense that their educational content is planned by the individual agency's staff to meet the needs of a segment of the public known to be interested in that particular community service. The programs are uncoordinated, they overlap, they fail to provide many needed services — flaws are easy to find. But these varied community art programs are educating, and have been educating, a large segment of the American population in art.

COMMUNITY EDUCATION
LEADERSHIP IN ART EDUCATION

The comparative absence of community-wide coordination among the various art education agencies is a major challenge to community education leaders. Hundreds of thousands of individuals may be benefiting from active participation in art experiences, but many millions of individuals are not learning to hear and see and feel art. These "many millions" are people of all ages living in all kinds of communities; coordinated community programs in art should be meeting their learning needs.

The implications of all the foregoing seem clear. The search of people today for something better in their lives; the efforts of researchers to find a way to help people improve the quality of their daily living; the possibilities in art; the tremendous but scattered community resources for individual participation in art — these conditions imply that community art resources must meet more adequately the specific needs of all the people. The resources are there. Community-wide coordination can improve them and make them more readily available.

Leaders of community education programs should, therefore, be knowledgeable about the specific opportunities for instruction in art. They should make certain that representatives of the art interests of these communities are involved in community education advisory, planning, and coordinating councils. And when community education leaders talk with the representatives of the various educational forces in their respective communities, they should make sure that they are convincing in their support of strong art components in the comprehensive plan for community education. Only when the leaders of community education believe in the necessity of an adequate learning experience in art education will the special values to be found in art become available to all the people.

Improvement in Three Steps

Directors and other leaders of the community education process can improve people's access to the values of art by taking these steps: (a) coordinating the various community resources in art education; (b) infiltrating the learner's range of comprehension with exciting, new ideas and perceptions from art; and (c) supporting great teaching.

A broadly conceived community education in art can make a particularly vital contribution to individual youth and children and to adult men and women; and by improving the quality of life for individuals, such a program will improve society as a whole. Vital community education in art will start where the people are, and then it will move from an emphasis on learning skills for recreational purposes to an emphasis on practicing creative skills as a means of growing in aesthetic perception and human insight. Instruction will become a process of helping a student have meaningful encounters with art.

But the current scene confuses both laymen and educators. Even though a large and vital role is being played by the various art-related agencies in a community, the role is difficult to see from one person's point of view. People tend to equate the word "art" with the form they know best whether that be a performance by a neighborhood electronic band, a landscape painted by a seventeenth-century European artist, or a handcrafted bowl carved from a burl of black walnut. And community educators must remember that they, too, are people. If many of them find the current art scene confusing, that is to be expected. They will need to do some learning while they join with other educational leaders in the community to plan better art opportunities for the learning of other citizens of the community.

Community education leaders will have to face also the fact that existing programs lack, in many cases, vitality, depth, comprehension of what art is all about. They are a beginning. They are often plentiful enough and large enough to serve many more people than they are serving. If these assets can be used to provide learning experiences of better quality, real improvement will have been gained.

The following three steps, taken patiently and seriously, can make a far-reaching difference in the effectiveness of the art opportunities now available. In fact, they can make a significant difference in the educative opportunities available in any area of interest. The steps are discussed under the headings *coordinate, infiltrate,* and *support.*

Coordinate. A community education administrator who cooperates with other community leaders in planning and coordinating the complex educational offerings in art that are available in an urban community will be providing a valuable service to the agencies and to the people. Coordination brings double benefits. The separate programs of the art-related agencies and of other educational agencies, including the schools, will be strengthened; and at the same time, the total program of community education in art for all the people will be stronger. Mutual planning tends to result in a balanced and effective use of all resources.

Some coordination will be found to exist before community education leaders enter the situation. For example, a symphony orchestra usually cooperates with the music department of the city school system in providing special programs for young people. Similarly, the school art department and the art institute or museum in many cities work together on an annual exhibit of art objects created in school classes. The educational program of the Battle Creek school system (Michigan) has, for approximately half a century, been coordinated with the community's public library and its museum; and the school builds a portion of its regular program around a publicly-owned farm and camp.

Further coordination can be worked out as experience reveals new opportunities and as feedback shows the kinds of programs that are most useful to the community. Coordination should work to the long-range benefit of all the agencies and all the people of the community — and experience shows that it does.

Infiltrate. Infiltration is an old and respectable technique in education. Learning must start where the learner is, but unless an influence outside the learner excites his imagination and offers him new paths to follow, the learner will progress very little from his earlier level of knowing.

John Dewey expressed the thought in the following statement written in 1910: "Teachers who have heard that they should avoid matters foreign to pupils' experiences are frequently surprised to find pupils wake up when something beyond their ken is introduced ... [p. 221]." Then he advised a careful balance of the far and the near, adding, "Too much that is easy gives no ground for inquiry; too much of the hard renders inquiry hopeless [p. 222]."

All learning proceeds most satisfactorily when it is supported by a reasonable balance of "the near and the far." This balance needs to be reasonable for each individual student, of course. Fast-paced study programs that are geared to "the near" knowledge and understanding of the more able students in a class will not be geared to "the near" of the less able ones. The desirable balance leads each student into the excitement of real learning. That is teaching — knowing how to infiltrate the new, harder, more stimulating material for maximum learning by each student.

In the same way groups of people who make up a community must start where they are in solving community problems; then they must depend upon insightful leaders to help them see and move toward new possibilities. Leaders will infiltrate the new, harder ideas carefully as people are ready for them. A problem in planning community-wide education for all the people could well test the best leader's ability to infiltrate. But experience convinces that broadside attack is seldom the most effective way to help people see new possibilities; patient, sympathetic, knowledgeable infiltration of new ideas works better.

Support. Teachers themselves seem often to see their role as smaller than the tremendous thing society assumes they can and will do. Education, in the final analysis, depends on teachers. Society believes that teachers, aided perhaps by assistant teachers and teaching machines, can take any group of people at their various starting levels, stimulate all their imaginations, and lead them all to learn. And, amazingly enough, great teachers can. Wise community education leaders will keep in mind the almost miraculous thing that great teachers are able to do; and, as administrators, they will support the work of teaching with helpful administrative housekeeping, supportive planning, meaningful in-service education, and a modest ration of expressed appreciation.

Arranging Encounters with Art

Maslow emphasized the need in human life for aesthetic perceiving and creating and for aesthetic peak experiences. Community education in art has a unique opportunity to help people meet such needs. Some students are ready to express — and need to express — in their own amateur fashion the creative combinations that spring up from the depths of their own unique vision. Community educators are responsible for bringing the right resource to bear on that need. Perhaps it will be a class in painting at the community art center; perhaps a seminar at the community college; perhaps lessons from an artist-teacher who lives in the community. The "encounter with art" may be the result of a list of educational opportunities which the would-be student sees in the local newspaper or it may be the result of his visit to the community education office – and a few minutes of advisement there. In either case, planned community education is responsible for an encounter with art.

The aesthetic experiences that are expected from encounters with art are rather mysterious to the uninitiated. For example, when students draw a sphere, they learn to see that sphere in new perspective. After they have drawn and painted scenes from nature, they see their surroundings as they had never seen them before. It is reasonable that educators should ask what kind of thing aesthetic experiences are, and it is also reasonable that artists should try to tell them.

Robert Henri, an artist and teacher in New York around the turn of the century, left fragments of his teachings in the form of a small book, *The Art Spirit* (1923). One fragment read, "The object of painting a picture is not to make a picture – however unreasonable this may sound. The picture, if a picture results, is a by-product and may be useful, valuable, interesting as a sign of what has past. The object, which is back of every true work of art, is *the attainment of a state of being, a state of high functioning, a more than ordinary moment of existence* [p. 159]."

Stanley Burnshaw (1970) quoted descriptions of personal experiences in the writing of poetry as reported by many different poets. An Eskimo poet, Orpingalik, told an ethnologist in the mid-twentieth century, "We get a new song when the words we want to use shoot up of themselves [p. 53]." John Keats was reported to have said, "My judgment is as active while I am actually writing as my imagination. In fact all my faculties are strongly excited and in their full play [p. 67]."

Ben Shahn, an artist of the American mid-century, wrote in 1957, "If any single kind of value or evaluation has tended to survive the many tides and reversals of taste, belief, and dogma, I imagine that value consists in some vague striving for truth. . . . Of course the separate truths achieved are not final; they represent only the moments of enlightenment. I believe that it is such moments of enlightenment that are formulated and perhaps preserved in art [pp. 126-127]."

Henri (1923) on one occasion spoke of art as a "noting of the existence of order throughout the world. . . . I find that the moment order in nature is understood and freely shown, the result is nobility . . . it is a vision of orderliness that enables the artist along any line whatsoever to capture and present through his imagination the wonder that stimulates life [p. 144]."

Aesthetic experiences are a subject of considerable interest among artists. Bruner (1962) described questioning several of his artist friends on the subject of a creative second wind — a point when the object took over. He found that all of these artists understood what he was talking about (p. 25).

Each student, whether he has lived six years or 75 years, is a person capable of growing through new perceptions and experiences. Each student can benefit, according to his ability to receive stimuli through his senses, from personal encounters with art. Most students are not and will not become artists. They know, however, that something in them insists upon trying new things. They seek teachers who will help them grow. Able teachers have insights beyond the skills they claim to teach; they know how to lead human beings beyond their first limited requests for help. They know how to open doors for those who never before knew the doors were there.

The mystery of this process is captured in an essay, originally delivered in 1962 as the fifth John Dewey lecture, by archaeologist and literary stylist, Loren Eiseley. As a teacher he spoke of the Shelleys, the Shakespeares, the Newtons, and the Darwins of our world who produced, out of widely differing lives, great thought, music, art — transmissible but unique. He added, "If we, as ordinary educators have the task which Dewey envisioned of transmitting from these enrichers of life their wisdom to the unformed turbulent future . . . their luminosity must encompass our minds. their passions must, in some degree, break through our opaque thoughts [p. 219]."

A wise teacher not only arranges encounters with art for his students; he expands his own understanding of art by experiencing

311

personally the values of aesthetic perception. He does not, of course, have to be an artist. It is enough that a teacher know and communicate to students his respect for art, his knowledge of the possibilities of unique perception through art experiences.

In his work with students a teacher avoids passing judgment upon an art experience. In art there is no right or wrong. When Beethoven offers his vision of beauty and truth through the performance of an orchestra of interpretative artists, the listener is enveloped in the entire presentation of beauty and truth. That is the listener's art experience. When a student studies Brancusi's delicately sculptured "Bird in Space," he enters into another aesthetic experience; he shares, according to his ability, the sculptor's vision of soaring freedom, of spiritual flight. And after a student has "lost" himself in his own vision of snow in the tall pines, painting through many intense hours to capture the cold, the wind, the silence in brush strokes and color on his canvas, his experience is a part of his growth. A teacher can help the student improve his painting technique, but the art experience − the encounter with art − is the student's own. Such encounters with art help a student find himself as a unique person.

●　●　●　●　●　●　●　●　●　●　●　●　●

Art is recommended today for a central place in education because experiencing art helps people to grow, to see, to know. As people learn to see truth more clearly, they can respond more accurately to personal problems and to societal problems.

Rich art resources exist in our communities. People of all ages are searching for enlightenment which can be found, in part, through experiencing art. But the people need better help from educators than they are getting today. The recommendation that education help people make art a more central aspect of human life views education as a continuing, pervasive, constant factor in life. Schooling provides one large segment of educative influence, but not all of it. The educative assistance envisioned must be broader than schooling.

The implications of this recommendation are significant for community education. As the process that achieves effective use of all contributing community forces in the education of all the people, community education is the process which can make art more effective in people's lives.

CHAPTER XIII

**SPECIAL EDUCATION IN
COMMUNITY EDUCATION**

SPECIAL EDUCATION
IN COMMUNITY EDUCATION

MORVIN A. WIRTZ
AND
MAURICE F. SEAY

Even though thousands of technical articles and books have been written on the subject of the education of the handicapped, little has been written to guide curriculum consultants, community educators, and school boards and superintendents through the intricacies of organizing and operating that part of education known as "special education." To set the perspective for the potential interface of community education and special education, it is necessary to examine practices which, in many instances, have grown like Topsy, and which have not been evaluated to any great extent as they grew.

For the past fifty years or more, professional special educators have been expanding programs, usually by bifurcation, and usually with reasons which seemed perfectly valid at the moment; but the expansions have become a professional trap from which there seems to be no escape except to start still more programs. The result has been the development of an amazing complex, called by the name "Special Education." Here are special classes, resource rooms, integrated programs, itinerant programs, special consultants of various types, orientation and mobility specialists, social workers, psychologists, child development specialists, supervisors, and directors. Each category of professionals has its own training program, certification, and, in many instances, a complicated financing formula. All of this is done in behalf of the handicapped — who have been categorically divided to the point where one wonders who is responsible for the individual as an individual. Each of these categorical areas has its coterie of professional specialists who have a wide variety of professional aspirations and perspectives.

On the obverse side of the coin are those general educators who insist that special education is not needed because, they claim, they are taking care of all handicapped children in regular classrooms. One can only wonder how they manage to convince the parents of children such as the severely cerebral palsied that they should do "something" with their children other than send them to schools. It is obvious that they cannot be cared for, much less educated, in regular classrooms. These children have frequently been excluded even from those schools which have specialized programs.

Is it any wonder, then, that community educators who attempt to understand the various needs and services for the handicapped find the welter of options overwhelming? Or that they find it difficult to know where to start?

This puzzling situation can be resolved by considering special education within the framework of the community education concept. Special education, ideally, is a phase of community education because community education is a process that concerns the total program of education in a community. Special education, as part of a community education program, does not lose its identity. It does, however, respond to (a) coordination, both internally among the many special education subdivisions and externally with the other phases of a total educational program; (b) cooperative planning, and (c) adopting some of the basic principles of community education — principles such as the use of local resources as instructional material.

What Is Special Education?

There is nothing magic about special education. Rather, special education is a strict adherence to the principle of individualizing education, capitalizing on strengths, and minimizing weaknesses. For example, the only thing one crippled child might need is the provision of a ramp instead of a step, or a desk which has been modified to conform to his physical condition. A principle to remember when thinking about special education is that physical facilities are expendable, human beings are not. All decisions must be made on that basis. Often an unusually successful service in special education is the result of a minor change in teaching method. The following illustration shows how even a small change in practice can accomplish a large educational benefit: A standard method of teaching reading in first grade uses experience charts. These are usually created for groups of children. But for children with severe language problems, the charts are created for each individual child so that his level of language is his only concern while the teacher systematically injects new concepts. There is nothing magic about that. The application of the principle, however, is sometimes difficult because teachers, in general, are taught to teach to groups and not to individuals.

There are many agencies in any given community which provide services to the handicapped. One of the difficulties in building educational programs for the handicapped is to attain a degree of coordination between these services so that the recipients and their families are not torn between conflicting philosophies and programs. During a handicapped child's school life, those responsible for special education should be knowledgeable of all other services in the community for the best interests of the child. This statement appears to be particularly pertinent at this time as more and more states move to mandatory special education and to the requirement that special education provide services to an increasingly wide age span. Many states at this point are mandating that the schools work with all handicapped children between the ages of 0 and 25. This trend will have an influence on the relationship of community education and special education. The role of the community educator will tend to be that of coordinator of agency services, those of the schools and of the various special education agencies, during the time the handicapped individual is the legal responsibility of the school system's special education department. In the case of the older handicapped person, the role of the community educator would continue to be coordination with the emphasis shifting from the state-required programs to the direct services of specialized agencies and the adult or continuing education most appropriate to the individual. Examples of this coordinating role follow in later sections of this chapter.

Who Should Be Served?

The provision of direct service would, of course, take into account the generally accepted categories of handicapping conditions. These categories include all of those individuals who deviate from the norm to the extent that they cannot participate in, or profit from, the programs usually offered or who would require some modification in such programs for participation. The traditional categories in the professional literature of special education are as follows: slow learners, educable mentally retarded (or handicapped as used in some states), moderately dependent mentally retarded, trainable mentally retarded, custodially mentally retarded (severely mentally retarded), crippled or orthopedically handicapped, blind, partially sighted, deaf, hard of hearing, asphasic, brain-injured, neurologically handicapped, perceptually handicapped, emotionally disturbed, learning disabled, speech handicapped, and combinations of these lumped together as multiply handicapped.

There is, however, a simpler way to program for these individuals; that is to consider the intellectual deficit, the sensory deficit, or the emotional deficit they may have. Community education leaders are in an enviable position to utilize this approach because, at the present time, this approach is not hamstrung by state laws and regulations. For example, a recreational crafts program would be equally appropriate for the mentally retarded, hearing impaired, and crippled. Only minor modification in a basic plan would be necessary to accommodate these groups, and that modification could be accomplished without reference to any category.

There is growing concern in this country over the increasing specialization of categories; however, because of state laws and regulations, it is extremely difficult to modify present practice. Even though in programming it is necessary to be concerned with such things as blindness and deafness, the major concern should not be over presently-used categories. These categories are based on medical rather than instructional models. Rather, the concern should be over how individuals can best be served by instruction based on their intelligence, their sensory skills, and their emotional stability.

DIRECT SERVICES PROVIDED AS PART
OF A COMMUNITY EDUCATION PROGRAM

This section will be divided into two parts, the first dealing with participation of the handicapped in "regular" programs and the second dealing with the provision of special programs for the handicapped.

Participation of the Handicapped in "Regular" Programs

A major problem which faces handicapped people in the United States is the negative attitude of normal people toward them. The psychological explanations of this unfortunate barrier have been the subject of several research projects; attitudes in this area and their change are worthy subjects of a more humanitarian kind of education. Lippman comments on this problem in the following comparison of attitudes toward the handicapped in Europe and the United States:

> Attitudes toward the mentally retarded . . . are a part of a larger attitudinal pattern . . . . But although I "learned" the lesson in 1967, it has taken several years for me to understand it. I have only recently absorbed the reality of the indivisibility of social attitudes. The rejection and infantilization of the mentally retarded, the thoughtless erection of architectural barriers against the physically disabled, the resistance to the recovered mentally ill and former convicts, the denigration of mothers who must accept public assistance to feed their children, the contemptuous treatment of older men and women who may no longer be completely self-reliant in our complex society — all are part of the attitudinal "set" in the United States which is so different from the respect for human interdependency that I saw in Europe, especially Scandinavia [1972, pp. xi, xii].

Samuel Laycock, in his teaching about attitudes toward the handicapped, indicated that there are three levels of acceptance of the handicapped. One is an outright rejection; another is intellectual acceptance; and a third is an intellectual and emotional acceptance of the handicapped as fully participating citizens. Very few individuals would admit to an attitude of outright rejection and would job, and a larger place in society. However, when it comes to implementing this philosophy, the population in general is unwilling to

319

do more than make a contribution to the solicitor who comes to the door for the March of Dimes or the Muscular Dystrophy Association. What is needed in this country is a true acceptance of handicapped individuals for the contribution they, themselves, can make. This kind of acceptance would make possible the participation of many handicapped people in all facets of life — including the regular programs of the educational agencies of their communities. The following example illustrates the application of this point.

A young man in St. Louis was employed by a school district to operate an offset press. He came from a large, greatly disadvantaged family and had spent eight of his twelve years in school in a class for the mentally retarded. After he had received some basic instruction on the operation of the press, the superintendent arranged for him to attend a large technical high school to learn more about the operation and maintenance of the equipment. The young man was so successful in this program that he returned to the technical school and enrolled in a course which would teach him about making photographic plates for the press. Again he had remarkable success, considering the fact that he had been classified as mentally retarded throughout most of his school life. Some time later he expressed interest in helping with the maintenance of the electronic gear used by the school district. Again he was sent to school where he completed a basic course in electronics and even built his own testing equipment. Thereafter he was responsible for maintaining all of the electronic equipment of the school, including such machines as tape recorders, projectors, and electronic page turners. About this time, he married the salutatorian of his high school graduating class. Today this young man has a fine position with an automobile company.

With encouragement and the availability of training facilities, many young persons from disadvantaged groups can become outstanding achievers. Other individuals who start in the categories of the handicapped can, with similar encouragement and training, become productive members of society rather than society's victims. Educators of young handicapped children carry an awesome responsibility for each child's ultimate opportunity. They must recognize the danger of labeling children too rigidly, of placing them in an educational track which is stultifying rather than stimulating and satisfying.

Still another example involves a young blind man who worked as an assistant to an official in the United States Office of Education. He was extremely intelligent and had the benefit of a good elementary and secondary school education at a private school for the blind. He then attended college where he obtained a bachelor's and master's degree. In spite of his obvious talents, employers were reluctant to give him employment commensurate with his skills. When he was finally accepted for employment in the Office of Education, he was given responsibility for doing legislative research. Readers would read the bills and he would catalog them, both in his mind and in his files. When his employer asked him for information, this man would quote the details of the bill under discussion and would then proceed to pull the bill from his file. Because he had had training in mobility, he was able to travel on official business; many times he traveled alone across the entire country. Without all the educational opportunities made available to him, and without an employer who was willing to give him an opportunity to prove himself, this man would have remained unemployed, or at best, underemployed. He was truly a product of education in the community education concept; he had received a coordinated and balanced blend of services from private and public agencies made effective through individual interest and assistance.

There are several models which might be examined for the insight they can give to community education leaders. The first of these is the recently enacted mandatory participation in vocational education. Many handicapped children are participating in regular vocational education programs with support from staff in special education. The support may be minimal as in the case of a staff member's helping a vocational instructor understand the nature of the individual's handicap. An attitudinal change is usually the major need in this kind of help.

A second model is that of the National Technical Institute for the Deaf. This is a federally financed, school-operated program in cooperation with the Rochester Institute of Technology. In this program, deaf individuals are given training in highly skilled technical programs with the only support being that of counseling and a dual communication system which is provided by the staff in special education. Although many of these deaf individuals are retarded academically, this handicap does not prevent them from participating in the regular programs of RIT satisfactorily because there is nothing wrong with their intelligence, and with the supportive services available, they are able to survive academically and profit from the programs.

Special Community Services for the Handicapped

The following are examples of services which might be made more readily available to the handicapped through the community education process. It must be remembered that these examples are discussed within the frame of reference of the legal responsibility, mentioned before, which has been placed upon the schools. Duplication by the schools of services that are already adequate through community special services agencies would be expensive and irresponsible. Community-wide cooperation through an educational planning and coordinating process (called community education) would seem to be a workable answer.

Some of the suggestions made here are not known to have been tried in community education programs, but in each instance the suggested arrangement would be compatible with both the philosophy of community education and the needs of handicapped individuals.

Rehabilitation teaching for the blind. One of the recent developments in services for the blind is known as "rehabilitation teaching." Western Michigan University is preparing teachers to work in this program. These teachers are trained to work with recently blinded individuals on the skills necessary to function in their own environment. Items such as reading braille, self-care, eating, cooking, and minor household maintenance are included. Presently, these services are offered (where available) under the jurisdiction of an agency serving the blind. However, such services could be offered through the schools, especially in communities where no other agency makes the services available. Instruction could be carried on in small groups and would serve a two-fold purpose: (a) the teaching of skills directly to the blind individuals, and (b) the social contact of the blind with other individuals in the schools. The comparatively normal social contacts would tend to lessen the feeling of isolation experienced by many newly blinded individuals.

Orientation and mobility training for the blind. Another service which is usually considered the responsibility of agencies serving the blind is that of providing orientation and mobility training. Although this has seldom been offered as part of a school program, the advantages of doing so are clear. The skills would be taught in a comparatively normal social situation. If part of the blind person's mobility training is aimed toward helping him move from his home out into the broader community, "going to school" is obviously a helpful procedure in itself. The specific training is in the use of the long cane to move around the community independently. This training and the necessary rehabilitation teaching are two areas which would require skillful coordination between the regular instructional agencies and the special agencies serving the blind — a type of coordination which can be and should be within the range of the community education process.

Lip-reading and skill maintenance for the deaf. One of the problems of the deaf, and particularly of those who have been deafened later in life, is that of learning where to obtain training in the use of lip-reading and in the maintenance of speech skills. The maintenance of speech skills is also an essential need of those who have been deafened at an earlier age and who have received earlier training in oral communication. Periodic monitoring of speech is necessary if the deterioration of these skills is to be avoided. This is a task which has been taken on, to some extent, by community agencies. In communities where the service is available, the process of community education would help the resources meet the needs; in other communities the process of studying needs and resources should lead to a development of the necessary services. Another skill which is desperately needed by many deaf individuals, even those who have gone through oral programs, is that of manual communication.

Volunteer interpreters for the deaf. The deaf who have gained oral and manual skills still need the support of the community. Many volunteers serve as interpreters for the deaf. Such people are available when a deaf person, without sufficient oral communication skills, meets an emergency such as becoming entangled with the law, needing to understand a contract, or needing help in a relationship with the Internal Revenue Service.

The same thing can be said about the need for having volunteers to work with the blind, but in this instance the service would revolve around converting standard reading material to braille and making acceptable recordings of existing printed materials. Half a dozen volunteers are needed, as a rule, to keep a blind child in a regular integrated program in the schools.

But these volunteers must be trained. People are available who can do this training — the need again is for coordination, for a community-wide planning process that can use available resources to solve community problems. Often the staff members of special education agencies have organized their own program to teach the necessary skills to volunteers. If, however, this training for volunteer service were coordinated through the organizational and administrative structure for community education, the trained volunteers would be available to the broader community — to deaf and blind adults as well as to school-age children and youth.

Recreation for the handicapped. One area of service in which several agencies now participate is an area of service which has been in very short supply for the handicapped. It is recreation. The more severely handicapped who cannot participate in the usual organized recreational activities need assistance particularly. Summer camping would be particularly helpful to crippled children. They are frequently excluded from school camping programs because of the fact that when it is easiest for them to go camping — when they would not have to worry about clothes, wheelchairs or crutches being mired in mud, and all the other hazards of camping — the schools are not in session. However, a coordinated community education program could meet this special need.

Organizing dance groups for the trainable mentally retarded, or organizing wheelchair volleyball and basketball for the physically handicapped would be two examples of special programs which could be parts of the community education enrichment programs, using the facilities of special recreational agencies or of the schools. Here again, the potential is limited only by the imagination and creativity of the handicapped themselves and the community educators who would be able to marshal the forces necessary to carry on the program.

Need for coordination. Community educators are key figures in marshaling all educational forces in the community and can bring to bear on the problem of providing coordinated services for the handicapped. It is a rare community that does not have agencies such as the following, all of which have something to offer the handicapped: (a) schools, both public and private, (b) area skill centers (or other vocational education facilities), (c) vocational rehabilitation services, (d) private trade schools, (e) local associations for the retarded children or an Easter Seal Society, (f) Jewish Employment Vocational Services, (g) service clubs such as the Lions, Rotary, and Optimists, (h) churches, and (i) industrial establishments. The services of each agency would be improved by community-wide planning, and the impact of their services upon the community could be greatly increased by coordination.

Unfortunately, it must be recognized that there is a great deal of empire building and protecting among the various services for the handicapped. The community educator, however, should be able to establish a rapport by offering to help meet the needs of these agencies; then reciprocal arrangements should be a natural outcome. By avoiding the position of always asking for cooperation, the community educator can encourage cooperative effort as a two-way street on which everybody gains. One technique which has been found useful by those leaders who engage in such coordination is to actively seek and accept positions on governing and advisory boards of those agencies which provide services for the handicapped.

Upgrading job skills. A very real need of the handicapped is to have a place where they can be retrained for upgrading in job skills. This need is particularly great among the educable mentally retarded who may have gone through their schooling under a false diagnosis, and who are then locked into unrewarding jobs because they do not have the training necessary to move upward. Many individuals, even though they have completed their formal schooling, have not yet reached the level of their full potential. A comprehensive community education program should offer them an opportunity to continue their education, including in it appropriate vocational training. If the concept of lifelong education is to be meaningful, it must include opportunities for the handicapped as well as for all the other people.

The community educator might well be in communication with employers who regularly employ the handicapped to determine what job skills would be necessary for various kinds of job improvement; then he could bring together the local community agencies providing these skills and the people who need them. He also has access to state and federal agencies. He might arrange for a federal manpower training program through the United States Department of Labor to be the basic element of the program; the students would be selected by vocational rehabilitation counselors (bringing in federal and state involvement) while modifications in instructional methodology would be designed by special education staff from the local community education program. Local industry often provides tools and equipment for such a project.

The management of involved coordination arrangements requires a great deal of administrative skill on the part of the community educator. He has to be constantly on the alert for new and changing authorizations at the federal, state, and local levels, and he has to make his voice heard on behalf of the community when such changes are under consideration.

Older handicapped people. In two previous instances mention was made of older handicapped people. As our population grows older, a larger percentage of adults will be described as having handicaps such as failing vision, faulty hearing, and physical infirmities. Any community education program which includes the geriatric group must include activities for the handicapped. Already "Older Citizens Clubs" are listed among the activities offered by many enrichment programs of community education. Such social activities are needed; the "Clubs" should make sure that they are available to handicapped "older Citizens."

Special education programs for older handicapped people which can usually be made available through the community education process are described in the following items:

1. Teach those with failing vision how to read braille or to use an Optacon (a new electronic instrument which converts printed or written material to tactual stimuli using braille characters).

2. Provide training in lip-reading to those with failing hearing. One could also organize a hearing-aid service where aids are not only fitted, but the recipients are taught how to use the aids successfully. There is much evidence that many older people who are fitted with hearing aids do not use them, but put them in a drawer, the reason being that they have never been taught to use the devices properly, or have had their aspiration level raised unreasonably.

3. Find a physical educator in the community who has had some training and experience in adaptive physical education. Work with him to organize a series of recreation activities such as swimming, conditioning exercises, volleyball, and bowling, which are adapted to the specific needs of the physically infirm. For those who are too infirm to take part in active recreation, arrange table games, art, music, and craft activities; allow for selection by individuals and arrange for adaptation to individual limitations.

Most of these suggestions require little or no special equipment; however, attention should be given to such things as table heights, chairs which provide adequate support, materials which are within easy reach, and ramps to accommodate those with ambulation problems. It should hardly need to be said that such activities must be scheduled on the ground floor of buildings without elevators. If elevators are used, the controls should be within reach of a person in a wheel chair and of a person who cannot rotate his arm fully. Lavatory facilities should be near the activity area, and at least one of the stalls should be adapted for use by persons in wheel chairs.

Buildings constructed for public use today, in most states, must be free from architectural barriers to the handicapped. Assistance in evaluating a building is available from personnel in the special education departments of government, a director of the United Cerebral Palsy Association, and a director of the Easter Seal Society — which is the name for local chapters of the National Society for Crippled Children and Adults, one of the agencies that played a major role in the enactment of legislation dealing with architectural barriers.

The major significance of programs for older handicapped people lies, probably, in the impact such programs can have on the mental health of the participants. Hundreds of articles and television programs have been produced to portray the loneliness of our "senior citizens." The devastation which a handicap adds to that loneliness can hardly be imagined by normal persons. Without question, programs such as those described will add new dimensions to the quality of life for a significant segment of any community.

The examples and suggestions given in this chapter are only illustrations of what might be done in a given community. One helpful starting technique is the community survey. The community educator, in cooperation with the staff members in special education, should plan a special survey of the handicapped or combine this survey with a more general community canvass. After determining the number of handicapped persons needing and desiring services, the names may be grouped by age level and interest. Planning usually proceeds rapidly after this start has been made.

In coordinating special education services and activities, the community educator must remember that educators in the area of special education have specific legal authorities and constraints under which they must operate. For example, Title III and Title VI-B of the Elementary and Secondary Education Act at the federal level, and state laws and regulations mandate certain provision of services to the handicapped in schools; intermediate school district regulations or county regulations also govern certain services; and of course local board policies have their governing power. Such a welter of laws and regulations can, and do, reduce the degree of flexibility leaders can exercise in developing community-wide educational and service programs for the handicapped.

Since the educator in special education tends to be more confined by laws and regulations than is the community educator, the community educator can make the first overture to the agencies serving the handicapped and usually his doing so is greatly appreciated.

● ● ● ● ● ● ● ● ● ● ● ● ●

The provision of a fully implemented program of education for the handicapped requires a coordination of school and other educational agency resources with the resources of the special education agencies of the community. As the needs are found, the varied resources are used in a balanced community-wide program of services to meet them.

The handicapped probably have more agencies serving as advocates for them than any other segment of society; the role of coordinator takes on added dimensions when working with such a large and dedicated group of organizations. Larger communities would be wise to consider employing a member of the community education staff who has a background in special education and whose major function would be the coordination of all community education for the handicapped.

CHAPTER XIV

THE ROLE OF THE COMMUNITY COLLEGE IN COMMUNITY EDUCATION

THE ROLE OF THE COMMUNITY
COLLEGE IN COMMUNITY EDUCATION

PAUL R. HEATH
AND
MAURICE F. SEAY

A community college leader, Stanley Wall, was speaking of community college work in 1973. He said, "The job is getting done because we've learned that the tap root of a community college won't support growth without a lateral root system of community involvement [Quoted in Hunt, p. 22]."

For many years, two-year post-secondary schools were referred to as "junior colleges." As late as 1972 their national organization, The American Association of Community and Junior Colleges, was entitled "The American Association of Junior Colleges." What caused the name change? Is there something in the idea of "community" that can explain the phenomenal growth of community colleges?

The Carnegie Commission Report, *The Open Door Colleges* (1970, p. 3) indicates that the rapid advance may be due to open-admissions policies, the geographic distributions of campus sites in the various states, low tuition rates, the variety of programs offered to undecided youth, and finally, the opportunity for working adults to upgrade their occupational competence. This Report failed, however, to recognize the strength of the direct relationship of the community college in the community which it serves.

There is meaning — even though it may be an enigmatic meaning — in the fact that the adjective "community" has replaced the word "junior" in describing this relatively new form of higher education. The name "community college" reflects an emphasis upon a two-way relationship in which the college serves the community and the community serves the college. In this remarkably compatible two-way relationship, the college is concerned with meeting the needs and problems of the community and the community serves as a storehouse of resources, as a vital part of the college instructional laboratory.

Most community college leaders accept the idea of a two-way relationship between community and college. The writers of this chapter, however, are proposing an extension of this principle of community involvement by suggesting that the community college play an enthusiastic leadership role and cooperative membership role in a consortium of agencies organized for the purpose of coordinating community educational activities — a phase of the process of community education.

The Need for Community Coordination

The necessity of coordination of community educational services has become particularly critical because community college districts have been superimposed over several local school districts. An example of this situation can be found in Michigan. In this state the problem is compounded by a plan for the regionalization of public education — a plan which involves intermediate school districts. The problem, of course, is that each local school district attempts to meet the educational needs of its constituents; then the district organization discovers that the citizens have another major, state-oriented educational agency which is also trying to serve their educational needs. If the services being offered are completely different, problems will not be particularly noticeable, although some of the advantages of cooperation will be absent. If, on the other hand, two or three institutions are offering similar programs, duplication will exist, waste will occur, and friction may develop.

In the example taken from Michigan possible areas of redundancy and conflict would include: (a) the adult enrichment programs of several different community educational agencies; (b) the various community programs for senior citizens; (c) the post-secondary technical vocational programs; and (d) the various physical education and recreation programs of the several agencies. There is also a great amount of overlap, duplication, and waste in the multiplicity of educational services provided by the YWCA and the YMCA, proprietary schools, private colleges, churches, the in-house educational programs of business and industry, the various governmental services, and hundreds of other agencies. The constant struggle by the smaller agencies to survive, and by the larger ones to protect their service perimeters has contributed to the prevalent condition of disjointed, ineffective community efforts toward meeting human needs.

The writers are suggesting that the community college is in a strategic position to advocate a special community-wide organizational structure designed to provide coordination and to fill gaps in the community's educational program for life-long learning. The leadership role that is being suggested stands in marked contrast with the assembly-line role that often results from the institutional struggle to produce more and more human credit hours.

An example of cooperative action. A pioneering step toward area-wide coordination was taken in 1973 in one Michigan area when the community services staff of the area community college cooperated with twelve community education directors, employed in twelve different local school districts. Group process functioned in behalf of a larger community.

An ad hoc committee administered details as the community education directors and college representatives shared plans, discussed new ideas, and resolved problems. New leadership emerged. The group identified new areas of concern and solutions were proposed. An area survey was made to obtain grass-roots data on the educational needs and resources; cooperative programs were planned and activated to fill the gaps where needs identified in the survey were not being met by identified agency resources.

Significant progress was made by this cooperating group of institutional forces in other areas of educational service. For example, (a) area programs were published in a minitabloid and distributed through the local newspaper; (b) common registration procedures, including common starting dates, were established for all the cooperating school districts including the college; (c) facilities were shared without charge; (d) instructional talent living in various parts of the area was identified and shared by the various districts; and (e) support services, including teaching equipment and library resources, were made available to each of the cooperating organizations.

A detail of the plans worked out for sharing supportive services serves to illustrate the practicality of the plans. The ad hoc committee and other representatives of the area-wide educational agencies discussed the need for more dissemination of information about the educational services that were available to the citizens of the area. They also discussed the fact that an area vocational skills center was teaching students from all the cooperating districts the skills of public communication — including the operating of printing presses. Using the process of fitting available resources to a recognized need, a community education process with which this group was becoming quite familiar, the committee appealed to the vocational skills center for help with publications and publicity. That center was happy to have the project as a learning activity, parents were delighted to receive fact sheets and minitabloids which their teen-agers had told them were in production, and the area educational services received the needed publicity.

Continuing needs. A sincere trial of cooperative action is an excellent way to discover the location of weak spots in community-wide coordination. Two of these spots are, perhaps, worth mentioning in the hope that as the community education process develops, such weaknesses will be removed.

The first weakness was observed in the usual pattern of representation of community agencies on the local-school-district advisory councils. The area community college was seldom represented. Certainly the lack of representation was an oversight on the part of community education directors and other educational leaders — and it is equally certain that representation on all the community advisory councils within a college area could tax the time and energies of college staff members — yet the weakness was there. A community college should be represented in the comprehensive planning and decision-making for education that takes place in its area. Through such representation each college would gain immediate feedback on its college activities, a liaison with other educational agencies, and the opportunity to achieve a better understanding of community-wide needs and resources.

A second weakness appeared in the absence of active participation in community education by the four-year colleges and universities of the larger community immediately surrounding the community college service area. Community education involves a balance and a use of all institutional forces in the lifelong education of all the people. That concept of education includes the four-year colleges and universities. Their specialized educational functions can be recognized at the same time that their community-wide services become better understood by the people who are to be served by them — and who are paying for them. And, from the viewpoint of the four-year colleges and universities, there should be an honest need to know the local communities they serve in order to make their services fit more exactly the existing, up-dated needs.

A 1972 study (Heath) reveals certain needs for higher education beyond the two-year community college level, needs which could be met more adequately. This study found that 28 percent of the community college graduates from Southwestern Michigan College, Lake Michigan College, and Kellogg Community College discontinued their educational programs upon completion of their community college degree. There was also an indication that more than 25 percent of those who began a four-year program failed to complete their university requirements (p. 42). These nontransferring community college graduates were not substandard students — a fact indicated by their college grade-point averages which were almost identical to the averages of the transfer graduates. These data lead to the conclusion that there are academically capable adults in every community who do not have an opportunity to reach their maximum potential because of a lack of services from institutions of higher education in their geographic area.

Senior colleges and universities have tended to overlook a real need in the local communities of their service areas. Some kind of representation on community education councils could help them provide a complete package of programs in higher education.

There are, however, some innovative programs which are indicative of new practices in higher education. For example, in Muskegon, Michigan, the local community college has instituted and coordinated an external degree program by planning the course offerings in cooperation with the four-year colleges and universities in the area. It is now possible for a Muskegon resident to complete a baccalaureate degree program without moving, physically, to a university campus in order to meet residential requirements.

An external degree program, such as the cooperative one described, is a step in the right direction. It is based on the idea of a consortium of colleges planning programs together. However, this plan does not meet all community needs for higher education. The four-year colleges and universities are still not actively involved in the grass-roots approach of meeting with local community educational directors who, in turn, have established contacts with business, industry, social agencies, YMCA directors, community college, other educational agencies, and governmental leaders to identify their communities' education needs. A senior institution enjoys the favorable publicity from press statements to the effect that they support lifelong learning, and that they have established an external degree program, but a real commitment requires money, personnel, and courage enough to change a pattern.

The time has come for all educators to cooperate; to gain a comprehensive view of the educational needs and resources of each community, including the vertical articulation of K-12, post-secondary, and graduate education, and also the horizontal articulation of educational resources mentioned in Chapter One. The time has come for all educators to coordinate their services in order to assure balanced opportunities in lifelong learning for the citizens of every community.

The rapidly changing and developing educational needs do, indeed, call for community colleges to play an enthusiastic leadership role and a cooperative membership role in a consortium of community agencies. How does this role fit the current image of the purposes of community colleges?

The Purposes of a Community College

Statements regarding the purposes of the community college reflect the history of the institution. Two writers on the subject provide an illustration of the similairity of views in this area. Harlacher (1969) lists five "purposes" and Myran (1969) lists five "functions" of the community college.

Harlacher's purposes are:

1. Preparation for advanced study (transfer).

2. Occupational education (terminal).

3. General education.

4. Guidance and counseling.

5. Community services [p. 3].

Myran's functions are:

1. Transfer function.

2. Vocational/technical function.

3. Student personnel services function.

4. General education function.

5. Community services function [p. 9].

The authors of this chapter suggest a new understanding in terms of general program objectives. This approach to the identification of the major purposes of the community college would result in eliminating two of the items listed by Harlacher and Myran. According to the program objectives, the purposes of the community college are in fact, three. They are:

1. The transfer purpose.

2. The occupational career purpose.

3. The community services purpose.

337

The transfer function is a primary purpose serving the preparatory need of students who desire professional or baccalaureate degree programs. The vocational/technical function is a primary purpose (more often stated today as occupational career education) serving the need of students who desire a two-year preparation for entering a vocation. The community services function has emerged in recent years as a primary function of the community college which accepts its role as one of the educational agencies in a local community.

Student personnel services (including counseling) and general education are actually part of the program which is developed to meet the three primary purposes. A brief analysis of the nature of each of these supportive functions will reveal the difference between them and the three primary functions.

Student personnel services are supportive services. The activities usually associated with student personnel are guidance and counseling, admissions, registration, financial aid, health services, placement, and miscellaneous services which facilitate the educational accomplishments of students. These services are provided for all students regardless of the program they may elect. They are necessary to the provision of a community college curriculum for students who elect to transfer to a senior college or university and for those students who choose a vocational program. They are also necessary to a program of community services in which students are involved.

Similarly, general education should permeate the transfer programs, the career programs, and the community services programs. General education does not stand by itself. The day when people went to college to get a degree in "general education" is over. Very few students actually enroll in a general education curriculum. They find that the requirements of the job world call for evidence of more specialized education. However, students need to be exposed to the many values of general education, and it is to be hoped that such exposure will kindle a hunger for more of the benefits of general education.

There are, of course, other important supportive functions. Sound financial procedures support all programs. Good housekeeping is necessary if primary programs are to be successful. The supportive services of an instructional materials center (including a library) certainly are essential to the achievement of all the purposes of an educational institution. Such supportive functions are essential to achievement of the three primary purposes.

The three primary purposes of the community college should not be thought of as separate entities, but as functions which should be integrated, or at least merged with much overlap. An example of this merging can be taken from the area of occupational education.

For years the two-year vocational/technical programs were referred to as "terminal programs." The Heath Study (1972, pp. 42-43) showed, however, that more than 30 percent of the graduates of occupational programs transferred to four-year colleges and universities for additional higher education. Obviously, "terminal programs" are not terminal. And how could they be? The use of that term indicated the failure of earlier educational leaders to realize the simple fact that learning is lifelong.

What happened to the other 70 percent of the graduates of occupational career programs? Community education asks that question and proposes to find the answer to it. As a part of community-wide education, the community college is now asking that question. The developing answer is that a large proportion of the population of every community is in need of continuing education. Every citizen should have the opportunity to "plug in" and "plug out" of programs at any level according to his motivation and ability.

An adult should be able to enroll in a community-service, off-campus adult education welding class, and after experiencing success in that class, to enroll in a two-year occupational mechanical technology curriculum. And, if he has the necessary motivation and capabilities, he should be able to transfer to the university for completion of some type of baccalaureate engineering degree program. Later, he should be able to "plug in" to a refresher course or a retooling experience which will bring him up to date in his field. Along with his maintenance of his vocational competence, he should have a choice of opportunities to increase his general education. The poverty of

American society in the more humane attributes of civilization is an indication that this type of adult education is greatly needed.

A closer look at the three primary purposes of the community college will show how a specific college can contribute to the total educational program of its service area. In other words, the role of the community college in community education grows out of its basic institutional purposes.

Transfer programs. Our society has been, traditionally, a credential-oriented society. Baccalaureate degrees, master degrees, specialist degrees, medical degrees, and doctoral degrees have become valued ends of college and university programs. The transfer programs of community colleges — and the rapid increase in the number of such colleges — have provided opportunities for great numbers of citizens to complete the first two years of various baccalaureate degree programs.

The transfer program is a valuable service to the people of the college's service area. From the viewpoint of the community college, however, the transfer function has proved to be somewhat restrictive. Senior institutions have been slow in accepting two years of course work from the community college, often insisting upon an examination of course syllabi, of instructional credentials, and of common learning experiences. Course requirements set up by senior institutions have had the effect of discouraging community college use of community resources as part of the student learning experiences in instructional programs.

Such restrictiveness, however, is waning. Credit for this fact is due both the senior institutions and the community colleges; both groups have responded according to their individual leadership and the societal milieu within which they operate. In the seventies, the efforts of many years are beginning to bear fruit.

One concrete result of such efforts in Michigan is an articulated agreement among two- and four-year colleges in the state which guarantees that community college graduates with an Arts and Sciences Associate Degree will not be required further coursework in general education upon being admitted to the senior institution. Only courses in the major-minor sequence are to be evaluated at the senior college. This agreement was developed by the Michigan Association of Collegiate Registrars and Admissions Officers (MACRAO).

The MACRAO agreement marked the first major recognition that each community college should develop its own education requirements in English, social science, science, and the humanities. As a result of the agreement, community colleges will be able to use more relevant community experiences as part of the academic curriculum. This state-wide recognition of the maturity of the community college should encourage innovation on the part of Michigan community colleges, and it should set a stimulating example for other institutions of higher education throughout the nation.

Spurred by their additional freedom in carrying out the transfer function, community colleges in Michigan are looking more realistically toward their communities. Leaders realize that there is no longer any logical reason why community concert and lecture series, public art exhibits, symphony performances, and community theater groups cannot be learning laboratories for community college humanities courses. Neither is there any reason why sociology students should not be introduced to community social problems by involvement with a local social service agency — and make their learning experience more vital by relating the real-life experience to textbook theory. Thus could learning experiences multiply in quantity and vitality for students of political science involved with city and county government. Certainly, students of communication, business art, and journalism would benefit from becoming involved in work at newspaper offices, TV studios, radio stations, and advertising agencies. The list could go on until almost all of the activities of a given community would be listed as learning resources. The students would gain; the community would gain. Staff members of the community college would become increasingly skillful coordinators of educational needs with educational resources.

In case the foregoing paragraph sounded like a dream for the future, a few specific examples of innovative use of community resources in the transfer programs of certain Michigan community colleges are described in the following six paragraphs:

1. Monroe Community College, located in the southeastern part of the state, offered (a) a class called "Introduction to Teaching" which required 60 hours of supervised intern experiences to be gained in the surrounding community; (b) a group of English classes which were taught in the high school

for students who had already met high school requirements; (c) a seminar on gerontology which demonstrated real insight into the problems of aging and the aged — and developed programs out of the seminar which were taken to various parts of the community.

2. Grand Rapids Community College developed a "biological ethics" course which was made available to the citizens of the community, assisting them in exploring various aspects of social and legal codes governing biology in contemporary society and relating to such controversial issues as abortion and drugs. The college also conducted a "Have Text — Will Travel" series of which one course was "Psychology for Major Industrial Firms" taught at plants with workers given time off their jobs to attend the sessions.

3. Jackson Community College (a) offered freshman and sophomore classes Monday through Saturday at the State Prison; many inmates who started educational programs in the prison continued them on the college campus after their release; (b) offered classes to senior citizens in city housing developments; and (c) monitored water quality in Jackson County as part of a college sponsored environmental program.

4. Lansing Community College developed (a) educational institutes for religious groups, such as Sunday School teachers, which emphasized teaching methods, psychology of learning principles, and instructional technology; and (b) overseas tours which were related to transfer course work.

5. Kellogg Community College in Battle Creek (a) developed practicums and independent student projects with local social agencies to provide volunteer assistance to the work of the agency while the agency, in turn, provided tuition cost as incentive for the volunteers; (b) coordinated the development of 13 area extension centers to work with public school organizations in serving the people of their districts; and (c) experimented with a program using the "College by Newspaper Program" and cable TV as distribution centers for course work.

6. Two other community colleges in Michigan should be mentioned briefly for the following innovative programs they have developed: (a) Oakland Community College introduced a "Step Ahead" program which took college-level courses into the high school at the end of a regular school day as a service to advanced high school students. (b) Glen Oaks Community College developed a project called "Far Out" which involved the use of six off-campus centers to serve isolated rural areas.

Occupational Career Education. The increasing technological orientation of our society has increased the need for two-year certificate programs in fields of study which range from agriculture through aircraft operations, accounting, marketing, retailing, banking, insurance, real estate, textile design, heavy industry, and the entire health-related group of occupational areas. Occupational career education is no longer thought of as a two-year program only. The two-year graduates of this program frequently continue their education at a university.

Recruitment and admission of community college occupational career students is still directed, for the most part, toward the eighteen-year-old high school graduate. A need for occupational education on the part of other members of the community does exist. For example, the older adult frequently needs educational assistance at a time of unemployment, for general job upgrading, and, especially in the case of women who have given up work outside the home while their children were young, an educational program that will enable them to go back into the work of their choice.

While recruitment and admission procedures should be directed toward citizens of all ages, the needs of all citizens will not always be met by courses provided on the campus of the community college. Frequently the college staff will serve in an advisory and coordinating capacity, helping the citizen who has come for a special kind of education to find the community educational resource best suited to his needs.

An area Vocational Center and Kellogg Community College have cooperated in the development of a series of learning modules for common occupational programs. The modules were based upon performance objectives, and the two professional staffs articulated Vocational Center and College programs to avoid duplication and overlap. It was possible for students to be enrolled in both institutions at the same time. Facilities and staff were shared in a true community education approach to a common need.

A few other specific examples indicate that the process of community education is being used by many community colleges. (a) Muskegon Community College developed a Credit Manager Workshop and other workshops on management by objectives for business and industry. (b) Southwestern Michigan College offered Small Business Management Coursework in an attempt to upgrade local groups. (c) Charles Stewart Mott Community College introduced programs in Auto Emission Controls, Traffic and Transportation Management, and Safety in the Construction Industry. (d) Kellogg Community College enrolled 45 people in a Probate Assistant Program, started a Traffic Management Program, and expanded an ongoing program to include six-month programs in clerk-typist skills and drafting. (e) Macomb Community College trained 120 persons as industrial sewing machine operators for the specific purpose of qualifying for employment at the Ford, Chrysler, and General Motors trim plants. (f) Lansing Community College designed a Child Services Program to train students for paraprofessional positions in mental wards and hospitals.

Community Services. Harlacher (1969) mentioned that ". . . community service is still an emerging function of the community college. Audible and written support for the community services program tends to outstrip the number of visible, constructive local programs [p. 42]." A major problem, in the slow emergence of community services lay in the fact, according to Harlacher, that presidents, deans, and faculty members treated the program as a secondary function of the college. Great progress, however, has been made in this area since that statement was written. In fact, considering the slow rate of academic change, the progress is phenomenal.

A good example of what is being done in the area of community services is the work usually called "extended services." In Michigan practically every community college has extended its campus throughout the college service district. Several extended services have been mentioned in the specific examples given under the heading "Transfer Programs." For example, the teaching of college-level courses in a high school at the end of the school day is an extended service.

The dialogue which precedes the setting up of "outreach programs," the kind that go into hospitals, business establishments, and industrial firms, for example, is an important communication link between community and college. It is the kind of factor in community services that sets the tone of the relationship between community and community college.

Extended service and outreach programs change the role of the professional teacher from an all-knowing, authority figure to a manager of learning activities. Such programs also encourage the use of teaching resources in the community. For example, a "teacher talent pool" may be developed in the college service area — a device which often benefits former teachers and would-be teachers living in the community as much as the citizens to whom they will teach their specialty.

And teaching does not have to take place in a classroom with a minimum of ten students. For years American parents have employed music teachers who live in the local community to teach their children the rudiments of music. Instruction, usually in piano, proceeded on an individual basis and continued until a particular performance level was reached or until the arrangement was dissolved. Such a tutorial method of meeting specific instructional needs offers many possibilities in community education. The community services function of the community college would act as the catalytic agent bringing need and resource together — and providing the administrative and communication services that would enable the citizens of the community to know the educational opportunities existing in their neighborhoods.

Gaps exist between the known needs and the available resources in any community. Various educational agencies may either compete or cooperate in filling the gaps. The needs, most of which have not been met — or are being poorly met — are suggested in the following list:

1. The elderly and aged, particularly in public housing developments, need recreation and health-related physical education exercise programs.

2. The housewife, who is often confined to the home except for a few of the hours between nine and two o'clock, needs neighborhood educational programs, possibly offered at the elementary school.

3. On-line factory workers need courses during lunch hours or immediately after work — or, in plants where company management sponsors worker education, during company time.

4. Unemployed workers need appropriate classes which would be available as part of their unemployment benefits.

5. Professional and semiprofessional people need retraining or specialized training from time to time to maintain competencies in their fields.

6. Low income families, identified by social agencies, need educational experiences related to basic family living problems; the experiences could be associated with such problems as inflation, family planning, and recreational opportunities.

Community services as a function of the community college is cast in a leadership role in many community situations. The same principles of leadership will apply to members of the community services staff that apply to the community education director and other community education leaders. They are discussed in Chapters Four and Five. The leadership role should be used to help both college and community meet problems with a flexible, adaptable, and innovative approach. The leadership exercised through the community services program will draw college and community together in a cooperative use of the community education process.

● ● ● ● ● ● ● ● ● ● ● ● ●

The role of the community college in community education is a combination of service and leadership. A community college provides service to its community as it carries out its three primary purposes: (a) meeting the transfer needs of citizens of the community, whatever their age; (b) providing the citizens with needed occupational career education; and (c) providing and coordinating community services. And it provides leadership when it carries out these three functions with imagination, innovation, and enthusiastic purpose.

The combination of these two roles might be called *cooperative membership*. Perhaps cooperative membership in the group made up of all the agencies which provide the total educational program of the community is the key to the role of the community college in community education.

CHAPTER XV

UNIVERSITY INVOLVEMENT
IN COMMUNITY EDUCATION

UNIVERSITY INVOLVEMENT
IN COMMUNITY EDUCATION

GERALD C. MARTIN
AND
MAURICE F. SEAY

Universities are becoming increasingly involved in the dissemination and implementation of the community education concept in the United States. This involvement is concentrated primarily in university centers for community education, most of which receive some financial assistance from the Mott Foundation.

In 1955, the Mott Program of the Flint Board of Education and Eastern Michigan University developed a graduate study program in community education. A basic goal was to prepare community education coordinators and other staff personnel for leadership positions in Flint's elementary and secondary schools and in the Flint Community Junior College. A second goal was to prepare descriptive and text materials for implementing the community education approach to learning. A third was "to stimulate the community education concept in higher education institutions throughout the nation [Seay, 1972, p. 201]."

This graduate study program was located on the campus of Eastern Michigan University. Since its inception, over 400 persons have completed the master's degree with a major in community education. These graduates are now in strategic leadership positions in Flint and throughout the country.

In addition to leadership training, the graduate study program at Eastern Michigan University has disseminated and implemented the community education concept through publications and conferences. For example, this program has been instrumental in the production of more than 150 publications, ranging from leaflets to monographs, with an aggregate distribution of more than 50,000 copies, and since 1955, the University has hosted or sponsored over 120 conferences, seminars, and workshops in community education.

REGIONAL UNIVERSITY CENTERS

The idea of establishing regional university centers, which would in turn sponsor cooperating university centers, grew out of the successful experience at Eastern Michigan University. Sixteen regional university centers are listed below with the dates of their establishment:

1963-64	Northern Michigan University
1965-66	Alma College
1966-67	Ball State University Florida Atlantic University Western Michigan University
1967-68	Arizona State University Brigham Young University
1969-70	Eastern Michigan University

1970-71	Connecticut State College
	(transferred 1972-73 to
	  University of Connecticut)
	San Jose State College
	(renamed California State
	  University)

1971-72	Texas A & M University
	University of Alabama
	University of Virginia

1972-73	University of Florida
	University of Missouri

Cooperating centers, sponsored by the regional centers, receive less support from the Mott Foundation, are funded over a period of fewer years, and serve a smaller geographic area. These cooperating university centers, all established since 1971, are located at the following universities: California State University (Northridge), Miami University, Colorado State University, the University of Georgia, the University of Vermont, and the College of St. Thomas.

The geographic spread of these university centers for community education assures considerable nationwide dissemination and implementation. And the trend toward increasing interest in community education throughout the nation would indicate that other universities will become involved by the establishment of new centers.

Factors Affecting the Establishment of Centers

In assessing the values of these university centers and in planning the establishment of new centers, the results of a study completed in 1972 are worthy of consideration. Douglas M. Procunier concluded that the following factors are prominent in the conditions necessary to the successful operation of a center for community education: (a) proper leadership, (b) a philosophical commitment, (c) an evident need, (d) financial support, (e) adjustable operating policies, (f) basic service capabilities, (g) intra-university communication, (h) university traditions, and (i) adequate office space. The following brief comment on each of these factors is adapted from the Procunier study.

Only when proper *leadership* is available should a university (or college) consider establishing a center for community education. Adequate leadership must, of course, be available for the center in the form of an able director and staff. An attitude of support for the center must also be assured from the leadership of the institution and the department within which the center is to operate. The leaders within

353

the professional ranks of the university must also be supportive. Lack of support from any of these categories can handicap a center; such a lack can even lead to a center's failure.

Related to the factor of center leadership with support from the institution's leadership are the two factors of philosophical support and evident need. The *philosophical commitment* to community education on the part of the person who is to act as director must be particularly clear, coherent, and sturdy. Needless to say, the educational philosophy of the host institution must be reasonably compatible with the concept of community education.

These philosophical commitments will develop additional strength when they are found in conjunction with an *evident need* for the proposed center. The institution should have in evidence a definite need, identified at the departmental level, which will lead to philosophical and financial support for the proposed center and to good working relationships with the educational field that surrounds the university.

Any institution considering the addition of a community education center to its program must recognize the necessity of providing certain institutional capabilities that will support the effective functioning of a center. *Financial support* is necessary for center salaries and the expenses related to the services given by a center. Institutional *operating policies* must be adjusted to insure the smooth functionong of a center within the structure of the institution. *Basic service capabilities* which a center will need from the institution include accreditation, undergraduate programs in education, graduate programs in education, rapport with the communities to be served, and flexibility in these services to meet a center's changing needs.

A center will also need a free flow of *communication* between the members of its staff and the staff members of the various academic and service departments which are to be associated with the center. The institution should have a history of strong performance in the field of higher education. A community education center draws strength from institutional *traditions* such as the maintenance of high standards of instruction and the steady pursuit of worthwhile research.

A center can function more effectively if it is housed in adequate, strategically located *office space*. The physical location of a center within the institution is more important than the quality or volume of space. An ideal arrangement is a clustering of the offices of departmental chairmen, other professors, and center personnel; a team approach to leadership in community education is facilitated by such proximity of the persons involved. Ideally, the center being located in a university would be placed in the college of education of that institution. Here the dean of the college would be able to encourage a dissemination of the community education concept throughout the college and a cooperative attitude toward the center on the part of all department heads. Such rapport will be more easily established, of course, if the director of the center functions well in a staff relationship.

Organizational Patterns

The established community centers reveal a variety of organizational relationships to their universities. For example, four centers, each considered by evaluating groups to be highly successful, are directly responsible to different categories of administrative authority. In one case, the director of the community education center is directly responsible to the dean of the college of education and has a working relationship with the department heads and, through them, with the departmental faculties. At another university the director of the community education center is directly responsible to one department head within the college of education and has a working relationship with other department heads and, through them, with their respective faculties.

Considerably different is the organization at a university where the director of the center is directly responsible to the dean of continuing education, maintaining working relationships with other colleges through their respective deans. In still another university, the director of the center is directly responsible to the head of the department of recreation education, maintaining clear working relationships with each of the other departments in the college of education and with the deans of the other colleges of the university.

An advisory council, with different types of representation, serves each center. In most cases the members are university administrators and instructors whose professional interests are related to education and community service. These representatives of the university provide an informal, functional link between the community education center and its university host; thus, the advisory council helps to make the diverse organizational patterns equally effective in actual operation. Since advisory lay and representative councils are so necessary for community education programs (as recommended and described in Chapter Seven) it is very important that the advisory council for a university center represent a successful use of this method of increasing involvement and making better policies.

Purposes of the Regional University Center

While each regional university center is unique in its operation, all of the centers have common purposes. Five general purposes were listed in the 1971 Mott Foundation report as common objectives of regional university centers. They are:

1. Disseminate information on community education.

2. Provide consultant service in all phases of community education.

3. Generate and supervise training programs for current and potential community education personnel.

4. Give assistance to school districts in setting up community education programs.

5. Provide leadership and assistance in evaluation.

No two of the centers are identical. Each has its own characteristics, its unique problems, and its varying geographic and demographic considerations. Each center, therefore, has its own specific goals and objectives. The following list of goals and objectives was developed by the staff of the Community School Development Center at Western Michigan University.

GOAL I: Provide Consultant Services and Assistance for School Districts

OBJECTIVES

1. Provide consultant services and assistance by working with key people in communities where a community education program is nonexistent.

2. Provide consultant services and assistance by making available speakers and programs for boards of education, administrators, teachers, P.T.A.'s, etc., interested in the community education concept.

3. Provide consultant services and assistance through printed materials explaining both the community education concept and the services available from the center.

4. Provide consultant services and assistance in determining the desires and needs of the community.

5. Provide consultant services and assistance in the development of objectives for the school district's community education program.

6. Provide consultant services and assistance to other local agencies and organizations as their services relate to the overall community education program.

7. Provide consultant services and assistance to help the school district secure a qualified community school director and other community education personnel.

8. Provide consultant services and assistance in budgeting for the community education program.

9. Provide consultant services and assistance in developing the financial base for the community education program.

357

10. Provide consultant services and assistance by conducting visitations to school districts currently operating a community education program.

11. Provide consultant services and assistance to school districts in the evaluation of their community education programs, based on predetermined goals and objectives.

12. Provide consultant services and assistance by advising persons interested in pursuing a career in community education.

GOAL II: Provide Preservice Educational Opportunities for Community Educators, Lay Personnel, and Students

OBJECTIVES

1. Provide preservice educational opportunities through the inclusion of units on community education in the undergraduate and graduate teacher-preparation programs.

2. Provide preservice educational opportunities in community education at the undergraduate level by designing and supervising undergraduate experiences, e.g., utilizing a portion of the semester during which prospective candidates are in directed teaching experiences and are in schools with successful community school programs.

3. Provide preservice educational opportunities by designing offerings in community education at the graduate level.

4. Provide preservice educational opportunities by designing graduate short-term preparation, e.g., utilizing the facilities of existing community schools and the National Center for Community Education.

5. Provide preservice educational opportunities by arranging internships to provide on-the-job experience for individuals preparing to be community school personnel.

6. Provide preservice educational opportunities through internships at the university center for doctoral interns who wish to become university center directors.

7. Provide preservice educational opportunities through internships at the university center and community schools in the service area for master's interns preparing for careers as community education leaders.

GOAL III: Provide In-service Educational Opportunities for Community Educators, Lay Personnel, and Students

OBJECTIVES

1. Provide in-service opportunities through the planning and direction of graduate work for individuals interested in community education.

2. Provide in-service opportunities by conducting regular scheduled community education oriented graduate classes, seminars, and/or workshops, with the opportunity to earn college credit.

3. Provide in-service opportunities through area short-term community education programs at the request of community school directors and others to meet specific training needs.

4. Provide in-service opportunities through off-campus community education classes throughout the service area.

5. Provide in-service opportunities through the encouragement of participation in regional, state and national workshops and conventions in community education.

GOAL IV: Promote Evaluation and Research in Community Education

OBJECTIVES

1. Promote evaluation and research by assisting area school districts in the evaluation of their community education programs.

2. Promote evaluation and research through establishment of new models of community education throughout the service area.

3. Promote evaluation and research by lending assistance in the development of dissertations and theses related to community education.

4. Promote evaluation and research through continuous self-evaluations as well as quarterly and annual assessments of the university center.

5. Promote evaluation and research through involvement with state and national research agents.

GOAL V: Disseminate Community Education Information

OBJECTIVES

1. Disseminate community education information by writing, editing, publishing, and distributing newsletters and other materials of advice and assistance to the development of community education on a regional, state, and/or national basis.

2. Disseminate community education information by preparing, editing, and distributing audio-visual materials depicting the need for and achievements of community education.

3. Disseminate community education information by seeking television, radio, and press coverage of community education throughout the service area.

4. Disseminate community education information upon request to the State Department of Education and/or other political bodies to aid them in the promotion, initiation and financing of community education programs.

GOAL VI: Promote the Community Education Concept at University

OBJECTIVES

1. Promote the community education concept through involving a maximum number of university staff in seminars and workshops, as well as in the university center operation, to make the university's approach to community education a multi-disciplinary approach.

2. Promote the community education concept through the utilization of faculty members on the Community Education Development Center's Advisory Committee.

3. Promote the community education concept through the development of community education units for use by the faculty at both undergraduate and graduate levels.

4. Promote the community education concept by providing community education resource people and materials for classroom utilization by university instructors.

5. Promote the community education concept through the organization of in-service workshops and seminars for university faculty members.

6. Promote the community education concept through service on university committees.

7. Promote the community education concept through use of the university news media.

GOAL VII: Assist in the Expansion of the
Community Education Concept at State and
National Levels

OBJECTIVES

1. Assist in the expansion of the concept at state and national levels through soliciting the cooperation of other institutions of higher learning to implement community education programs in their respective colleges or universities.

2. Assist in the expansion of the concept at state and national levels by developing further the cooperating university center idea and helping selected sites become full service community education units.

3. Assist in the expansion of the concept at state and national levels through cooperating and sharing ideas with other university centers.

4. Assist in the expansion of the concept at state and national levels through participation in workshops sponsored by other college and university community education dissemination centers.

5. Assist in the expansion of the concept at state and national levels through participation in the evaluation of other college and university community eduaction dissemination centers.

6. Assist in the expansion of the concept at state and national levels through involvement in the selection and training of interns at the National Center for Community Education.

7. Assist in the expansion of the concept at state and national levels through contributing to state and national publications.

8. Assist in the expansion of the concept at state and national levels through attending and speaking at professional meetings to promote community education.

9. Assist in the expansion of the concept at state and national levels through encouraging membership in professional organizations related to community education.

Evaluation of the Regional University Centers

An evaluation of each center is conducted each year. The listed goals and objectives of the center are taken as the basis for evaluation; a group of several persons, each well acquainted with the concept and process of community education, is asked to participate. Members of this group are often drawn from the university personnel, center staff, the center's advisory council, community education directors in the region served by the center, school superintendents in the region, personnel from various national and state organizations, representatives of professional education associations, Mott Foundation representatives, and the directors of other regional university centers.

Table 15-1 shows the first two of a long list of items which make up the evaluation form used by the regional center at Western Michigan University.

The headings of Table 15-1 indicate that evaluation of the WMU center is based upon the center's stated goals and objectives. Two questions are asked in relation to each item: (a) Of what importance is this objective for a university center? (b) How satisfactorily did your university center accomplish this objective?

Financing the Regional University Center

The majority of the existing regional university centers have been financed at the time of their establishment by a combination of funds granted by the Mott Foundation and supplied by the university. The university funds may be a contribution from local resources or may come from other special funding sources. This university portion of the total support of a center, however, increases rapidly as compared to the Foundation portion; as time goes on, the center becomes an increasingly integral part of the university operation.

Table 15-1

Evaluation Form: Community School Development Center
Western Michigan University
Kalamazoo, Michigan

Explanation of rating values:

   I means "insufficient information to make a valid judgment."
   0 means "not at all."
   1 means "very little."
   2 means "a moderate amount."
   3 means "a substantial amount."
   4 means "a very high degree."

GOAL I: Provide consultant services and assistance for school
districts.

Of what importance is this objective for a university center?	Objective	How satisfactorily did your university center accomplish this objective?
4 3 2 1 0 I	A. Provide consultant services and assistance by working with key people in communities where a community education program is non-existent.	4 3 2 1 0 I
4 3 2 1 0 I	B. Provide consultant services and assistance by making available speakers and programs for board of education, administrators, teachers, PTA's, etc., interested in the community education concept.	4 3 2 1 0 I

(Continued for seven goals and their 49 objectives.)

General Factors Influencing the
Functioning of Regional University Centers

Many aspects of the factors which affect the successful establishment of a new center continue to be involved in the successful functioning of a working center. Able leadership, commitment to the concept of community education, adequate financial support, and intra-university communication are essential factors.

Several additional factors, however, assume increased importance as a center builds up its program of services, expands its field of operations, and becomes a more integral part of its own university. The directors of the regional university centers agreed, in 1972, that the following factors contribute to the continuous successful functioning of regional university centers:

1. Reinforcement of the concept of community education both within and outside the institution through the work of a center staff, the work of other university personnel, and through the effect of policies established by both organizations.

2. Strengthening of informal, nonbureaucratic techniques of operation within a center, in its relationships with its university, and in the discharge of center responsibilities to the field of community education.

3. Clarification of roles. The roles of the center and of the director of the center need to be defined carefully in order to minimize conflicting expectations from the partners in financial support, the university and the foundation.

4. Integration of the action growing out of acceptance of the concept of community education: (a) community education needs to be made an integral part of the curricular offerings of the university; (b) research in the field of community education needs to be promoted by the university; (c) evaluation of community education programs needs to be made an integral part of the university-level education evaluation; (d) service to community education, as performed

originally by a center, needs to become an integral part of university service to the educational agencies of its region.

5. Integration of the personnel carrying out the action. Center personnel, for example, should be members of the university staff with the accompanying remuneration, privileges, and responsibilities.

6. Flexibility in institutional and center operation which will facilitate change.

7. Strengthening of all lines of communication: (a) those between university administrators and the center; (b) those between professional educators and community education centers; (c) those between various community education centers; (d) those between institutions engaged in similar endeavors in community education; (e) those between a university's power structure and the sources of financial support for community education [adapted from Sandberg and Martin, 1972, pp. 47-48]

The growth of community education in Minnesota offered the nation an example of simultaneous development of many factors contributing to the successful implementation of the community education concept. A cooperating regional center was established at the College of St. Thomas in 1972-73. At the same time Minnesota's educational, legislative, and societal leaders acted to bring into a supportive focus several conditions in the state educational scene. These conditions included the following: (a) a supportive commitment to the concept of community education from the State Department of Education; (b) legislative enactment of support with funds for community education; (c) a supportive commitment from professional education organizations and the establishment of a state-wide community education association; (d) a well-organized system of public schools which encouraged a variety of ongoing programs; (e) supportive commitment from public school administrators and school boards; and (f) the commitment of an institution of higher learning to the concept of community education which was accompanied by a willingness to provide resources for the further development of community education.

The Minnesota experience offered encouragement to many individuals and institutions to believe that cooperative action can accomplish more than separated individual actions. The simultaneous achievement of several supportive actions correlated with the opening of a cooperating regional center did accomplish a significant level of success for both the center and the region it served.

THE NATIONAL CENTER FOR
COMMUNITY EDUCATION

The need for leaders in community education grew rapidly through the fifties. In the early sixties an inter-university program was developed in Michigan to help meet the need. The Mott Foundation has given financial assistance since 1963 to an inter-university clinical preparation program – a consortium of seven Michigan universities with headquarters in Flint, Michigan, and bearing the general title of National Center for Community Education. The seven universities which compose this consortium are Michigan State University, the University of Michigan, Wayne State University, Western Michigan University, Central Michigan University, Eastern Michigan University, and Northern Michigan University.

Since 1963 the seven Michigan universities have provided the disciplinary and degree capability for leadership training at the graduate level. The Flint school system has served as a clinic or laboratory for leadership internship experience; and the Mott Foundation has provided $5,000 and $8,000 fellowships to support selected interns during a one-year period of study at the masters or doctoral level. By the end of the first decade of its work, the National Center had made possible the participation of approximately 600 graduate students at the masters and doctoral levels.

The one-year period of study is designed to provide each intern with the opportunity to gain knowledge, experience, and a credential or degree. In recent years short-term programs and special institutes have been added. Well over a thousand leaders and prospective leaders in community education participated in these special programs during the years 1963-1973; some participants earned graduate credit and others attended as an in-service experience provided by their employer.

The Director of the National Center for Community Education wrote in 1972, "The NCCE is a leadership development center, a clearinghouse, a service agency, a human resource, and an initiator of exemplary programs and experimental projects. . . . [The NCCE] is concerned with preparing leaders who plan, organize, and manage educational resources to provide an opportunity for each citizen to achieve his life goals [Bush, p. 201]."

ROLE OF THE UNIVERSITY IN COMMUNITY EDUCATION

The period of the fifties, sixties, and early seventies brought the American university into direct contact with the community education concept. Not only have regional university centers, cooperating university centers, and the National Center of Community Education emphasized the training of leaders and dissemination of the idea, but the professional literature and the work of professional associations have brought a more general awareness of the concept of community education to the top levels of educational intellectualism. What will grow out of this association is yet to be determined. Professors in the colleges of education in practically all American universities are aware of the concept as increasingly influential; many of them are increasingly interested in the community education process and are becoming acquainted with various programs of community education.

Students bring to their university classes, as part of their general background, their former experiences in community education programs and their curiosity about the concept. Some of the students bring with them an active, contagious enthusiasm for the concept.

The same societal pressures that are causing communities to see the process of community education as hopeful for the improved solution of human problems are causing universities to look beyond their campuses into their surrounding communities. Many state universities — particularly those which started as land-grant colleges — recognize a familiar theme: the concept of education for all the people of a community is not too far removed from the concept of service through higher education, to all the people of a state. More recently, the confrontations with angry youth, with disenchanted taxpayers, and with pressure groups representing minorities have brought all universities to have more accurate perceptions of their real communities and of the needs — and expectations — of the people living in those communities.

Russell G. Mawby, President of the W. K. Kellogg Foundation, made the following statement in his article, "A Foundation Executive Views the Future of Continuing Education:"

But I also sense a readiness today in academia to consider, explore, and test new concepts and approaches. This readiness is evident in such developments as the Carnegie Commission's report, "Less Time, More Options," and the Newman Report; the Commission on Non-traditional Studies; and widespread interest in such ideas as the open university, the external degree, and a university without walls [1971, p. 69].

● ● ● ● ● ● ● ● ● ● ● ● ●

The reappraisal of higher education, demanded by the people who support and who use the products of American colleges and universities, appears to be getting under way. New consideration must be given to the old, isolationist relationships among research, instruction, and field services; a new comprehension must be developed in regards to the interaction between higher education and other educative institutions. Colleges and universities must acknowledge the continuousness, the comprehensiveness, and the immediacy of the role of education.

CHAPTER XVI

**THE ROLE OF PROFESSIONAL
ASSOCIATIONS IN COMMUNITY EDUCATION**

THE ROLE OF THE PROFESSIONAL ASSOCIATIONS IN COMMUNITY EDUCATION

DONALD C. WEAVER
AND
MAURICE F. SEAY

By its very nature community education requires a concerted effort among all persons and agencies interested in improving the quality of life in the community. Therefore, the community educator must work cooperatively with a multiplicity of professional agencies and associations each interested in some aspect of education in the community. It is important for the community educator to know the interests and concerns of those agencies most directly involved with community education; hence, this chapter reviews briefly the roles of various professional associations as they relate to the improvement of community life and to the role and function of the community educator.

The National Community School Education Association

Founded in 1966 by a small group of dedicated community educators, the National Community School Education Association (NCSEA) now serves over 2000 professional and lay members. At the time of its founding the stated purpose of the Association was "to promulgate and promote more effectively the community education concept." However, since 1966 a number of other organizations have become actively involved in the promulgation and promotion of the community education concept with the result that the NCSEA has turned its attention to other issues of concern to its membership. Such matters as the following are currently being considered by the NCSEA and are likely to receive increasing emphasis by the Association in the immediate future:

1. *Need to increase membership in the Association and to improve services to the members.* While membership in the Association has been open to anyone interested in promoting the community education concept, the membership is comprised primarily of professionals — those members who view the NCSEA as their prime professional organization.

   Services to members include: (a) consultative services; (b) research and special publications; (c) the NCSEA *News* (bi-monthly); (d) a subscription to *The Community Education Journal;* (e) a membership directory; (f) community education information and dissemination service; and (g) a national convention.

   Efforts to influence legislation favorable to community education depend for their success upon a strong organization of professional people dedicated to the improvement of community education services. The NCSEA must, therefore, continue to promote membership in the Association and must make every effort to expand services to its members as the need for such expansion becomes apparent.

2. *Demand for improved communication among the membership.* At the time of its inception, the NCSEA membership was limited to a relatively small geographical region which permitted regular and frequent face-to-face communication among the members. Today the membership is national in scope with all the consequent problems of wide-ranging membership. The Association must strengthen lines of communication for the simple purpose of keeping abreast of what is happening in the professional field. Further, the

longer a professional organization continues to exist, the more likely its members will have something of consequence to say to each other. As each community educator practices, he develops implementation strategies which should be shared with his professional colleagues. Constant efforts are required on the part of the Association, to assure a reasonable degree of professional intercourse among the members of the NCSEA.

3. *Urgency for attention to research and publication.* The kinds of research needed in the field of community education and suggested strategies for promoting it are discussed in Chapter Seventeen. It should be noted here, however, that the professional organization must be concerned with three matters as they relate to research: (a) that priority be given to those matters considered urgent by the membership, (b) that research done in the field of community education be based upon sound theory and (c) that the results of research be disseminated to the membership.

Only recently has the NCSEA given attention to the research needs in the field of community education — the first National Research Symposium on Community Education was held in 1971. Several specific recommendations emanating from that symposium were referred to the Research Committee of the NCSEA and most of the recommendations have since been implemented. Such action and the general interest in the findings of research among the professionals in community education would indicate that the promotion of research and the publication of research findings will become a major concern of the NCSEA in the years ahead.

4. *Recognition of the advantages of state, regional and institutional affiliates.* Provision is made within the by-laws of the NCSEA for state, regional and institutional memberships. Because affiliate memberships are of manageable size to facilitate communication, promote research and provide in-service training programs, the affiliates are important adjuncts to the work of the NCSEA. The NCSEA is likely, therefore, to place increased emphasis upon the development of additional state, regional and institutional affiliates.

5. *Pressure for standards of professional performance for the community educator.* Until recently it had been possible to recruit community educators from among experienced teachers and administrators thus assuring educational experience in positions of community education leadership. However, present and future demands for personnel capable of providing leadership in community education make necessary an increasing amount of recruitment from among candidates with limited training and experience. Such a trend requires that the profession develop standards of professional performance for the community educator. The logical organization to provide the leadership for developing and enforcing such standards is the NCSEA.

The evidence cited above would indicate that the NCSEA faces a difficult but exciting future. Those individuals who serve as community educators should consider joining the NCSEA and its affiliates as a major step they can take in determining the direction to be followed by the community education profession. The future of individual community educators as well as that of the entire community education movement may well depend upon a viable organization through which professional matters can be promoted and adjudicated.

Organizations with Complementary Functions

Three organizations provide some of the professionals who work in communities with services which supplement and complement those services provided for community educators through their own professional organization. They are: (a) American Association for Health, Physical Education and Recreation; (b) National Recreation and Park Association; and (c) National Association for Public Continuing and Adult Education.

Historically, community education has promoted with particular diligence a variety of activities in the areas of health, recreation and adult education. While promotion of such activities is considered a legitimate part of a community education program, it is not the intent of those operating the programs to usurp the prerogatives of professionals in the fields of health, recreation, and adult education. As Totten and Manley (1969) have indicated, "The schools [when an integral part of a community education program] attempt only to strengthen the work of other agencies, not to duplicate it, and the schools use the services of the various agencies to enrich the school program [p. 57]." Hence, the community educator views such organizations as the American Association for Health, Physical Education and Recreation, the National Recreation and Parks Association, and the National Association for Public Continuing and Adult Education as allies in his efforts to bring the best in health, recreation and adult education to the community. Each of these organizations makes available through its publications many years of research and practice in the improvement of community services.

Supporting Agencies

Four organizations, in addition to the NCSEA, actively support community education. They are: (a) the National Congress of Parents and Teachers; (b) the Big Brothers of America; (c) the United States Jaycees; and (d) the North Central Association of Colleges and Secondary Schools.

The National Congress of Parents and Teachers (PTA) has long been recognized for its efforts to improve the quality of education in this country. It is not surprising, therefore, that the PTA should adopt, at its National Board of Managers meeting in September 1971, a resolution supportive of community education. The term used is "community school," but the comprehensive concept implied in the following statement is that of "community education:"

> The PTA recognizes that the learning process is a continuing one, that it is lifelong and involves the total community. The community school provides learning opportunities for all people of all ages at all times. The philosophic principle that the public schools belong to the people may become a reality under the community school program, as people of all ages — preschool, schoolage, and adult — make the school a part of their lives by continuing participation in programs of their own choosing. The community school may be the vehicle for realizing the full potential of every individual.

> The community school makes maximum use of all available resources, both human and material, in carrying out its program. It

develops its curriculum and activities from continuous study of people's basic needs, and involves citizens in that development. It integrates insofar as possible the community's educational, social, physical, recreational, and health programs for children, youth, and adults.

By extending its services around the clock and throughout the year, the community school makes maximum use of school facilities.

The human interaction inherent in the community school concept could provide a basis for strengthening family life, improving interpersonal relations, and working toward identifying and solving community problems. Because educational problems today are so complex, the total community must be involved in seeking solutions.

It is, therefore, desirable that PTA's at every level work to promote and develop the community school program.

The PTA resolution is of particular significance because it comes from the organization which is universally recognized as the one committed to the improvement of education for *all* children and youth. Also worthy of note is the fact that there was considerable "grass-roots" involvement preceding and preparatory to the adoption of the resolution. Community education literature abounds in examples of successful campaigns resulting from appropriate involvement of people; the developments leading up to the adoption of the PTA resolution provide community education with still another example of successful involvement processes in the selling of an idea. Beginning at the state level as early as 1968, PTA representatives were discussing the merits of community education and planning for action in that field. In 1969 the PTA's Commission on Individual Development began the promotion of community education – a campaign that resulted in the drafting of a statement which formed the basis for the resolution adopted in 1971. Each step in the carefully planned process leading up to the actual adoption of the resolution involved literally hundreds of people. Thus, in one comparatively low-key action, the PTA informed many of its members regarding community education, provided educational leaders with an exemplary case of grass roots involvement, and called nationwide attention to the fact that the prestigious PTA was taking an official position supportive of community education.

While the focus of Big Brothers of America is upon a specific problem within American society — the absence of a father in the lives of many boys during their formative years — its program is of particular significance to the community educator as he attempts to meet the needs of fatherless boys in the community. The community educator is assured ready access to the services of the association inasmuch as the Big Brothers of America have long recognized community education as a logical vehicle for implementing the program within the local community.

At its meeting in March 1972, the Board of Directors of the United States Jaycees adopted the following resolution in support of community education:

Whereas public schools are owned and maintained by the people and most often represent the largest single investment of tax money in a community, and

Whereas schools are most often strategically located in communities and possess facilities and equipment which are adaptable for broader community use, and

Whereas the traditional use of schools for the purpose of educating young people six to eight hours a day, five days a week, 36 weeks a year is a luxury the citizens of any community can no longer afford, and

Whereas the problems facing our citizens today as they attempt to adjust to a changing society are so great that no one organization can continue to operate independently of other organizations, and

Whereas no single cohesive strategy for the development and utilization of community resources, especially for youth, the poor, the alienated, the handicapped, the minorities, the aged, and the nonparent has been established, and

Whereas the philosophy of community education provides that "master plan" by expanding the traditional role of the school from that of being a formal learning center for young people to a community human development center which provides self-improvement activities to all segments of the population on a schedule that is virtually around-the-clock, around-the-year,

Therefore be it resolved that the United States Jaycees extend their national support for the further development and expansion of the community education philosophy as it seeks, through the medium of the community school, to promote the increased use of existing school facilities, equipment, and personnel for educational, recreational, social, cultural, and civic activities in response to community needs and wants as determined by the people through their local community school staff and its local community council.

The resolution by the Jaycees provides concrete evidence of the high regard of the businessman for community education. Further, the resolution supporting community education at the national level provides the community educator with a valuable entree to the businessman at the local level.

The North Central Association of Colleges and Secondary Schools has demonstrated considerable support for the community education movement in recent years. Through its Commission on Research and Service, a special committee has been named to develop programs and materials in the field of community education. This committee has produced materials and provided programs for member schools throughout the region of 19 states served by the Association.

Related Organizations

Six of the large national education associations are particularly helpful to community education. They are (a) the National Education Association, (b) the National Association of Elementary Principals, (c) the National Association of Secondary School Principals, (d) the American Association of School Administrators, (e) the Association for Supervision and Curriculum Development, and (f) the National School Boards Association.

The activities of most professional education associations are germane to the work of the community educator; hence, one could justifiably include all professional education associations in a listing of related organizations. However, the organizations listed are those generally recognized as providing services and publications which deal with areas directly related to the work of the community educator. The community educator should, therefore, familiarize himself with the work of these and other organizations in their operations at the national level as well as with their extensive work within individual communities.

Local Counterparts

Each of the six "related" national professional associations discussed above has its counterpart in a state or local association. While official recognition by the parent organization at the national level is important to the development of public understanding and enthusiasm for the community education concept, the state and local associations are the source of specific aid to the process of community education. The community educator should become familiar with the personnel and programs of each of these associations at the state and local levels. Realistic cooperative programming at these levels is a necessity for successful community education.

Cooperative Efforts to Promote Community Education

While national policy statements such as those of the PTA and the Jaycees open the way to cooperative efforts, they do not insure cooperative planning among professional organizations. Enterprising community educators take the initiative themselves and capitalize upon opportunities to test the viability of such policy pronouncements. One effort at establishing working relationships, which was made by the NCSEA, illustrates the kind of action that can eventually strengthen all community education. The Executive Secretary of the NCSEA sent a letter to the organizations serving complementary and supportive roles, as well as to the related organizations listed above, inviting official participation in a national conference on community education in April 1973. The purpose of participation, as stated in the letter, was to develop "a positive liaison with other national organizations . . . by better understanding each other's goals and objectives."

The activities of the NCSEA to promulgate and promote the community education concept are of prime concern to the community educator. Although its influence in the beginning was regional in nature the NCSEA now provides leadership to both professional and lay members interested in improving the quality of community education across the country. The NCSEA recognizes:

1. A need to increase membership in the Association and to increase service to members.

2. A demand for improved communication among the membership.

3. An urgency for attention to research and publication.

4. A recognition of the advantages of state, regional and institutional affiliates.

5. A pressure for standards of professional performance for the community educator.

In addition to the NCSEA, several professional associations provide services which are complementary to the work of the community educator. Such organizations as the American Association for Health, Physical Education and Recreation, the National Recreation and Parks Association and the National Association for Public Continuing and Adult Education work cooperatively with the community educator to improve community services in the areas of health, recreation and adult education.

A number of organizations have pledged support for the community education movement nationally. Such organizations include the National Congress of Parents and Teachers, Big Brothers of America and the United States Jaycees. Also working cooperatively with the NCSEA in the field of community education are such organizations as: the National Education Association, the National Association of Elementary Principals, the National Association of Secondary School Principals, the American Association of School Administrators, the Association for Supervision and Curriculum Development, and the National School Boards Association.

While policy statements by national professional associations pledging support for community education are important to the promotion of the concept across the country, the community educator must capitalize upon opportunities to implement action programs involving those associations at the local level if such pledges are to result in specific activities to improve the quality of life in the community.

CHAPTER XVII

RESEARCH IN COMMUNITY EDUCATION

RESEARCH IN COMMUNITY EDUCATION

DONALD C. WEAVER
AND
MAURICE F. SEAY

Community educators recognize that the viability of the community education concept is strengthened by research which tests the assumptions inherent within the concept. They also recognize the difficulty of accomplishing research in areas of community-wide education and social interaction. The same difficulties afflict many other areas of education. For example, career education is in great need of the tested findings of research; so also is the concept of "the open classroom." The problem of developing techniques that will support meaningful research in the broad, more complex areas of social interaction is a problem facing modern civilization.

Granting, then, that action in meeting the needs of people must continue even while researchers seek to prove the assumptions upon which the action is taken, this chapter will take a brief look at efforts — early, current, and prospective efforts — to seek that proof. Three factors that have had a deterrent influence upon research in the field are discussed. And, finally, a theoretical model of community education is offered with the suggestion that research needs may be inferred and current assumptions and practices may be tested by using such a model.

Early Efforts

The community school movement of the thirties, forties, and early fifties was an experimental movement (as explained in Chapter Two). The majority of the experiments were not well structured for purposes of evaluation, but many of them were carried to a conclusion, the results were documented, disseminated, and used in a variety of valuable educational programs. The results of this experimentation have been a major factor in the development of the concept of community education which today is widely accepted in the United States — and in many other countries.

The grass-roots, almost naive, nature of some of the reports of these early experiments can mislead sophisticated observers to conclude that such experimentation had nothing to do with research. Certainly the hypotheses were not called by that name nor were the findings published in the research quarterlies of that day. In a study like that of the Parker District High School, however, the teachers and administrators set out to achieve certain carefully planned, heretofore untried educational objectives. They had some of the best consultative service available at that time from the Southern Association of Colleges and Secondary Schools. As the faculty wrote their report of the study, they noted reasons for their successes and their failures; and in conclusion they wrote, "We are now able to see additional and better ways to accomplish our aims [p. 79]."

A few experiments of this period were evaluated according to a carefully structured plan. Among them were the Sloan Experiment in Kentucky (see Chapter Two) and the Community School Service Program in Michigan (see Chapter One).

A description of the measurement program incorporated in the original plans for the Sloan Experiment in Kentucky was published in 1944. That report explains that (a) relatively isolated experimental and control schools were selected for their similarity in community background, type of pupil and teacher, and stability of populations; (b) the educational programs of the experimental schools were changed in only one respect — especially prepared instructional materials relating to diet were made available, together with printed suggestions as to their use; no changes were made in the programs of the control schools; (c) three types of measurement were applied at appropriate intervals; (d) the results obtained from the experimental schools were compared to those obtained from the control schools (Seay & Meece, pp. 14-15). Among the results established by this measurement program were the anticipated improvement in diet and a measurable improvement in reading skills, especially in the areas of comprehension and vocabulary.

The original plan of the Community School Service Program, sponsored by the Michigan Department of Public Instruction, contained the following plan for evaluation: (a) collect base-line data at the beginning of the experiment; (b) collect certain data by means of cumulative records; and (c) collect data from "spot studies" made periodically and at the end of the experiment which "will serve as indices for measuring change in school and community [*An Evaluation and Community Study Pattern,* 1947, p. 5]."

While such experimentation was never considered in-depth research, it was a part of the process of developing a concept. Community education has come through that period to the place where its leaders can now study its lack of formal theory, its lack of sophisticated research, and begin to remedy those lacks.

Deterrents to Research

Deterrents to research are plentiful in most areas of complex social interaction, and community education is even more beset by such factors. Three of them are discussed here as illustrative of the general problem.

1. In their efforts to be practical, community educators have often rejected opportunities to contribute significantly to the knowledge in the field. In many communities the adoption of the community education concept has been viewed as a means to the resolution of practical problems considered

389

crucial by the community. Those involved in initiating programs, therefore, concentrated their efforts upon borrowing tested practices and strategies which promised fairly certain results rather than developing and testing their own approaches to the resolution of problems.

The borrowing of practices from such exemplary models as that provided by Flint, Michigan, illustrates the misuse of what might otherwise have been an excellent laboratory experience. Thousands of visitors to the Flint laboratory each year return to their home communities to transplant practices observed in Flint. Needless to say, such practices are not always successful in a new setting. However, in the absence of adequate theoretical framework against which to test, the cause of the failure cannot be determined. A community usually sees the situation as a failure of community education, not the failure of a transplanted practice. Had the laboratory been used to examine the community education concept itself − to generate hunches or hypotheses to be tested − and had the mechanics for testing been established and used, meaningful data would have been available to prevent the trial of an unsuitable practice.

Such testing of practices need not be limited to one center. Community educators, by committing themselves to the importance of research in the field, can be collecting valuable empirical evidence as a result of their daily practice.

2.   Contributing to the lack of research in the field of community education is the comparative absence of theory development. Inasmuch as Chapters One, Two, Three, and Four are devoted to a discussion of community education theory, this chapter is enabled to limit comment to the fact that if research is to contribute to the development of the community education concept, such research must emanate from a systematic framework of beliefs about community education. Chapter Four is concerned primarily with the problems and the necessary steps to be taken in developing a theory of community education. It is sufficient to note here that the need for such development is recognized.

Research in a field needing extensive development of theory results in the testing of unrelated hypotheses and does little to contribute to a systematizing of beliefs in that field. In a special issue of *Phi Delta Kappan* devoted to community education, Weaver (1972) attempted to present a case for theory development as follows:

An examination of the literature reveals few attempts at systematic theory development. One of the first attempts to look critically at community education was that published by the National Society for the Study of Education in 1953. It attempted to define and analyze the concept and to summarize the related research. However, most recent publications in the field have been more descriptive than definitive, more promotional than analytical, and more practical than theoretical. This is not intended to disparage either the quality or the impact of such publications but to indicate the present status of theory development in the field. The time has come when one does expect to see a greater effort to account for successes and failures by using empirical data derived from the testing of hunches and/or hypotheses emanating from a supportable rationale.

Primary factors contribute to the urgency for theory development in community education. The first is the rapid rate at which the concept is being disseminated nationally. The second is a general social malaise within American society which has created a demand for accountability. Citizens concerned with the quality of education in this country deserve some assurance that support of legislation to adopt and fund community education programs will effect improvements not realized through existing educational processes. In its present state of development, community education theory cannot provide such assurance. I believe it is now possible to develop sound theory — theory which will vindicate Mott's faith in community education as a means of resolving social and educational problems and persuade the American public that the

391

concept is worthy of public support. Satisfactory demonstration of community education demands more attention to theory and less attention to practice.

> Certainly, the community educator must be concerned with both theory and practice. In his field, as in any other, the theory to which he subscribes suggests hypotheses to be tested; the results of such testing confirm or deny the validity of his practices. The community educator either confirms or modifies his theory based upon results of the testing of hypotheses suggested by the original theoretical position. Hence a practice which does not emanate from sound theory of operation is of doubtful value to the community educator [p. 154].

Indeed, attempts to test the philosophical concepts of Dewey (1916) failed, in part, due to lack of theory. Early proponents of Dewey's philosophy attempted to imply appropriate practice directly from the complex philosophical pronouncements of Dewey without first having developed and tested a systematic framework of assumptions and hypotheses emanating from his philosophy. The results were unsatisfactory since attempts to test practices so derived resulted in a distortion of what Dewey had to say about community education and probably contributed to the ultimate demise of "progressive education."

3. Colleges and universities have contributed relatively little in the way of substantive data based upon systematic study in the field of community education. A prime source of empirical data in most areas of education is the doctoral dissertation. However, since there have been few professors of education in universities across the country whose major area of interest is community education, relatively little effort appears to have been made to stimulate students to do their research in this field. Some definitive studies have been conducted by doctoral students — primarily by those students serving as interns in the National Center for Community Education. Results of such studies are on file in the NCCE in Flint, Michigan, but unfortunately, the findings have not been widely disseminated.

Current Status

Three documents intended to compile published works in the field are of interest to the student of community education. A chronological bibliography of articles and books dealing with community education published prior to 1953 was prepared by E. Olsen and published by the National Community School Education Association (1970). A bibliography entitled *Research in Community School Education* (B. Olsen, 1970) lists materials published from 1954 to 1970. An *Annotated Bibliography of Books and Pamphlets* (Totten, 1972) includes selected materials dealing with community education spanning the period covered by both of the previously cited bibliographies. The Totten work includes a list of 15 unpublished doctoral dissertations dealing with community education written between 1950 and 1971. Also of interest to the student of community education is a review by Brackett (1972) of the books written in the field of community education. Forty-three books are reviewed including two not released by the publisher at the time the materials were reviewed. The reviewer has indicated the significance of each book for the field of community education and has related the contribution of each author to the current social milieu.

With the exception of the 15 doctoral dissertations cited by Totten and doctoral dissertations along with some masters theses included by B. Olsen, most of the works cited are descriptions of experiences of practitioners and observers in the field. While such observations are of interest to community educators, they are, nevertheless, observations; and as such, they do not contribute to the research data base in community education. It would appear, therefore, that doctoral dissertations have made the greatest contribution to research in the field of community education in the recent past and that they are likely to continue to be a prime source of substantive contributions in the future.

However, if doctoral dissertations are to be maximally effective in providing research data to the community educator, two actions are required:

1. Some agency such as the National Community School Education Association must coordinate the efforts of doctoral students around topic areas. Present attempts at research via the doctoral dissertation result in piecemeal attempts to answer isolated

393

questions rather than deliberate efforts to test assumptions and hypotheses emanating from a particular theoretical position. Professors knowledgeable in the field will be engaged in developing theories of community education and will stimulate their students to test those theories much as the staff at the University of Chicago encouraged research based upon the Getzels theory of the school as a social system following its development in 1957. During the 10 years following its introduction in 1957, scores of studies, including many doctoral dissertations, were conducted to test the social systems model. Similar attempts to do intensive investigation into one facet of community education are required if such efforts are to contribute to the theory development in the field.

2. A vehicle must be found through which the results of research can be disseminated to all interested members of the profession. It is doubtful that one out of ten community educators in this country is aware of the findings of Becker (1972) as they relate to perceptions of the community educator by his professional peers. Yet, the implications of this study and other similar investigations, including the study by Johnson (1973), have considerable bearing upon the competencies required of the community educator and the training appropriate to his position. Some means must be found through which the results of such investigations can be disseminated. Ideally, an organ developed by an organization such as the National Community School Education Association would be devoted to abstracting and disseminating such information.

Prospects for Research

Three recent developments show promise for increased research in community education in the future:

1. A research component in the National Center for Community Education. For the first time in the history of the Mott Foundation sponsored Center, a research component has been funded and staffed. The Research Division of the NCCE is charged with the responsibility of promoting research in the field, conducting research studies and disseminating the results of such

studies. Because it is an integral part of other NCCE activities, namely, the leadership training program, the Research Division is in a unique position to stimulate and coordinate research efforts among doctoral students. (Seventy doctoral students study for a year at the NCCE as part of their preparation for community education leadership positions.) The staff at the NCEE communicates regularly with members of the National Community School Education Association and with dissemination centers in colleges and universities across the country which provides further opportunity to stimulate, coordinate, and disseminate research.

2. A Research Symposium sponsored by the NCSEA. In April of 1971 the first national Research Symposium on Community Education was held at Ball State University to identify needed research in community education and to develop a master plan to encourage and implement research in the field. Symposium results have been published by the NCSEA in a publication entitled *Needed Research in Community Education* (1971). The master plan developed as a result of the symposium included contacts with doctoral students studying at the National Center for Community Education to promote interest in increased research. As a result of those contacts, there has been a significant increase in the number of doctoral dissertations investigating problems directly related to community education.

3. Increasing concern regarding the skills required for satisfactory performance as a community educator and the attendant problems of qualifications and training required to enter the field. In an earlier discussion of leadership training in Chapter Five the fact was mentioned that, while there are presently no generally accepted criteria of performance for the community educator, there is a growing interest in the development of such criteria. Obviously, investigations into the skills associated with successful performance will be required before credentialing standards can be established.

Evidence of the increasing concern for the qualifications of the community educator is the number of doctoral dissertations completed and in process dealing with this issue. Since 1969 four doctoral dissertations, Hadden (1969), Decker (1971), Becker (1972), and Johnson (1973), have dealt with issues related to the

395

performance of the community educator; and there are a number of studies currently under way dealing with similar issues. It seems reasonable to assume that as the number of professionals devoting full time to community education increases there will be an attendant increase in pressure for standards of performance in the field. Such pressures seem likely to produce an increase in the number and quality of doctoral studies devoted to issues related to professional performance.

Needed Research

Students of community education who are interested in exploring areas of needed research should secure a copy of the national Research Symposium results published by the National Community School Education Association under the title *Needed Research in Community Education* (1971) – a document mentioned in the preceding section. Areas of needed research identified by the symposium can be grouped under four main questions as follows:

1. What are appropriate goals and functions of community education? There is still considerable divergence of opinion among both practitioners and writers in the field regarding what community education is intended to accomplish. Minzey and LeTarte (1972) emphasize "process" goals of community involvement and action as contrasted with "program" goals of promoting more classes and activities within a community education program, while Totten and Manley (1969) consider the "program" roles of organizing, coordinating, supervising, and administering activities within the school as the prime function of community education.

   As indicated earlier, alternate models need to be developed and tested to determine the impact of various approaches to community education. It is altogether possible that, as Minzey and LeTarte (1972) imply, both "program" and "process" functions are appropriate under certain conditions. However, until both "program" and "process" oriented models are developed and tested under reasonably controlled conditions, decisions will continue to be based upon limited observation and experience; and the question of the appropriate thrust of community education will go unresolved.

2. Does community education accomplish the goals it purports to achieve? A plethora of claims for its efficacy by proponents of community education may be found throughout the literature — claims ranging from an increase in the use of school facilities by adults to a guarantee of the good society. Yet, faced with the challenge to substantiate their claims with data gathered under conditions of reasonable objectivity, the proponents of community education admit that much more substantive evidence is needed.

To be sure, the absence of such data does not negate the claims of many that the community education approach holds promise for the resolution of the educational and social problems facing the society. On the other hand, to convince those unfamiliar with the concept that the concept does indeed hold promise for the resolution of such problems requires more than mere belief on the part of its proponents. Convincing evidence is needed, and such evidence must be collected by practitioners in the field where there are on-going programs and processes aimed at meeting specific goals. Colleges and universities can provide assistance with the techniques of design and data collection, but such data should be based upon real programs and processes in real communities involving real people.

3. What are the variables associated with successful community education programs? Most community educators are aware that the outcomes from efforts to implement community education programs and processes are affected by such factors as the socio-economic level of the community, inter-group conflicts within the community, the attitude of personnel in schools and in other educational agencies toward community involvement, community attitudes toward education, and the value orientations of those being served. Yet many community educators behave like the proverbial leader who, having lost sight of his goal, redoubles his efforts. While recognizing that there are givens (variables) present in every community which are related to the success or failure of efforts to implement community education, many community educators apply and reapply the same model to every situation.

The history of efforts to implement community education in large urban centers illustrates the futility of such practices.

Doherty (1972) expresses the potential for community education in the large urban centers as follows:

> The American "City of the Seventies" is the antithesis of what we aspire to. It is bankrupt, dirty, crime-ridden, drug-infested, racially isolated, educationally inept, lonely, de-humanizing, and decaying. At the same time, American cities represent much of the best in American culture (theater, music, libraries, art institutes, universities, ethnic enclaves, etc.). And they are home to a growing percentage of minorities and to the old and the poor; they are a fading hope for a diminishing number of middle-class Americans who see real advantage in the population mix and life style of city living.
>
> While by no means a panacea for the complex political, economic, and social problems related to urban survival, the concept of community education can be a major factor in providing meaningful alternatives to the tedium, loneliness, and purposelessness characteristic of many urban residents who find themselves on society's bottom rung [p. 187].

Undoubtedly, community education has great potential for improving conditions in the large urban centers of this country. However, with a few notable exceptions, there are not many success stories resulting from attempts to apply community education models to large cities (Provus, 1973). Yet, recent issues of the *Community Education Journal* are replete with descriptions of successful attempts to implement community education in small and medium-sized communities. Most unsuccessful attempts to establish community education programs in large cities have utilized models which had been applied successfully in small and medium-sized communities. Based upon what we know from unsuccessful attempts to implement a community education model in large cities, it should be possible to design a model which, when tested in the large urban setting, would reveal isolated variables which make failure inevitable; and it should then be possible to redesign the model to account for those variables. Such efforts to develop and test models appropriate to the urban setting are imperative if community education is to contribute to the resolution of the critical social and educational problems related to the survival of the city.

4. What are the personal and professional qualifications of the community educator? Ideally, research would be conducted to determine the goals of community education and to delineate the variables bearing directly upon the success of the community educator before attempts are made to specify the skills required on the job. However, to delay investigation of the leadership skill requirements would seriously hamper efforts to develop new programs in the field. At least some attempt must be made to secure tentative answers which provide direction to the development of training programs for community education. As already indicated in the discussion of leadership for community education, new programs are being established throughout the country at an accelerative rate, which means that training programs must be developed immediately to train leadership for the future. Therefore, investigations must proceed on all fronts at once with high priority given to coordinating the findings wherever relationships are believed to exist.

Becker (1972) has projected further research needs related to the qualifications of the community educator as follows:

> Further study should be carried out along similar lines of this study to determine: (a) student perceptions of the Community School Director and (b) community perceptions of the Community School Director.

> The interest of the field would be furthered if studies concerning the position of the Community School Director within the school structure were carried out. Studies on the effect of age, experience and background of the Director and their relation to his perceived effectiveness would be of great service.

> In the final analysis, the Community School Director's role as a leader is of paramount concern if the community education effort is to be successful [p. 86].

The discussion of leadership skill requirements in Chapter Five referred to technical, conceptual, and human skills as essential to satisfactory performance as a community educator; also included were suggested components of a training program designed to insure development of those skills.

The Model As a Means of Generating Research

An investigation to determine goals and functions of community education conducted by Weaver in 1972 is described in Chapter Five. The model presented here is based upon data gathered in that study; sources of the data included group interviews with 245 community educators in 20 university centers across the country. The model is not intended as exemplary but rather as illustrative of the kind of model needed in the field of community education to systematize the concept and to develop testable hypotheses.

As indicated earlier, productive research is possible only after beliefs about the particular phenomenon under investigation have been systematized. It is from the systematized framework of beliefs about a particular phenomenon — that is, from the theory — that a researcher is able to develop hunches to be tested. The model is a graphic representation of the theory, and it expedites the process of generating hunches or hypotheses to be tested. The results of all testing generated by the particular theoretical position are fed back into the model, thus contributing to modification of the theory and the development of a new, more viable model.

The theory (model) attempts to account for all the elements in the situation based upon what is known to date, the outputs expected of the system, and the dynamics of the interactions within the system which produce the outputs. Further, the model must generate testable hypotheses. Given such restraints upon the theorist, it is not surprising that most fields of study are short of theorists. Community education is no exception.

Indeed, the field of community education is in need of a more systematically developed theory — a need demonstrated by the fact that research efforts tend to be sporadic and limited to areas of concern to the individual investigator. The development of models based upon what is known to date will go far toward meeting this need. The testing of hypotheses generated by the models can then lead to modification or confirmation of the original theoretical position.

For example, a model is needed which takes account of all the elements in the large urban center as they relate to the implementation of a community education program. Such a model would include the outputs to be expected from a program in the large city and the dynamics of the interactions required to produce the desired outputs in that setting. It would then be possible to test the model under varying conditions within the large urban center and, on the basis of such tests, to develop a new model which would take into account the variables in the urban setting. The new·model, when applied in the urban setting, could reasonably be expected to produce the desired outputs.

The model, shown in Figure 17-1, is illustrative of the kinds of models needed in community education. A brief description of the elements in the theory and a list of testable hypotheses generated by the theoretical position follow. For further information regarding the details of the investigation which produced the data upon which the model is based, the reader is referred to a manuscript prepared by Weaver and produced by the NCSEA entitled *The Emerging Community Education Model* (1972).

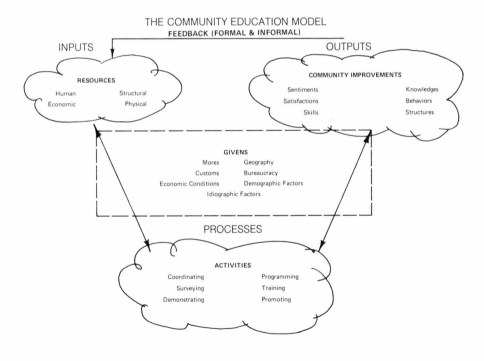

Figure 17-1
A Community Education Model
based upon a National Study of Community Education Goals (Weaver, 1972)

The model, shown in Figure 17-1, assumes the outputs (community improvements) to be classified within six categories: sentiments, satisfactions, skills, knowledges, behaviors, and structures. It is assumed that any function of community education known to date is aimed at accomplishing one of the six outputs included in the model. To accomplish the stated outputs, the community educator engages in six kinds of processes (activities): coordinating, surveying, demonstrating, programming, training, and promoting. As he organizes to produce the desired outputs, he must select appropriate inputs (resources) including human, economic, structural, and physical resources. The dynamics (interactions) present in the community education situation are illustrated by the arrows indicating that interventions at any point in the system automatically affect other elements in the system. For example, a change in desired outputs automatically affects the processes and inputs required to reach the desired outcome.

Further, the model provides for feedback indicated by the arrow from outputs to inputs. Modifications in inputs or processes are possible based upon feedback regarding the quality of outputs. The community educator benefits from feedback obtained through structured surveys of community members (formal) as well as from unsolicited comments of those toward whom the outputs of the system are directed (informal). The community educator must take account of certain givens present in every community — factors which may affect any dimension of the model. Those givens included mores, customs, economic conditions, geography, bureaucracy, demographic factors, and idiographic factors.

Two questions remain:

1. Of what use is the model to the practicing community educator? The model provides a means by which the community educator can conceptualize his job. He is providing activities and allocating resources to effect community improvements daily, but he has no conceptual framework within which to analyze what is happening. The model provides a reminder that every time an activity is provided or a resource is allocated, he must take account of the givens in his situation. He is further reminded that systematic feedback from those who receive community education services makes possible improvements in those services. The community educator who utilizes the model to look at his job is aware of the

interrelatedness of all aspects of his work and realizes that action taken in one area is likely to affect all other elements within the model. The model does not prescribe answers to specific procedural questions; it merely provides a conceptual framework through which the community educator may view his job more objectively.

2. Of what use is the model to the researcher? The model is essential to the work of the researcher because it depicts the theoretical framework of the theorist. The model specifies the essential elements within the theory and demonstrates the relationship of those elements to each other. Hence, the model suggests to the researcher possible hypotheses to be tested. The model suggests many testable hypotheses, seven of which are stated below:

Hypothesis 1. To the extent that the community educator is limited to programming as an activity, outputs will be limited to skill, knowledge, and structural improvements.

Hypothesis 2. Highly developed conceptual and human skills on the part of the community educator are related to success in coordination, demonstration, and promotion activity.

Hypothesis 3. Knowledge and skill outputs depend for their success upon economic and physical inputs.

Hypothesis 4. Sentiment and satisfaction outputs depend for their success upon human and structural inputs.

Hypothesis 5. In the large urban center the extent of freedom permitted the community educator in selecting the appropriate processes and inputs will determine the extent of success in effecting community improvements.

Hypothesis 6. Programming in the face of opposing community givens increases negative output in the form of sentiments, satisfactions, and behaviors.

Hypothesis 7. Highly developed technical skills are related to success in surveying, training, and programming activity.

Until efforts are made to promote the development of theories from which to test assumptions about community education, research in the field will continue to be haphazard and sporadic. Colleges and universities interested in promoting community education must develop models intended to test assumptions about community education and must encourage programmatic research based upon those models. Such efforts should produce a body of knowledge which can be used to demonstrate the efficacy of community education to all who would improve the social and educational status of communities throughout this country.

LIST OF REFERENCES

Albig, W. *Modern Public Opinion.* New York: McGraw-Hill, 1956.

American Association of School Administrators. *Educational Administration in a Changing Community.* Thirty-seventh Yearbook of the AASA. Washington, D.C.: AASA, 1959.

An Evaluation and Community Study Pattern for the Community School Service Program. Lansing, Mi.: State Department of Public Instruction, 1947.

Art Education. Sixty-fourth Yearbook of the National Society for the Study of Education. Chicago: NSSE (distr. University of Chicago Press), 1965.

Art in American Life and Education. Fortieth Yearbook of the National Society for the Study of Education. Chicago: NSSE (distr. University of Chicago Press), 1941.

Barnard, C. I. *The Functions of the Executive.* Cambridge: Harvard University Press, 1938.

Becker, W. E. *A Study of the Leadership Effectiveness of the Community School Director.* (Doctoral dissertation, University of Michigan) Ann Arbor, Mi.: University Microfilms, 1972. No. 73-6788.

Berelson, B., & Steiner, G. A. *(Eds.) Human Behavior* (shorter ed.) New York: Harcourt, 1967.

Bernays, E. *The Engineering of Consent.* Norman, Oklahoma: University of Oklahoma Press, 1955.

Bettelheim, B. A personal vision. In *Art.* New York: The Museum of Modern Art, 1964.

Biddle, W. W., & Biddle, L. J. *The Community Development Process.* New York: Holt, Rinehart and Winston, 1965.

Boles, H. W. *The 3R's and the New Religion.* Midland, Michigan: Pendell, 1973.

Brackett, P. C. The literature of community education. *Phi Delta Kappan*, 1972, 54(3), 205-210.

Brown, C. E. Emerging priorities for continuing education. In National Society for the Study of Education, *The Curriculum: Retrospect and Prospect.* Seventieth Yearbook, Part I. Chicago: NSSE (distr. University of Chicago Press). 1971.

Bruner, J. S. *On Knowing*: Essays for the Left Hand. Cambridge: Harvard University Press, Belknap Press, 1962.

Burnshaw, S. *The Seamless Web.* New York: George Braziller, 1970.

Bush, D. O. The National Center for Community Education. *Phi Delta Kappan,* 1972, 54(3), 201.

Carnegie Commission on Higher Education. *The Open Door Colleges.* New York: McGraw-Hill, 1970.

Clapp, E. R. *Community Schools in Action.* New York: Viking Press, 1940.

Clark, H. F., & Sloan, H. S. *Classrooms in the Military.* New York: Bureau of Publications, Teachers College, Columbia University, 1964.

List Of References

Clark, H. F., & Sloan, H. S. *Classrooms on Main Street.* New York: Teachers College Press, Teachers College, Columbia University, 1966.

Clark, P. A. If two and two and fifty make a million. *Community Education Journal,* 1971, 1 (1), 7-9.

Cohen, E. J. Education and learning. *Annals of the American Academy of Political and Social Science,* 1967, 373, 79-101.

Coleman, J. S. Community disorganization. In R. K. Merton & R. A. Nisbet (Eds.), *Contemporary Social Problems.* (2nd ed.) New York: Harcourt, Brace, 1966. Pp. 670-722.

Community Education: The Florida Community School Act of 1970. Report fiscal year 1971-72 and interim progress report fiscal year 1972-73. Tallahassee, Fla.: Department of Education, 1972.

Coyne, J., & Herbert, T. *This Way Out.* New York: Dutton, 1972.

Curriculum Handbook for School Executives. Arlington, Va.: American Association of School Administrators, 1973.

Cutlip, S. M., & Center, A. H. *Effective Public Relations.* New York: Prentice-Hall, 1952.

Decker, L. E. *An Administrative Assessment of the Consequences of Adopting Community Education in Selected School Districts.* (Doctoral dissertation, Michigan State University) Ann Arbor, Mi.: University Microfilms, 1971. No. 72-16,412.

Demos, C. On the decline of authority, *International Journal of Ethics,* 36, 250. Cited by K. D. Benne, *A Conception of Authority.* New York: Bureau of Publications, Teachers College, 1943, P. 4.

Dewey, J. *School and Society.* Chicago: University of Chicago Press, 1900.

Dewey, J. *How We Think,* Boston: D.C. Heath, 1910.

Dewey, J. *Democracy and Education.* New York: Macmillan, 1916.

Dewey, J. *Art As Experience.* New York: G. P. Putnam's Sons, Capricorn Books, 1958. (Originally published in 1934.)

Doherty, D. J. Community education: an urbanologist's view. *Phi Delta Kappan,* 1972, 54(3), 187-188.

Douglas, W. O. *Points of Rebellion.* New York: Vintage Books, 1970.

Drummond, H. D. The staff of the community school. In National Society for the Study of Education, *The Community School,* Fifty-second Yearbook, Part II, Chicago: NSSE (distr. University of Chicago Press), 1953.

Durant, W., & Durant, A. *The Lessons of History.* New York: Simon and Schuster, 1968.

Edman, I. As education. In *Art.* New York: The Museum of Modern Art, 1964.

Educational Policies Commission. *Strengthening Community Life: Schools Can Help.* 1201 Sixteenth Street, NW, Washington, D. C.: National Education Association and the American Association of School Administrators, 1954.

Eisenstadt, S. M. Social institutions: the concept. In D. L. Sills (Ed.), *International Encyclopedia of Social Sciences.* Vol. 141 New York: Macmillan, 1968. Pp. 409-421.

Eiseley, L. The mind as nature. In L. Eiseley, *The Night Country.* New York: Charles Scribner's, 1971. (Originally published as the fifth John Dewey Society Lecture, 1962.)

Eisner, E. W. Research on teaching the visual arts. In R. M. W. Travers (Ed.), *Second Handbook of Research on Teaching.* Chicago: Rand McNally, 1973.

Everett, S. *The Community School.* New York: D. Appleton-Century, 1938.

Farquhar, R. H., & Piele, P. K. *Preparing Educational Leaders.* Columbus, Ohio: University Council for Educational Administration, 1972.

Fisher, T. H. Educational evaluation in perspective. *The Michigan School Board Journal,* 1973, 20(6), 14-15.

Fitzgerald, S. E. *Communicating Ideas to the Public.* New York: Funk & Wagnalls, 1950.

Gant, G. F. Education in the use of natural resources. In National Society for the Study of Education, *American Education in the Postwar Period.* Forty-fourth Yearbook, Part I. Chicago: NSSE (distr. University of Chicago Press), 1945.

Getzels, J. W. Administration as a social process. In A. W. Halpin (Ed.), *Administrative Theory in Education.* Chicago: Midwest Administration Center, University of Chicago, 1958.

Gibb, J. R. *In Search of Leaders.* Washington, D. C.: American Association of Higher Education, 1967.

Goodlad, J. I. The future of learning: into the 21st century. *AACTE* (American Association of Colleges for Teacher Education) *Bulletin,* 1971, 24(1), 1, 4.

Goodman, P. *Growing Up Absurd.* New York: Knopf (Vintage), 1962.

Graubard, A. *Free the Children.* New York: Pantheon, 1973.

Graves, C. W. Deterioration of work standards. *Harvard Business Review,* 1966, 44(5), 117-128

Hadden, M. T. *An Analysis of the Emerging Roles of the Paraprofessional School-Community Aide with Implications for Strategies of Social Change in Disadvantaged Areas.* (Doctoral dissertation, University of Michigan) Ann Arbor, Mi.: University Microfilms, 1969. No. 70-4095.

Hagerstrand, T. Diffusion: The diffusion of innovations. In D. L. Sills (Ed.), *International Encyclopedia of the Social Sciences.* Vol. 4. New York: Macmillan, 1968, Pp. 174-177.

Halle, L. J. *Sedge.* New York: Praeger, 1963.

Halpin A. W. *Theory and Research in Administration.* New York: Macmillan, 1966.

Hanlon, J. M. *Administration and Education.* Belmont, Ca.: Wadsworth, 1968.

Hanna, P. R. The community school and larger geographic areas. In National Society for the Study of Education, *The Community School.* Fifty-second Yearbook, Part II. Chicago: NSSE (distr. University of Chicago Press), 1953.

List Of References

Harlacher, E. L. *The Community Dimension of the Community College.* Englewood Cliffs, N. J.: Prentice-Hall, 1969.

Hart, J. K. *The Discovery of Intelligence.* New York: Century, 1924.

Heath, P. R. *A Study of Nontransferring Community College Graduates from Selected Community Colleges.* (Doctoral dissertation, Western Michigan University) Ann Arbor, Mi.: University Microfilms, 1972. No. 72-31, 641.

Heckscher, A. The quality of American culture. In *The Report of the President's Commission on National Goals: Goals for Americans.* New York: Prentice-Hall, 1960.

Henri, R. *The Art Spirit.* New York: J. B. Lippincott, 1960. (Originally published in 1923.)

Henry, N. B. (Ed.) *American Education in the Postwar Period.* Forty-fourth Yearbook of the National Society for the Study of Education, Parts I and II. Chicago: NSSE (distr. University of Chicago Press), 1945.

Henry, N. B. (Ed.) *The Community School.* Fifty-second Yearbook of the National Society for the Study of Education, Part II. Chicago: NSSE (distr. University of Chicago Press), 1953.

Herzberg, F. The new industrial psychology. *Industrial and Labor Relations Review,* 1965, 18, 364-376.

Herzberg, F. *Work and the Nature of Man.* New York: World, 1966.

Herzberg, F. One more time: How do you motivate employees? *Harvard Business Review,* 1968, 48, 53-62.

Herzberg, F., Mausner, B., & Snyderman, B. B. *The Motivation to Work.* (2nd ed.) New York: John Wiley, 1959.

Hickey, H. W., VanVoorhees, C., & Associates, The *Role of the School in Community Education.* Midland, Mi.: Pendell, 1969.

Hicks, H. G. *The Management of Organizations.* New York: McGraw-Hill, 1967.

Hillis, R. *The Preparation and Evaluation of Instructional Materials on Community Agencies.* Bulletin of the Bureau of School Service, 10(4). Lexington, Ky.: University of Kentucky, 1948.

Hollander, E. P. Conformity, status, and idiosyncrasy credit. *Psychological Review* 1958, 65, 117-127.

Hollander, E. P., & Hunt, R. G. *Current Perspectives in Social Psychology.* New York: Oxford University Press, 1967.

Holt, J. *Freedom and Beyond.* New York: Dutton, 1972.

Holtville Consolidated School Faculty. *The Story of Holtville.* Deatsville, Ala.: Holtville High School, 1944.

Hottleman, G. D. Whose board? *Saturday Review of Education,* 1973, 2(3), 51.

Hovland, C. I., Janis, I. L., & Kelley, H. L. *Communication and Persuasion.* New Haven: Yale University Press, 1953.

Hunt, J. L. Education is environment-related and life-oriented. *Community Education Journal,* 1973, 3(4), 22-23.

Hyman, H., & Sheatsley, P. *The Current Status of American Public Opinion.* Twenty-first Yearbook of the National Council for the Social Studies. Washington, D. C.: National Education Association, 1950.

Illich, I. *De-schooling society.* New York: Harper, 1971.

Irwin, M., & Russell, W. *The Community is The Classroom.* Midland, Mi: Pendell, 1971.

Jay A. *Corporation Man.* New York: Random House, 1971.

Johnson, W. D. *Leadership Training Model for Community School Directors.* (Doctoral dissertation, Western Michigan University) Ann Arbor, Mi.: University Microfilms, 1973. (Numbering in process.)

Joyce, B. R. The curriculum worker of the future. In National Society for the Study of Education, *The Curriculum: Retrospect and Prospect.* Seventieth Yearbook, Part I. Chicago: NSSE (distr. University of Chicago Press), 1971.

Kellogg, W. K., Foundation. *Toward Improved School Administration.* Battle Creek, Mi.: The W. K. Kellogg Foundation, 1961.

Kerensky, V. M., & Melby, E. O. *Education II, the Social Imperative.* Midland, Mi.: Pendell, 1971.

Kyte, G. C. *The Principal at Work.* New York: Ginn, 1952.

Lasswell, H. D. *Democracy Through Public Opinion.* New York: George Banta, 1941.

Learning By Living: Education for Wise Use of Resources. Tallahassee, Fla.: Southern States Work Conference and The Committee on Southern Regional Studies and Education of the American Council on Education, 1950.

Leavitt, H. J. *Managerial Psychology.* (3rd ed.) Chicago: University of Chicago Press, 1972.

Lerbinger, O. & Sullivan, A. J. (Eds.) *Information, Influence, and Communication.* New York: Basic Books, 1965.

Lilienthal, D. E. *TVA: Democracy on the March.* New York: Harper and Brothers, 1944.

Lipham, J. M. Leadership and Administration. In National Society for the Study of Education, *Behavioral Science and Educational Administration,* Sixty-third Yearbook, Part III. Chicago: NSSE (distr. University of Chicago Press), 1964.

Lippman, L. *Attitudes Toward the Handicapped.* Springfield, Ill.: Charles C. Thomas, 1972.

Mager, R. F. *Goal Analysis.* Belmont, Ca.: Fearon Publishers, Lear Siegler, Inc., 1972.

Mahlmann, J., & Madeja, S. Art education. In W. J. Ellena (Ed.), *Curriculum Handbook for School Executives.* Arlington, Va.: American Association of School Administrators, 1973.

List Of References

Martin, Gerald. On community education models. *Phi Delta Kappan,* 1972, 54(3), 187.

Maslow, A. H. *Motivation and Personality.* New York: Harper, 1954.

Maslow, A. H. Some basic propositions of a growth and self-actualization psychology. In Association for Supervision and Curriculum Development yearbook, *Perceiving, Behaving, Becoming.* Washington, D. C.: ASCD, 1962.

Mawby, R. G. A foundation executive views the future of continuing education. In *New Life Styles for Continuing Education,* Proceedings for the 13th Conference for College and University Leaders in Continuing Education. East Lansing: Michigan State University, 1971.

Mayer, M. *The Schools.* New York: Harper, 1961.

McCloskey, G. *Education and Public Understanding.* New York: Harper and Row, 1959.

McCloskey, G. Planning the public relations program. *NEA Journal,* 1960, 59, 15-17.

McClure, R. M. The reforms of the fifties and sixties: A historical look at the near past. In National Society for the Study of Education, *The Curriculum: Retrospect and Prospect,* Seventieth Yearbook, Part I. Chicago: NSSE (distr. University of Chicago Press), 1971.

McClusky, H. Y. The school in the community. *Community Service News,* 1953, 11, 149-153.

Mead, M. Questions that need asking. *Teachers College Record,* 1961, 63(2), 89-93.

Melby, E. O. Approaches to role change in community education. *Phi Delta Kappan* 1972, 54(3), 172.

Michigan Format for Local Evaluation. Lansing, Mi.: Michigan Department of Public Instruction, 1973.

Michigan Policy for the Distribution of Community School Funds in Accordance with the Provisions of Section 96 of Act No. 258. Lansing, Mi.: Department of Public Instruction, 1973.

Michigan State University. Rationale and program model. In *Behavioral Science Elementary Teacher Education Program,* Vol. 1, sec. 2. Washington, D. C.: HEW, Office of Education, 1968.

Minardo, W. The right man for the right job. *Community Education Journal,* 1972, 2(5), 13-14.

Minnesota Guidelines for Community Schools Supplement. St. Paul, Minn.: State Department of Education, 1973.

Minzey, J. D., & LeTarte, C. *Community Education: From Program to Process.* Midland, Mi.: Pendell, 1972.

Moon, R. A. Their relationship to community agencies. In H. W. Hickey, C. Van Voorhees, & Associates, *The Role of the School in Community Education.* Midland, Mi.: Pendell, 1969.

Morphet, E., Johns, R., & Reller, T. *Educational Administration.* Englewood Cliffs, N. J.: Prentice-Hall, 1959.

Morse, H. T. The education of war workers and returned service personnel. In National Society for the Study of Education, *American Education in the Postwar Period,* Forty-fourth Yearbook, Part I. Chicago: NSSE (distr. University of Chicago Press), 1945.

Myran, F. A. *Community Services in the Community College.* Washington, D. C.: American Association of Community and Junior Colleges, 1969.

Nance, E. E. The community education coordinator. *Community Education Journal,* 1972 2(5), 52-55.

Nance, E. E., & Snapp, T. What next? *Community Education Journal,* 1973, 3(4), 12-15.

Needed Research in Community Education. Flint, Mi.: National Community School Education Association, 1971.

Olsen, B. K. *Research in Community School Education — A Bibliography.* Provo, Utah: Brigham Young University, 1970.

Olsen, E. G., & Others. *School and Community.* New York: Prentice-Hall, 1945. (Revised in 1954.)

Olsen, E. G. *School and Community — A Chronological Bibliography.* Flint, Mi.: National Community School Education Association, 1970.

Orchard View Community Schools, *Fact Booklet.* Muskegon, Mi.: Author, 1972.

Pappadakis, Nick. Financing Community Education. *Community Education Journal,* 1971, 1(2), 37.

Parker District High School and the Parker District Community: A Story of the Work of the Parker School and Community. Greenville, S. C.: Parker District Schools, 1942.

Paulston, R. G. (Ed.) *Nonformal Education: An Annotated International Bibliography.* New York: Praeger, 1972.

Paw Paw Schools, *Community Education: Report to the Board of Education.* Paw Paw, Mi.: Author, 1973.

Pfeiffer, J. W., & Sabers, D. *Attrition and Achievement in Correspondence Study.* Washington, D. C.: National Home Study Council, 1970.

Plumb, J. H. The great change in children. *Intellectual Digest,* 1972, 2(8), 82-84.

Poster, C. D. *The School and the Community.* London: Macmillan Education Lts, 1971.

Procunier, D. M. *An Analysis of Factors Necessary for Effective Innovation in Regional Community Education Dissemination Centers.* (Doctoral dissertation, Michigan State University) Ann Arbor, Mi.: University Microfilms, 1972. No. 72-30,032.

Provus, M. In search of community. *Phi Delta Kappan.* 1973, 54(10), 658-661.

Reimer, E. *School is Dead.* Garden City: Doubleday, 1971.

Rogers, C. R. Divergent trends in methods of improving adjustment. *Harvard Educational Review,* 1948, 202-219. Cited by the author, *Client-centered therapy.* Boston: Houghton-Mifflin, 1951, P. 490.

411

List Of References

Rogers, C. R. *Client-centered Therapy.* Boston: Houghton-Mifflin, 1951.

Samuelson, A. Relationships of the schools to other social and educational agencies. In National Society for the Study of Education, *American Education in the Postwar Period,* Forty-fourth Yearbook, Part II. Chicago: NSSE (distr. University of Chicago Press), 1945.

Sandberg, J. E., & Martin, G. C. Western Michigan University hosts national conferences of deans of education and university center directors. *Community Education Journal,* 1972, 2(5), 47-48.

Saxe, R. W. (Ed.) *Opening the Schools: Alternative Ways of Learning.* Berkeley: McCutchan, 1972.

Schramm, W. *The Process and Effects of Mass Communication.* Urbana, Ill.: University of Illinois Press, 1955.

Seay, M. F. Some principles of an educational program. In M. F. Seay (Ed.), *Adult Education: A Part of a Total Educational Program.* Bulletin of the Bureau of School Service, 10(4). Lexington, Ky.: University of Kentucky, 1938.

Seay, M. F. The community-school emphases in postwar education. In National Society for the Study of Education, *American Education in the Postwar Period.* Forty-fourth Yearbook, Part I. Chicago: NSSE (distr. University of Chicago Press), 1945.

Seay, M. F. The communtiy school: New meaning for an old term. In National Society for the Study of Education, *The Community School,* Fifty-second Yearbook, Part II. Chicago: NSSE (distr. University of Chicago Press), 1953.

Seay, M. F. Role of the four-year college and the university in community education. *Phi Delta Kappan,* 1972, 54(3), 199-202.

Seay, M. F. Threads running through the community school movement. *Community Education Journal,* 1972, 2(1), 16-19.

Seay, M. F. & Crawford, F. N. *The Community School and Community Self-Improvement.* Lansing, Mi.: State Department of Public Instruction, 1954.

Seay, M. F., & Meece, L. E. *The Sloan Experiment in Kentucky.* Bulletin of the Bureau of School Service, 16(4), Lexington, Ky.: University of Kentucky, 1944.

Shahn, B. *The Shape of Content.* New York: Random House, Vintage Books, 1957.

Sizer, T. R. In D. W. Cudhea, Life and Learning. *Saturday Review of Education.* 1972, 55(38), 34.

Skinner, B. F. *Beyond Freedom and Dignity.* New York: Knopf, 1971.

Stevens, B. A. The revival of handicrafts. In T. R. Ford (Ed.), *The Southern Appalachian Region: A Survey.* Lexington, Ky.: University of Kentucky Press, 1967.

Stoddard, G. D. As the measure of man. In *Art.* New York: The Museum of Modern Art, 1964.

Stodgill, R. M. Personal factors associated with leadership: A survey of the literature. *Journal of Psychology,* 1948, 25, 35-71.

Strang, R. Community schools and the people working together. In National Society for the Study of Education, *The Community School,* Fifty-second Yearbook, Part II. Chicago: NSSE (distr. University of Chicago Press), 1953.

Stufflebeam, D., & Others. *Educational Evaluation and Decision making.* Itasca, Ill.: F. E. Peacock, 1971.

Thelen, H. A. *Education and the Human Quest.* New York: Harper, 1960.

Totten, W. F. *Annotated Bibliography of Books and Pamphlets.* Flint, Mi.: National Community School Education Association, 1972.

Totten, W. F., & Manley, F. J. *The Community School.* Galien, Mi.: Allied Education Council, 1969.

Travers, R. M. W. (Ed.) *Second Handbook of Research on Teaching.* Chicago: Rand McNally, 1973.

Tyler, R. W. *Basic Principles of Curriculum and Instruction.* Chicago: University of Chicago Press, 1950.

Weaver, D. C. A case for theory development in community education. *Phi Delta Kappan,* 1972, 54(3), 154-157.

Weaver, D. C. *The Emerging Community Education Model,* Presidential address, The National Community School Education Association. Flint, Mi.: NCSEA, 1972.

Weber, M. The three types of legitimate rule. In A Etzioni (Ed.), *Complex Organizations; A Sociological Reader.* New York: Holt, 1961. Pp. 4-14. (First published in Preussische Jahrbucker, 1922.)

Wheelis, A. *The Quest for Identity.* New York: W. W. Norton, 1958.

Williams, C. S. Changes needed in school organization to provide educational opportunities for adults. In National Society for the Study of Education, *American Education in the Postwar Period,* Forty-fourth Yearbook, Part II. Chicago: NSSE (distr. University of Chicago Press), 1945.

United States Office of Education. *Bulletin No. 5.* Washington, D. C.: Government Printing Office, 1951.

Wurman, R. S. (Ed.) *Yellow Pages of Learning Resources.* Cambridge, Mass.: Massachusetts Institute of Technology Press, 1972.

Wynn, R. *Unconventional Methods and Materials for Preparing Educational Administrators.* Columbus, Ohio: University Council for Educational Administration, 1972.

Your Lakeview Schools, February, 1973. Battle Creek, Mi.: The Lakeview School District, 1973.

NAME INDEX

Name Index

SUBJECT INDEX

Accountability, 134, 185, 194, 207-231, 272-273, 391
Advisory councils
    leadership role, 150, 168, 171-186
    to facilitate accountability, 218
    with agency representation, 172, 175-178
    with lay representation, 172, 173-175
Aesthetic experiences, 285, 309-312
Agencies, 27, 28, 49, 53, 61-80, 101-102, 147-151, 189-194,
    209, 268-270, 298-301, 324-325, 373, 377-380
Agricultural Extension Service, 301
Alaskan Readers, 34
Alma College, 352
American Association for Health, Physical Education
    and Recreation, 376, 382
American Association of Community and Junior Colleges (AACJC),
    7, 331
American Association of School Administrators (AASA), 7, 120,
    178, 289-290, 380, 382
American Educational Research Association, 290-291
American Management Association, 137
Annual report, 255
Appalachian Adult Education Center, 192
Arizona State University, 352
Art
    as enrichment program, 295-298
    in community education, 285-312
    through community-wide resources, 298-306, 312
    through traditional presentations, 305
Articulation, 13, 14, 336, 340, 344
Association for Supervision and Curriculum Development, 380,382
Audio-visual presentation, 255-256

Ball State University, 352, 395
Battle Creek School System, 34, 308
Big Brothers of America, 377, 379, 382
Board of Education, 152, 156, 163, 171-172
Brigham Young University, 352
Business as art patron, 304-305

California State University, 352
California State University (Northridge), 353
Canadian Education Association, 120
Carnegie Commission, 332, 369
Catalytic agent, 13, 25, 167, 193, 345
Central Michigan University, 367
Charles Stewart Mott Community College, 344
Chicago Art Institute, 305
College of St. Thomas, 353, 366
Colorado State University, 353
Commission on National Goals, 303
Committee on Southern Regional Studies and Education, 38
Communication, 97, 106, 129, 173, 185, 212, 214, 235-257, 266,353, 354
Community
    lack of, 58-60

Subject Index

Orchard View community, 195
Organizational structure
    and social systems, 14-15, 60-63, 90-91, 147-168, 195-201, 213, 218
    and university-center relationships, 355-356
    core elements, 62
    elements of structure, 149-150, 172
    line relationship, 163-164
    staff relationship, 167
    survival elements, 62-63
    typical models, 163-166
    working elements, 62
Outreach delivery systems, 271-272, 345

Paraprofessional counselor, 267-268
Parker District High School, 35-36, 46, 388
Paw Paw Public Schools, 200
Pendell Publishing Company, 4, 5
Performance standards; criteria, 136, 395-396, 399
Phi Delta Kappan, 81, 161, 391
Philosophical commitment, 354
Polarization of viewpoints, 26-27
Popular art, 303-304
Power of education, 11, 202
Procedures, 40-41, 149, 178-182
Process, 3, 7, 11, 31, 40, 92-93, 113, 126-129, 143, 193, 201-203, 274-275,
    346, 368, 396
Professional education associations, 5, 373-383
Program
    activities to fill gaps, 152-153, 194-201
    as a comprehensive plan, 193-204, 220
    as a result of process, 148-149, 173, 201-203
    as distinct from process, 126-129, 396
    examples, 195-201, 341, 343, 344
    for counseling, 275-379
    for public communication, 252-257
    with enrichment classes, 295-298
Programming
    community-wide, 3, 134, 151, 156-163, 189-204
    for the handicapped, 317-328
    sample budget, 154-155
Progressive education, 20, 392
Project in Applied Economics, 32-34
Public communication
    as a part of community education, 219, 235-257
    basic functions, 248-252
    demonstrating, 129, 130
    preparing materials, 254-257
    principles, 239-242
    promoting, 129, 130
    responsibilities, 242-248
Public health units, 151
Publications
    bibliographies, 393

Subject Index

Technical skill, 133, 136, 141
Tennessee Valley Authority (TVA), 10, 22, 29
Texas A & M University, 353
Theory
    definition, 85-86
    development, 85-116
    lack of, 387-392, 400
    use of, 400-403
Traditions, 353, 354
Two-way relationship, 35-38, 332

United arts councils, 299
United Cerebral Palsy Association, 327
United Indian Tribes of America, 274
United States Jaycees, 377, 379-380, 381, 382
United States Office of Education, 38, 77, 320, 321
Universities
    center advisory council, 355-356
    center director, 355
    community education centers, 80, 351-367, 400
    participation of colleges and, 135, 351-369, 392, 395-396
University Council for Educational Administration (UCEA), 121, 122
University of Alabama, 353
University of Connecticut, 352
University of Florida, 353
University of Georgia, 353
University of Kentucky, 32
University of Michigan, 367
University of Missouri, 353
University of Vermont, 353
University of Virginia, 353
Urban center, 397-398, 400-401

Variables, 397, 398

Wayne State University, 367
Western Michigan University, 92, 141, 161, 215, 352, 356, 363
World War II, 11, 23, 73